Children and Television

DATE DUE

			PRINTED IN U.S.A.

In loving memory of Margaret Elsa Lemish

(January 13, 1912 – March 2, 2006)

Children and Television

A Global Perspective

Dafna Lemish

Blackwell
Publishing

BLACKWELL PUBLISHING

350 Main Street, Malden, MA 02148-5020, USA
9600 Garsington Road, Oxford OX4 2DQ, UK
550 Swanston Street, Carlton, Victoria 3053, Australia

First published 2007 by Blackwell Publishing Ltd

3   2008

Library of Congress Cataloging-in-Publication Data

Lemish, Dafna
  Children and television : a global perspective / Dafna Lemish.
    p. cm.
  Includes bibliographical references and index.
  ISBN: 978-1-4051-4418-6 (hardcover : alk. paper)
  ISBN: 978-1-4051-4419-3 (pbk. : alk. paper)

1. Television and children. 2. Television in education. 3. Television broadcasting–Social aspects. I. Title.

  HQ784.T4L35 2006
  302.23′45083–dc22

2006012514

A catalogue record for this title is available from the British Library.

Set in 10.5/13pt Minion
by SPI Publisher Services, Pondicherry, India
Printed and bound in Singapore by COS Printers Pte Ltd

The publisher's policy is to use permanent paper from mills that operate a sustainable forestry policy, and which has been manufactured from pulp processed using acid-free and elementary chlorine-free practices. Furthermore, the publisher ensures that the text paper and cover board used have met acceptable environmental accreditation standards.

For further information on
Blackwell Publishing, visit our website:
www.blackwellpublishing.com

Contents

Detailed Contents

Preface

Can one book fully and completely cover such a wide and complex terrain as the intersection of children and television from a global perspective?

Obviously it cannot. What it can do, however, is provide one scholar's account of the landscape, a map if you will of its typography with its shinning mountain peaks and hidden valleys, from the point of view of one person who has been climbing in this trek.

Accordingly, this book presents a critical analysis of the accumulated literature developed over the past fifty years on the relationships of children and television with a view to assisting contemporary researchers, students of media, television producers, policymakers, educators, and parents to understand the key issues that have been and should be studied, discussed, and confronted in terms of research, public policy, education, and production. The general structure of the book follows an earlier version of a textbook I wrote for the Open University in Israel (*Growing-up with television: The little screen in the lives of children and youth*, 2002, Hebrew). However, this book moves beyond conventional analyses of American and European-based studies, including my own earlier work, to present a broader, integrative analysis of research conducted all over the world on the interrelationships between television and children as a global phenomenon.

I have been studying children and television for 25 years in the USA, Europe, and Israel, as well as its complementary implications for the development of media literacy. I have read, taught, conducted research, written about it, and presented my work in numerous scholarly as well as professional settings. I take pride in being in a unique position to bridge two complementary research traditions to children and television: The American tradition of developmental psychology with a general emphasis on the individual child, effects studies, and quantitative methodologies; and the European tradition of sociology of childhood and cultural studies with its general emphasis on sociological and cultural issues, and the application of qualitative methodologies. My education and experience in both traditions allows me the privileged position of integrating them into a more holistic view of the field that is not biased by either tradition.

I bring with me to this work, as to anything else in my professional and personal life, a feminist worldview and set of values. What I mean by this is a special concern and interest for issues of equality and diversity, a critical view on the constructed nature of all social life, and an ethics of care. Within the framework of my own research, the feminist worldview has stimulated a rethinking of traditional binary oppositions related to children and media: The distinction between childhood and adulthood, the separation of children's public and private lives, rational and emotional reactions to media, cultural constructions and developmental theories, and the like. I have also taken very seriously an understanding of the power hierarchies that characterize relations between adult researchers and children investigated, and my own privileged position as a middle-class, educated, white female-academic.

A major characteristic of all feminist work is the commitment not only to contribute to research and social theory, but also to being a catalyst for deep social change. Indeed, the feminist perspective often criticizes contemporary social science for differentiating, rather than integrating knowledge and action and highlighting the emancipatory potential of their co-joint workings. I am therefore deeply involved with making academic knowledge accessible to the public through efforts at teacher training, development of media literacy curricula, appearances in the media, advising grassroots organizations, participating in exchanges with producers, and the like. What I have gained from these efforts occupies an important place in the following pages as well.

The task undertaken here is enormous and very ambitious. I approached this challenge with deep gratitude to many, many people who have contributed to my professional development and life throughout the years, too many to even attempt to name individually, but I am indebted to them all. A few who stand out as important "milestones" on my way have my deepest gratitude: to David Buckingham, Máire Davies-Messenger, Kirsten Drotner, Shalom Fisch, Maya Götz, and Sonia Livingstone, from whom I learned much about children and media as well as about the intricacies of cross-cultural research; to Aletha Huston, Mabel Rice, and the late John Wright who pointed the way to developmental traditions to the field; and to Ellen Wartella, who started it all with the first graduate course I took with her almost three decades back then and who has continued to fuel my interests since ... I hope that she would have considered this book as her textbook, if she was to teach that course once again.

To my colleagues and friends from the Feminist Scholarship Division of the International Communication Association, Carolyn Byrely, Cynthia Carter, and Karen Ross, for constantly reminding me of the meaning and responsibility of being a citizen of the globe, and the value of our daily work in attempting to make a difference within it.

I am grateful to my Israeli community of scholars and students for their cooperation, support, and insights as we live through the good times and bad times of life in Israel. In particular, to my research collaborators who have become intellectual partners as well as dear friends – Linda-Reneé Bloch, Akiba Cohen, and Chava Tidhar; and to the two more recent partners who have already enriched my work – Nelly Elias and Rivka Ribak. Special thanks go to Liora Gabay and Liora Weinhaber for their enormous administrative help and support.

I thank Cambridge University Press for permission to republish here six short quotes from Dafna Lemish and Mable Rice, "Television as a Talking Picture Book: A Prop for Language Acquisition," *Journal of Child Language* 13 (1986), pp. 251–74. © 1986 by Cambridge University Press.

I owe a great deal to Elizabeth Swayze, the editor of Blackwell, who believed in this project and in me from the very first exchange we held on it (New Orleans, May 2004) and to the production staff at Blackwell particularly Simon Eckley, Lisa Eaton, and Mervyn Thomas for their professional, efficient and friendly collaboration. Special thanks go to Amy Jordan for her constructive and insightful comments on an earlier draft.

To my children – Leeshai, Noam, and Erga, who were fortunate enough to watch television in several places on the globe, and who never fail to challenge, inspire, delight, and surprise me – for stimulating my research following their own development from infancy to adulthood.

And finally, to Peter Lemish, my multi-dimensional life-time partner: the most intellectual, original, critical yet loving reviewer and editor one can hope for, I am grateful (among other things on my too long a list to mention) for keeping me intellectually and personally constantly on the tips of my toes ...

This book is for a better television for children.

Introduction

Why are children and television a global issue? Why in the era of media convergence should there be focus on television? Why a specific concern with the audience of children? Let us start our joint journey into the exciting field of study of children and television by confronting these three central challenges embedded in the title of this book.

Why Global (Is it)?

Children and television is a global issue for a variety of compelling reasons. First, children of both genders and all ages, races, religions, classes, and geographical regions of the world watch television on a regular basis, enjoy it tremendously, and learn more about the world from it than from any other socializing agent. A phenomenon so pervasive and central in children's lives is bound to be of great interest to anybody involved in and/or concerned about their world – students, parents, teachers, scholars, politicians, professionals, policymakers, concerned citizens, in short, all of us.

There is very little else that can be claimed with such confidence that is an experience shared by most children in today's world. At the beginning of the third millennium, children are being raised in a great variety of social arrangements: by dual parents, single parents, divorced parents, uni-sex parents, communal parents, no parents. Furthermore, regarding the existential nature of their lives, we can say that not all children are literate or go to school for that matter; they speak hundreds of different languages, eat different foods, play different games, wear different cloths; they face very different challenges in their daily lives; they have different dreams and aspirations for their future; but all this having been said, almost all of them watch television.

In short, television is the one of most shared and homogenizing mechanisms of children's lives today throughout the world. Whether they have their TV in their bedroom, share the family set in the living room, or watch it in the classroom or the community center, it is part of the taken-for-granted everyday experience of most children. They may be watching it lying in bed, while playing on the rug, eating their dinner, doing homework, or playing the computer – but still, they are watching it. Very few other cultural phenomena have such a magnitude of penetration, and even fewer have achieved global status.

Television has global status, too, because very similar debates over television's role in the lives of children have emerged worldwide. The introduction of television and its diffusion since the middle of the twentieth century has been accepted dialectically, in all societies in a very similar manner to the way other communication technologies that preceded it have (e.g., books, newspapers, radio, films) or those that followed it (computers and the Internet). On the one hand, there were high hopes and great expectations for television to enrich children's lives, stimulate their imagination and creativity, widen their education and knowledge, encourage multicultural tolerance, narrow social gaps, stimulate development and democratization processes. On the other hand, there was also great anxiety about the ability of television to numb the senses, develop indifference to the pain of others, encourage destructive behaviors, lead to a deterioration of moral values, suppress local cultures, and contribute to social estrangement. This ambivalent stance in regard to the medium of television – as a "messiah" on one hand and "demon" on the other – has been discussed widely in public debates in every culture that has absorbed the medium. Most pronounced are concerns over the effects of television violence on children, as well as the potential harm of exposure to sexual portrayals, the effects of advertising on consumer culture, and the more general concern over children's passivity and social disengagement. Media debates, public forums, parents and community newsletters, legislative bodies' hearings, educational leaders, broadcasting policymakers – all contributed to these popular debates framed as "moral panics," exerting public pressure on governing institutions. Countries that can afford to do so allocate public funds to research institutions in search of more definite and conclusive answers to the nagging question: "What is television doing to our children?"

Indeed, the field of "television and children" has become a global research interest of scholars, mainly in psychology, media studies, sociology, and education. Their varied disciplinary homes have made a great deal of difference to the kind of theoretical underpinnings they brought to their studies, the questions posed, the research method applied, and naturally, to the kind of findings they came up with and their interpretations. Further, in this respect, the academic field concerned with the reciprocal relationships between children and television reflects in large degree the changes that have taken place in the various disciplines nourishing this scholarly field, in general, and the study of mass media, in particular. Psychology, the most prominent of the approaches applied to this area, has focused on the individual child and a host of related issues, such as: social learning from television, the effects of television on behavior, development of comprehension of television content, or the uses children make of television and the gratifications they acquire from their viewing behaviors.

As the body of literature started to accumulate, mainly from the Western academic institutions, it became clear that the "strong effect" conclusion that assumes a unidirectional television effect on children is too over-simplistic. Other research demonstrated something that common sense and anecdotal data posited for a long time: children are not passive, proverbial "tabula rasa" upon which television messages leave their marks. On the contrary, children are active consumers of television. They react to, think, feel, create meanings. They bring to television encounters a host of predispositions, abilities, desires, and experiences. They watch television in diverse personal, social, and cultural circumstances that, too, influence and are part of their discourse and interactions with television. Thus, it became clear that asking "what do children do with television?" is just as important a question as "how does television influence them?"

This paradigm shift led to highlighting the need for cross-cultural research. Clearly, comparative research of this global phenomenon can illuminate many of the questions on the research agenda. Does televised violence affect children differently if they are living in a violent urban center in comparison to a tranquil isolated village? Are children more frightened by news coverage of war when they are growing up amidst armed conflict in comparison to children for whom war is a fictitious concept? Do children react differently to actors and actresses of European descent who appear in their favorite soap operas and situation comedies if they are living in a dominantly Euro-American society in comparison to African, Latino, or Asian ones? And what about consumerism – would children raised in rich consumer cultures amidst an abundance of products from which to choose interpret advertising differently then those with no financial resources or limited personal property? Pursuing such questions related to children and television has become a global endeavor for researchers to study as no single body of knowledge based on contextualized studies in one culture, be it as rich and diverse as possible, can provide us with the in-depth, multifaceted picture necessary to understand this phenomenon in its full global manifestation.

Children and television is an issue of global interest for an additional crucial reason. Today, children are part of a global audience that transcends local or even regional physical and cultural boundaries in consumption of television programs. As a global phenomenon, television promotes mainly what has been termed as "late modernity" values, typified primarily by commercialism, globalization, privatization, and individualization. This is "achieved" as a result of the fact that children all over the world watch, for example, American-produced cartoons, situation comedies, soap operas, action-adventure serials, as well as Disney-style and Hollywood movies. However, they also watch programs that come from other parts of the world; such as Latin-American tele-novellas; localized versions of the Japanese animated series *Poké-mon;* or the local co-productions of the American *Sesame Street* and/or the United Kingdom's *Teletubbies.* Worldwide, children complete their homework or chores to the sounds of popular music on MTV and fantasize on love and adventure over blockbuster movies broadcasted at a later time on their local channels. They cheer for their favorite sports team across continents and seas; follow the news of armed conflicts worlds apart; admire many of the same celebrities, collect their memorabilia, hang their posters, wear their T-shirts, follow their private lives in the magazines and websites. Visit any country in the world today and you will be able to strike up a conversation with local children by asking about their favorite television programs. You do not even have to know the language. Hand motioning to pictures and ads and mere mention of the names of global celebrities and popular programs will stimulate enough cooperation. At least some of them are bound to be those familiar to you from your own home television viewing or that seen in the homes of friends, neighbors, or relatives.

Obviously, the monies invested in children and television is a global business of enormous proportions and value. For huge entertainment corporations, children are not future citizens but first and foremost they are consumers. From such a point of view childhood is not a distinct period in the life cycle, one that should be attended to with compassion and responsibility. On the contrary, it is a distinct market opportunity. With a television set hooked to cable and/ or satellite dish, receiving programs fed by huge international commercial corporations over dozens of channels, the battle over the quality of the local channel is a battle over the quality of one drop in the sea. Thus, any attempts to develop or lobby for change in the content of television programs for children, for developing policy guidelines for broadcasting to them, and for fostering television literacy skills in the educational system – can not be undertaken in isolation. Concern for the quality of the relationship between *children and television* is a global issue and only global co-operative efforts are likely to make a substantial, enduring difference.

Why TV (Still)?

As has already become clear from this brief introduction, television cannot be studied in isolation. It is common nowadays to substitute the discussion of television with "screen" culture, in order to recognize the trend for convergence of various screen media: television, including cable and satellite connections, video recorder and games, computer games, the Internet, movie theaters, and even mobile-phone screens. They all share the predominance of the audio-visual system of signification, using similar codes and conventions to convey rich abundance of contents. Indeed, our discussion of "television" is deeply integrated with all the above forms. However, while computers in general and the Internet in particular have become the spearhead of research on children and media in the past few years, the following chapters will continue to focus specifically on the "good-old-and-familiar" television set.

There are several reasons why this is the case. First, computers and the Internet in particular, while diffused rapidly, are still the privilege of the minority of well-to-do, middle and high class children in developed countries. Second, while scholarly study of computer access has been extended beyond the limited focus on ownership of the hardware itself (i.e., who has a computer at home or has access to one in a public place?) to questions related to cognitive and motivational access (e.g., who has the knowledge as well as the linguistic and computer skills necessary to access the computer; who perceives the computer as relevant to one's own personal goals and future prospects and thus has the motivation to pursue computer use?).

Interestingly, television remains the dominant medium even in those cultures where computers have reached a high diffusion rate. Recent studies in both the USA as well as Europe suggest that children still spend significantly more time watching television than any other leisure activity; they prefer to turn to television as their "default" medium, when bored or lonely; they would rather have their own television set if they had a choice for their next birthday. Thus, at the time that these lines are being written, and probably for years to come, television is still the central medium in children's lives, with the computer lagging far behind.

However, focusing on television from a global perspective can also serve to illuminate the growing field of computer and Internet studies, for which television research provides a solid base. The same questions to be discussed in the following pages are still as relevant and applicable today for this rapidly advancing field of research as they are for television, and thus, by extension, can be applied to and compared with the still evolving research on "convergence." That is, we can say for now that the same theoretical foundations are nurturing this newly emerging field of research. Thus, there is much to be gained by establishing it on the foundations of 50 years of accumulated knowledge regarding television and children. It is from here that the new studies can spread their wings to new territories.

Why Kids (Only)?

Finally, although common discourse suggests that children are living today more and more in a world devoid of childhoods, with a constant blurring of traditional dichotomies such as adulthood and childhood as well as the public and private spheres, this book insists on continuing to treat children (up to age 18) as occupying a very unique time in the human cycle that deserves our special attention as well as the best of our resources and human investment. Studies of television and children are gradually becoming more sensitive to the existence of various approaches to the concept of "childhood," to its socially constructed nature, as well as to the various diverse dimensions that it encompasses: differences of gender, ethnicity, and class are gaining more and more prominence in addition to those related to children's age. All of these add new dimensions for understanding the already complex nature of the relationships between children and their favorite medium of television.

As we delve into the many issues involved, we find that the theoretical approaches developed to understand the nature and meaning of childhood have deeply affected the kinds of research questions asked and the kind of methods employed in an attempt to answer them. To a large degree, studies of children and television that dominated the field until the end of the twentieth century where *about* children: that is, children were tested for understanding the content of programs; they participated in experiments that measured its effects on them; surveys were conducted about the amount and kind of exposure they had to it; and the like.

The theoretical assumption of most of this research perceived adulthood as the end goal of children's development and the measuring stick of all their performances. Accordingly, children were perceived as deficient: they were unable to understand television content quite as well as adults; they were not yet immunized to its negative effects as were adults; unlike adults, they were naive and easily persuaded.

Furthermore, according to this approach, children were also under-stood to be inexperienced "subjects" of research who had difficulty accounting for their personal experiences and understandings of the medium of television. Such research, then, relied heavily on adults – caregivers, educators, parents, researchers – to be the reporters about children's inner worlds, their modes of making meaning, their viewing pleasures, and so on.

Recently, theories of culture and the sociology of childhood have challenged this assumption that children needed to be viewed in relation to the process of "becoming" fully grown adults. In its place, they suggested that childhood be assumed to be a form of "being" in its own right. Accordingly, this approach highlighted the need to allow children, in each stage of their development, to be fully recognized as having a unique personal voice that deserved to be listened to and understood with empathy. Research on children and television con-ducted through such an approach has been understood by a growing number of researchers to be the kind that should allow for studies that are as much *with* children and *for* children as they are *on* children. This theoretical and ideological turn has also lead to adopting a wider range of methodologies for studying children: in addition to surveys and experi-ments, there is a need for finding ways that facilitate a more active role of the children, as participants with an independent voice, such as in-depth interviewing, participant observation of their viewing of programs, play, etc. as well as analysis of their artwork and written accounts.

The TV (Book) Guide

The intellectual journey offered you, the reader in this book, will tune in right at the place where it is lived on a regular basis – in the home settings of children. Chapter 1 will examine the changes that have taken place in the role of television in the lives of families worldwide and the place it has come to occupy in children's leisure. Our discussion will address issues such as: How is television integrated in the everyday lives of children? What are the various roles that parents and siblings play in intervening in viewing habits: for example, in controlling amount of time devoted to television as well as type of contents viewed; mediating the messages; incorporating television in family communication patterns; and the like?

While family types and the social contexts in which children are growing up are extremely diverse, so are their individual personalities, cognitive skills and life experiences. Thus, in Chapter 2 we will explore the importance of such individual differences: What can we learn from the literature on various dimensions of children's development and their relevancy to the consumption of television? For example, how are children's attention and comprehension of television developed? What is the role that television's audio-visual "formal features" play in these processes? How do children learn to distinguish between the reality and fantasy dimensions of television content? How does the development of genre recognition, comprehension of narratives, characters and moral issues progress? What kind of emotional responses to television content do children display – such as fear? Further, we will ponder the issue of how much we know from research can be generalized to children as a homogenous group, across cultures and age groups versus how much of their relationships with the medium change as they grow and develop within particular contexts.

With the understandings gained in the first two chapters, we will be ready to tackle the much-debated issue of behavioral effects of television on children. Grounded in the general literature that perceives the vulnerability of children as a special audience, particular attention will be devoted in Chapter 3 to the question of the effects of television violence in both the short and long run. This discussion will include presentation of different hypotheses and research traditions; the effects of pro-social behaviors; the effects of television advertising on consuming behaviors, including shopping motivations, development of unhealthy eating habits, consumption of over-the-counter drugs and alcohol; and the role of advertising in parent–child confrontations. In addition, the chapter will address the debate over the effects of television (and pornography in particular) on sexual behavior of adolescents. The literature on the displacement effect of television within the leisure culture of children will be discussed, including issues such as television's effects on fantasy play and "addictive" viewing behaviors. While focusing on a review of these popular questions, we will keep a critical eye on important research questions: How valid are the methodologies commonly employed in studying these effects? How relevant are those questions to non-western societies? What are the issues of study that we have been seriously neglecting?

The study of behavioral effects of television is only part of the story. In our field, many questions have been posed that are concerned with influences of this medium on children's worldviews, values, and stereotypes. Thus, Chapter 4 focuses on the role of television in the cultivation of a worldview through a process of social and political construction of reality. How does television contribute to the construction of gender identities, sexuality, and body image as well as socialization to sex-roles? Does television foster a perception of the world as a mean and dangerous place in which to live? And, what is television's role in teaching us about "others" (we all have different "others", depending on who we are) – be they racial minorities in our society, persons with physical and/or mental disabilities, agesim? Does television play a role in helping children: "know thy enemy?"; in socializing them to the political world – to being involved citizens?; in socializing immigrant children into their host societies?; in formation of a global youth culture that transcends cultural and geographical borders? Is indeed, childhood disappearing in front of our eyes as many have been arguing?

The potential of television to teach has been recognized by formal institutions and educational systems around the world, particularly in regards to those less privileged. Televised "schooling" and educational television challenge many of our conventional assumptions regarding proper pedagogies. In this regard, Chapter 5 will include discussion of the relationship between television and formal learning: such as, what are the inter-relationships between viewing television, school perform-ance, and reading–writing literacy? Is television viewing related to lan-guage – as well as second language – acquisition? It will also proceed to discuss intended learning through educational television, focusing in particular on prominent cases, such as the world-wide research conducted on *Sesame Street* as well as educational programs for school-age children.

Chapter 6 discusses the application of all of the above in three distinct areas: a) media education – the rationale, curricula, and prac-tice around the world, both in formal institutions as well as informal parenting strategies; b) the development of broadcasting policy and regulations for children around the world, particularly regarding con-cern with issues such as broadcasting hours, inappropriate content for children, advertising practices, exposure of children on the screen, and sponsorships of quality programming; and finally c) the many public initiatives and activists' efforts at improving children's television and fostering global cooperation. These outstanding efforts highlight the value of cooperation between the worlds of academia and activism, both with their unique accumulated bodies of knowledge and person devoted to the betterment of the lives of children all over the world.

While these six chapters map the field of television and children in a logical and organized manner, such a presentation is somewhat misleading as clearly these issues are deeply interwoven and cannot be discussed independently of one another. Children are holistic human beings and need to be viewed as such: their cognitive development and learning do not stand independent of their social context or of their behaviors and worldviews. Therefore, in many ways, the book artificially fragments the field to facilitate the acquaintance of readers with this exciting field of study. Clearly, this "cake" could have been sliced differently as well. For example, we could have decided to pinpoint several central substantive topics (e.g., violence, advertising, fiction, news) and discuss each one of them from various angles. We could have followed age groups separately (e.g., babies, pre-school, elementary-school, middle-school children). We could have chosen other paths as well. What is offered here is but one way to organize the vast amount of accumulated knowledge. The book concludes with a brief review and discussion of the issues raised.

Painstaking efforts have been made to address the issues from as diverse theoretical and methodological points of view possible, as well as from studies conducted all over the world. This is no small under-taking, as much of the work is not accessible to English-speakers, myself included. Much important work has been published in professional and academic media in Spanish, French, German, Chinese, Japanese, and Arabic among other languages, with very little exchange between these isolated academic enclaves. One of my primary goals in making an effort to draw upon some of this non-English work is to initiate such intellectual dialogue, if only on paper for now.

I have used the proverbial "wide-brush strokes" in writing this book. As a result, specific details of research studies are not included in order to attain a more general, integrative view and to maintain the flow of the argument. Accordingly, bibliographic references are often cited together at the end of the discussion of each theme and appear as endnotes. Beyond their function to give appropriate credit to the authors upon whose work I draw and whose ideas and knowledge are discussed in the book, these citations primarily serve to point out directions for additional readings.

As you read the following pages you are invited to explore the field on various levels, choosing the one that fulfills your needs the best. You may choose to read the text alone, in its narrative style. You may want to pause and expand your knowledge and understanding by referring to the more informative and referenced readings suggested at the end of the book. In either case, I hope you will get as excited about this field as I am.

1

The Home of Television Viewing

Television Comes Home

Viewing television occurs mostly within the home, in a family context. It is so familiar that it is one of those areas of our life that we take "for granted" as part of everyday routine. Consequently, it is impossible to separate the study of children and television from the context within which it occurs – be it the physical conditions – the size of the set, the quality of reception, its location, the number of sets available, and the like; and the social conditions within which viewing takes place while engaging in other activities, in the presence of other family members, their use of television and the various influences on the children in the family. Further, viewing television is not only an individual act of one's choice, but often it is a result of adjustment, negotiation, compromises and imitation of others in the child's environment. What does viewing a particular program mean in such a rich context? Is it an active choice on the part of the child to watch television from among all the other activities available at the moment? Is it an active choice by the child to watch a particular program from among all other programs available at the moment? Is the child joining an older sibling's viewing choice? Does the child just happen to be around in the viewing area while an operating television set is on?

One social change that is a by-product of the transition to more modernized life has been the creation of family leisure time on one hand, and the growing emphasis on the home as a center of indoor life, on the other. Growing urbanization and concern for personal safety in the streets together with these trends create a fertile ground for the gradual growth of television's central role in family life. Clearly, this development is culturally dependent: many cultural differences may interact to create varied forms and amounts of television use. Longer school hours, warm weather, a safe rural neighborhood, active social life, child-labor, daily chores, quality of television reception, availability of channels – to name just a few – all play a significant role in shaping the centrality television has for children. In order to understand children growing up watching television in our own cultures, a comparison with others will enable us to see how the same phenomenon operates in different cultural contexts. Such a comparison is a necessary condition to building a more abstract universally applicable theory of the role television has in children's lives while recognizing and accounting for differences and diversity. Such a theory must account for such differences, at the micro-level, as the family's socio-economic status, parental occupation, income, education, and ethnicity; and, at the macro-level, structural issues that differ across cultures – national identity, historical background, underlying social or political conflicts, national goals, and characterization of the media systems available and their role in society.

More specifically, when it comes to television systems, there is wide variation from nation to nation in the historical development, shape of the media industry, the ideology embraced, the governmental, societal, and cultural mechanisms of control, preferred types of programming, tension between global and local forms of entertainment, and unique functions of and uses by audiences. It follows that understanding children's use of television in their everyday life is best analyzed as an interaction not only of individual, contextual, and social characteristics, but also of more general understanding of media as culturally situated.

Let us take, for example, a girl growing up in a society torn by a deep social conflict (such as between ethnic or religious groups) in which there is only one television station, which is owned by the dominant social group. News programs in this country are a central solidifying mechanism that serves to convey a sense of nationality that is highly revered by most viewers of the dominant group. Family members, perhaps some neighbors and relatives as well, may gather around the television set on a regular basis to watch the news program and argue as they do over the content broadcast. In this particular social context, the girl internalizes an understanding that television has both essential and ideological values, more far reaching than watching her favorite cartoon or comedy as a leisure activity. In comparison, a boy growing up in a relatively homogenized society that has not experienced overt conflicts, with a multi-channel commercial television in his room, in a culture in which viewing is regarded as a mindless pass-time accompanied by a reward system ("No TV until you have done your homework and cleaned your room!") may develop a very different attitude to television as a leisure activity.

Such cultural differences can be found not only between nations throughout major regions of the world, for example, Latin America in comparison with South Asia, but even within smaller geographical areas that seemingly have a lot more in common. A study of European children, for example, found that children growing up in countries that, historically, have been relatively more permissive in parenting style, such as Italy and Sweden, had higher private ownership of televisions in children's rooms, higher individual viewing and less parental mediation. In contrast, in France and Belgium, where parenting styles have been less permissive, television has been found to be a more integral part of the entire family and viewing took place more often in the presence of other family members. Thus, the contexts of television use and parental educational approaches seem to be part of a more complex and general pattern of cross-cultural differences including general attitudes toward the media, perceptions of the degree of privacy that should be granted children, division of space at home, availability of additional media, and the like.[1]

The way television in the family is integrated within more general ideological and cultural forces is demonstrated, for example, in differences in the socialization of children to television news that have been found in the USA and Israel. In middle class USA, families have adopted a defensive approach, trying to shield their children from a frightening world as it is often represented on television news. In Israel, however, middle-class parents encourage children to be involved in current affairs by offering a role model of regular news watching and by engaging in a discussion of the news during the broadcast. It seems that the norm of "good" parenting in middle-class homes in one society involves shielding children from the outside world while in another society just the opposite is the case: "good" parents are expected to encourage their children's involvement in their country's affairs through viewing television news.[2] From this example we can learn that children being raised in different societies are being socialized very differently to the role of news in a democratic society.

Another social dimension of interest regarding television viewing has to do with the diversity within each society itself, such as class differences. Unfortunately, much of the available research has been performed by – and on – middle class populations, as these are the ones most familiar and accessible to most researchers operating within academic institutions worldwide. However, several studies that focused on working class families in Western countries found that beyond income, education and occupational differences typical of such comparisons, there were also significant class differences in many aspects of family lives including their experiences in and approaches to child rearing, the different roles they take upon themselves in socialization of their children and the like. For example, "blue-collar" families in the USA were found to emphasize conformity, obedience, and adoption of conservative values in their children's education. In comparison, middle-class families emphasized motivations, affects, creativity and self-control. Such differences can have significant consequences on the role television occupies in the family. For example, do such differences shape strategies of parental viewing supervision, and if so, in what ways? What are the consequences of parents' employment experiences on viewing habits in the family? For example, allocation of time for various activities, too, has been found to be a social construction. Often working-class occupations involve strict time frameworks that leave the individual worker with little or no control over their schedule (e.g., a 9–5 job; a night shift; work around-the-clock during harvest season). In contrast, many middle and higher classes occupations allow more flexible time schedules and ideologies of efficiency and the view that "time is money." Such different conceptions of time are expressed not only in the allocation of time to various activities, including television viewing, but also in the ways in which time is "used." As a result, for example, parents from middle- and higher-class social groups who perceive time as a resource, express more concern over the time their children spend with television, perceive it as more "wasteful," and try to engage them in more pre-planned viewing than their lower-class counterparts – who tend to show less concern for time spent with the medium – to watch it more while engaged in a host of secondary activities, and to be more concerned about the actual content viewed.[3]

Sociological research dealing with the changes taking place in the modern family suggests that families in which both parents work are becoming less able to supervise their children's activities, resulting in their being left on their own which results in increased television viewing, in comparison with the situation several decades ago when a full time mother-home-maker was present to supervise children's after-school activities. However, this is also often the case for other forms of families as well, such as single-parent, immigrant, or working-class families. Such family situations are not as unusual as one might be led to believe based on middle-class grounded and oriented research, but compose a significant part of societies all over the world. When providing for a family's basic needs and striving to survive daily difficulties, worrying about children's TV viewing is hardly an issue of concern. Even parents who wish to be more involved in their children's viewing habits are forced, increasingly, due to their work schedule, to handle it through "remote control" by leaving clear instructions for the children, placing them in the care of family members, employing caretakers and babysitters, supervising them via phone-calls, and the like.

On many occasions, the main family gatherings occur around the television set, often at the end of a tiring day for all family members. In the USA, for example, the rapid diffusion of television during the 1950s and 1960s reached a saturation point in the 1990s when 98 percent of households owned at least one set and 65 percent owned more than one television. In the earlier period, viewing television was a family event for middle-class families who used to watch it together in their living rooms. Later, many American homes had dens or special TV rooms. The need to adjust to the centrality of this medium lead to several changes in behavioral patterns, including having dinners in front of the screen as well as changing bedtimes and associated habits. Changes in family structures, parenting styles, the need to juggle employment and child-reading missions, all brought about changes at the turn of the century in the place the medium of television plays in family life.[4]

Many researchers do not necessarily look at this form of family integration as a positive development. Some say that it hurts family life because of its routine, regular, mechanistic and ritualistic nature. While it forces family members to stay in the same physical vicinity, it controls their time together, and, so goes the argument, erases those unique family activities such as games, rituals, conversations, and the like. According to this critic, joint viewing of television takes place randomly, without planning. But what about those family events where viewing is a pre-planned, by choice, activity? What of the female bonding of mothers and daughters who view a romantic series together? Or the male bonding of fathers and sons while cheering on their favorite sports team? Or the nostalgic, cross-generational viewing of such programs as an old movie, a favorite comedy, a dramatic series, a special holiday event, or a political speech? In such cases and many others, television has the potential of being as much a stimulator of family integration as it is the other way around.

The introduction of smaller and more mobile televisions as well as those of better quality encouraged middle-and higher-class families to purchase additional sets. This trend resulted in the growing number of children who watch television on their own, often in their own bedrooms. The introduction of cable television as well as remote-control devices strengthened the trend of individual viewing. The result of this process is that in a multi-channel and multi-set environment, there are very few programs that attract all family members to come together for joint viewing.

While these trends are, of course, typical of developments of television viewing in Western societies and the more economically affluent segments in and outside of them, it is very different in cultures and sub-cultures with lower income levels, different dwelling conditions, and a more collective social orientation and value system. One way or another, television should be perceived as a central force in the complex social processes involving the many forms of family structures, goals and functioning all over the world.

The Role of Television in the Fabric of Family Life

Studying television viewing in its natural habitat, at home, is not a simple task. We do, of course, ask children – and their caregivers – about their viewing habits. We use surveys, conduct interviews by phone or face-to-face, and even ask them to fill in questionnaires in a school setting. They may (or may not) do their best to provide truthful and complete responses; they may (or may not) try to guess our intentions and provide what they perceive to be pleasing and socially accepted responses; they may (or may not) be able to be reflective over their own and other family members behaviors around the TV set. We also use data of television ratings provided by commercial and public companies in order to find out what children like to view, when, for how long, and with whom.

These are all very important sources of information and knowledge, yet they still leave us with a very incomplete picture of what viewing television in the home as a routine everyday experience is "really" like for children. To do so, we may wish to be invisible investigators, living in the homes of children all over the world, for long stretches of time, and gaining a first hand, non-intrusive experience with their lives.

Although researchers cannot be invisible, some have been able to become participant-observers of family life for a long enough period of time to be able to integrate comfortably into the fabric of family routines and so attain first hand understanding of their everyday "lives," including television viewing. First introduced into the study of television in the 1970s, ethnographies of family lives have slowly gained a following among researchers. These efforts are still disproportionately time consuming and limited in scope, yet extremely insightful and valuable. While reading the accounts and analyses provided by such studies, one stops to ponder: Is this the way things are happening in my family? Is this true for me as well? Do these issues resonate with my own reflections? Many of the findings reported below that attempt to answer these questions were gained through the practice of ethnographic research.

The social uses of television

One of the major contributions of such work was the realization that television serves many more functions and roles than those of providing entertainment or information.[5] The social uses of television are surprisingly diverse and can be generally divided into two groups: *structural* and *relational* uses. *Structural uses* of television are those that are non-content related and have to do with the mere use of the medium. For example, when television is used to provide background noise for routine household activities or a feeling that the house is "full" of people when a child is home alone. Television can also regulate much of a family's daily schedule: it can determine eating and bedtime hours, weekly routines and the like: when a mother encourages a resistant pre-schooler to take a nap by a tempting promise: "When you wake up from your nap, it will be time to watch your program;" or when a teen requests: "Let's have an early dinner tonight so I can see the soccer match." Running errands, scheduling social appointments and outdoor activities are often effected, directly or indirectly, by the television schedule.

Relational uses of television focus on the role of television in patterns of relationships between family members. For example, television can facilitate communication between them: to illustrate experiences, emotions or opinions, one may use a television character or scene. A familiar television episode can assist the child to gain access to a conversation as it provides an equalizing and common point of reference to all participants. Applying social knowledge and behaviors directly acquired from television in everyday situations confirms television's role as a social role model for imitation and problem solving, as much as for rejecting them. "I wish we could have solved our problems just like that ...," sighs the girl following "a happy ending" of the comedy she has been viewing. And, a father scolds his son, saying: "where do you think you are, in some television program?"

Viewing television as a family can facilitate conversation as much as it can depress it, depending on the circumstances. The viewing situation provides a common experience that brings the family together – in laughter, suspense, interest, as well as in physical expressions of togetherness, like body contact and hugging the child during viewing.

Avoiding interaction, too, is an important function of television for viewers. Television viewing and the attention it demands enables viewers to enjoy their privacy and to relieve social pressures for constant participation in conversation chats of an unpleasant nature. The child who seeks to unwind after a pressured day at school can watch a cartoon; a teen can wallow in melancholic feelings through viewing a sentimental movie; siblings seeking to separate themselves from the adults can do so by viewing pop-music. All of these family members use television viewing to demarcate the boundaries of their personal space.

Using television to demonstrate competence as well as to attain dominance in the family setting is a common form of social use, too. Controlling children's viewing, for example, is a clear marker of family hierarchy as is controlling the remote-control or managing the video-recorder. Family members may use television to assert their status in the family as well as to establish areas of expertise: for example, when they guess the plot's development, answer a quiz question correctly, or elaborate on the content of a news item.

On the other hand, the struggles over program choices are often a battle field representing the family's power-relationships: Do younger children have as much a say in selecting programs viewed as their older siblings? Research tells us that more often than not children join the programs viewed by older members of the family, than vice-versa. Do female family members have an equal chance of participating in and influencing program choice? Apparently not, as it seems that fathers dominate viewing in households studied. Does anyone have the power to veto viewing choices at his or her digression? Once again, it was found to be the father. Is there one person who has the power to say the final word? Here too, it was the father. Thus, as noted previously, we can learn a lot about parenting styles and gender relationships from the way families organize themselves around the set. Put another way, television viewing in the family is always contextualized within a particular social environment.[6]

Gender, in particular, above personal characteristics related to age and to social class, was found to be a central structural principle organizing many households' viewing styles. Men and women often describe their viewing habits and preferences in very different, often contradictory, terms. Understanding such differences, on the basis of the more general gender-related division of labor in the family, serves as an outstanding illustration of the need to understand children's television viewing within a social context and not as an arbitrary individual act. For most men around the globe, even in progressive societies in terms of gender-equality, the home is still viewed by them as a place of rest and leisure, a sanctuary from the public sphere in which they spend most of their days. For women, including the growing number employed outside the home, the *home* is an endlessly demanding work-environment. As a result of this substantial differ-ence, many men, as well as the boys who learn from their example, devote themselves to their viewing heartedly, while women, who are a model for their daughters, often approach viewing with feelings of guilt for the "waste of time" while multi-tasking with household and child-rearing chores.

Gender differences are visible in a variety of other viewing behaviors. While there is the danger of over-generalizing, there is substantial evidence that men (and teenager sons) are more often dominant in the making of viewing choices, particularly in cases of family disagreements; they are more in charge of the remote-control in the family setting; in doing so, they "zap" (i.e., quickly change from one channel to the other, often during commercials), "zip" (i.e., fast-forward program segments while watching a videotape), "graze" or "surf" (i.e., change from one channel to another, staying at each for a few seconds to explore or check the program) much more often than women (who often become so annoyed with this behavior that they prefer to leave the room); they view uninterruptedly for longer stretches of time; are more impatient with conversations while viewing; and have very   different viewing preferences.

Women, on the other hand, some of whom actually spend more time around an operating television set, perceive most of their viewing as a secondary, unplanned activity, often a wasteful one. However, they do admit that viewing a particularly favorite program, often an engaging romantic series when the rest of the family is absent, asleep, or otherwise occupied, is a special treat that they *allow* themselves. As in other domains of everyday life, women often chose to avoid conflict with other members of the family over their personal viewing preferences and pleasures, and retreat to realize their personal choices at other, more private, times. In addition, women tend to talk about their viewing with others more than men (with the exception of sports and politics), and chose to seek a male's help in operating television-related equipment, such as setting the VCR.

The latter finding has been explained as a result of a combination of at least two social trends: the historical conception of technology as a male domain, on the one hand, and women's choice to maintain this balance, on the other hand, by demonstrating "calculated-ignorance" regarding technology as a way to avoid adding another chore to their already abundant number of household responsibilities.

Feminist theories perceive such gender differences to be a result of deeply ingrained cultural constructions and social arrangements, rather than a simplified ascription to biological differences. Accordingly, boys and girls in all societies are socialized to prevalent sex-roles, in general, and internalize viewing behaviors that construct them, in particular, as "appropriately" female or male. Deviations from these norms are clearly more visible in families where mothers are educated, have higher

professional and economical status, and who are practicing more gen-
der-equal parenting styles.

Beyond quite universal gendered differences, family viewing rituals
are also grounded in a wider cultural environment and have culturally
specific characteristics. In different cultures, families arrange the physical viewing space differently, have different concepts regarding time
and its use, hold different age and gender power structures, and the like.
For example, adolescents in Asian countries (Taiwan, Korea and China,
in one study) were more likely to view television with their family
members, while the ones from the USA were more likely to view with
friends or alone. The concept of time, as another example, was interpreted and practiced very differently in Denmark compared to Pakistan
in the 1980s. As in many other countries during this period, so too in
Denmark television schedules were fixed and well known in advance,
and thus allowed for planning family meals around them. In Pakistan,
on the other hand, the concept of time was much more flexible and
non-orderly, irregularities in broadcast schedules were normative, so
that audiences were neither angered nor disturbed by them.[7]

The typical North American "TV-dinner" of ready to prepare and
serve frozen meals as well as "take-away" food or the culinary prepar-
ations for "Superbowl Night" (annual final match of the American
football games) viewing parties may seem quite odd to an outsider,
an Israeli for example. North American viewers, on their part, may be
completely perplexed by the loud argumentativeness that is part of the
"rituals" of viewing the news and political talk-shows in Israel. The
introduction of additional viewing technologies – such as the video
recorder, allowed adjustments to be made in family viewing habits and
power "hierarchies" and created new behavioral rituals – such as family
viewing times, recording schedules and responsibilities, preparation
and consumption of meals and the like.

We can conclude that children's viewing habits are not necessarily a
result of their own personal choice, but a result of complicated family
constraints. Children learn from their parents, older siblings, and other
significant people in their lives a variety of viewing habits, patterns of
use of the remote control, strategies for choosing programs, and appropriate gendered behaviors, all of which become part of their independent viewing repertoire.

Television viewing and communication patterns in the family

Television viewing, so we have seen, is integrated within the family's
general interpersonal communication patterns. However, we can go one
step further in distinguishing between different types of families based

on their communication patterns in order to examine how these affect their children's television viewing. Two central dimensions have been identified in the research: *social* orientation and *conceptual* orientation, with each family located on a continuum between low to high in orientation. Accordingly, families with high *social* orientation are characterized by encouraging their children to get along with other family members, to withhold as much as possible from engaging in confrontations, to depress anger, and to stay "out of trouble." The importance of preserving peace and quiet at home and avoiding hurting others' feelings are central values in the socialization processes of children growing up in these families. In contrast, families with a high *concept* orientation encourage an atmosphere of open communication, free expression of ideas and conceptual debates. Children in these families are exposed to different sides and perspectives on controversial issues and their parents encourage them to voice their opinions and to argue about them. The central emphasis in such families is on ideas, rather than on feelings.[8]

In studies attempting to distinguish between these general types of families, children are asked to rate the frequency of parental statements such as the following:

- How often do your parents say that children should give way in an argument and not irritate others?
- How often do your parents say that it is inappropriate for children to express anger during an argument?
- How often do your parents say that children should not argue with adults?

Children who respond to such questions with a high number of "frequently" or "very frequently" are raised in families with a more social orientation. In contrast, children who respond more often "frequently" and "very frequently" to the following questions are raised in families with a more concept orientation:

- How often does one of you have a different opinion from the rest of the family when you talk at home about issues such as politics or religion?
- How often do your parents say that it is important to express ideas, even if they are disliked by others?
- How often do your parents encourage family members to challenge the ideas and opinions of others?

The type of family orientation influences a wide variety of personality traits in children. Those growing up in typically social orientation families tend to be more cooperative, disciplined, expressive, and easy to be around, while children from concept orientation homes tend to be more argumentative and to provide facts and opinions, they are higher achievers at school, and more involved politically.

Interestingly enough, family orientation was found in the USA to influence children's viewing habits, as well. As a general rule, socially oriented families view television more, but are lighter consumers of news and current events programs. They perceive television to be primarily an entertainment medium and means of producing family solidarity. In contrast, children from high concept-oriented families, use television more as a source of keeping up-to-date with the news and much less for entertainment purposes. They are lighter television viewers, use it less for social purposes, and their parents are more involved in regulating their viewing behaviors. As a result, they are less exposed to television violence, identify less with aggressive characters, and are less involved in relating televised characters to their own life experiences.

Children who grow up in a variety of combinations of the two family orientations create varying types of typical communication patterns, including the use of media. Thus, television viewing habits and preferences are clearly not only an individual choice or personality trait, but are greatly affected by familial characteristics. In turn, the fact that families are also formed within a particular cultural setting, too, must be taken into account. For example, in collective-oriented cultures, such as more traditional ones, or those deeply divided by a conflict, where cooperation and conformity to the collective is more highly regarded and children are discouraged from expressing individuality and encouraged to fit in, we may expect social orientation families to be more of the norm and, as a result, stronger emphasis is placed on the social roles of television.

Parenting styles and mediation

What is the meaning of a joint family viewing or its absence? What are its possible consequences? What role do parents play as mediators between the world of television and that of children, either through direct intervention (by setting viewing rules and conversation, for example) or indirect influence (by providing role models for their children)?

The viewing "rules" that shape viewing habits of families worldwide are often informal and non-visible. When interviewing family members, researchers often find themselves raising issues that operate on a subconscious level in the family, revealing agreements that are embedded deep within everyday life that have never been actually discussed nor even spoken out loud. Therefore, it is not enough to interview just one family member. For example, children may be completely unaware of the viewing rules, followed or violated, that the mother may be explaining to an interviewer. This poses an interesting theoretical issue: since viewing television is such a routine, taken-for-granted activity, any attempt to formalize the norms involved in it may seem completely useless. Viewing "rules" are behavioral directives based on the family's general value and normative system, but they can also be easily overturned by them. For example, a family might have a rule that "no TV after 9:00 p.m." or "no TV during dinnertime," but may actually encourage their youngster to break these rules on occasion and join them for a viewing of a special media-event, a favorite program, or a cultural event.

Clearly, parents' involvement in their children's viewing may be related to at least three levels. First, is the level of "awareness and co-viewing:" the degree to which parents are around during viewing, are familiar with the content of the programs their children are viewing, offer their children role models of viewing habits, and even view with them. Second is the level of "supervision," also termed "restrictive mediation," which relates to the degree to which parents supervise and restrict the amount of television viewing of their children, viewing times and viewing content, and use viewing as forms of reward or punishment; and to what degree do they monitor secondary viewing behaviors (e.g., doing homework or eating while viewing)? Finally, "instructive mediation" level relates to the degree to which parents mediate between their children and the television content viewed – through conversation, explanation, value judgments, processing of emotions, understanding information, application of learning, critical evaluation and the like.[9]

One common way to study and to assess forms of parental involvement with children's viewing asks parents to rate their behaviors on scales. For example, the following statements can be rated on a five-point scale: from: "never," "rarely," "occasionally," "often," to "very often ":[10]

- My child is allowed to turn the television on without asking permission.
- There are several programs that our family watches together regularly.
- There are several programs that I encourage my child to watch on television.
- I encourage my child to watch during particular times of the day.
- I put limits on how much time my child can watch television.

- There are certain television programs that I forbid my child to watch.
- My child and I disagree on viewing rules.
- My child and I talk about specific television content.
- My child asks me to explain television content.

Responses to such questions help researchers map the different parental-viewing-interventions styles. Notice that viewing interventions do not necessarily mean restricting television viewing, as is commonly accepted. If we operate under the assumption that television has positive as well as negative potential for children, we should expect parental interventions to include encouraging certain viewing behaviors: calling children's attention to valuable programs, applying television content to everyday experiences, using viewing opportunities as a positive socializing force, and the like. How often do we hear parents telling their children: "Why don't you do your homework later – come watch with us this great program about …?"? According to most research reports – apparently parents do not make such types of comments very often.

Viewing television together with children has been demonstrated to be a desirable activity. In doing so, parents are able to assist their children to understand the medium of television as well as its content, to encourage them to internalize messages selectively and critically, to intervene immediately when children are exposed to objectionable content in their opinion, to handle emotional reactions of children, and the like. The fact that more and more children are engaged in individual viewing, in the privacy of their own room or when there is no adult supervision at home – denies them this possibility.

These three dimensions of potential parental intervention – awareness, supervision, and instructive mediation – are intertwined with parents' own attitudes towards television. Some perceive television to be a destructive force in their children's lives, even to the point of believing in the addictive power of the medium, and so take a protective position towards it. Others may see the positive sides involved in viewing television, and its role in providing entertainment, relaxation, and information to their children. Yet another group of parents may find that television assists them in the task of raising and socializing their children. While others my take a liberal stance towards their children's viewing, allowing them the freedom to determine their own viewing habits.

This kind of research emphasizes the importance of understanding the place of television in the lives of children as an integral part of the socialization processes taking place in the family as a social unit. For their part, parents derive their attitudes towards television from a much more general public discourse related to their perception of children's developmental processes and their own role as parents and educators. Research evidence suggests that parents who have more negative attitudes toward television are more likely to engage in various forms of mediation. Mothers who are more involved in child rearing to start with are usually also more involved in this form of parenting than fathers.

The attempt to find a delicate balance between the desire to protect children from the undesirable aspects of reality, such as violence, on one hand, and the desire to prepare them to handle the complexity of adult life, on the other hand, creates a dilemma for parents that has no easy solution. Setting clear viewing rules and guidelines are not going to resolve such a dilemma. This is an issue that is negotiated on a daily basis between the children and the parents, and between the parents themselves. Parents are aware of their inability to completely control their children's viewing and its influence on them. Many are not interested, willing to and/or able to assume responsibility for deciding what is good or bad for their children to view. Children, on their part, know from quite an early age what their parents' viewing expectations are and often echo them in their own responses to researchers' using statements such as, "too much television viewing can hurt your eyes" or "cartoons are bad for you."

Clearly, those attitudes cannot be viewed independently of the surrounding environment and the other leisure options available to children. Whether television viewing is perceived as "good or bad" for one's children is always a relative matter and, hence, the question is – compared to what? Compared to hanging out on the street in an urban slum area? To helping out in the fields or at home? To getting into trouble with armed soldiers or guerilla fighters? To taking guitar lessons in the community center? To playing soccer in the neighborhood playground? Television-related middle-class values of what is "good" or "bad" for one's children can be completely irrelevant or even a luxury in other social settings. A child of a lower income family with limited leisure options may do well spending time in front of television. Thus, perceptions of the value of television viewing as "good" or "bad" for children are clearly relativistic and culture-laden. Indeed, so is the mere posing of the question in a binary manner.

Let us also note that there is hardly any reference in the extant research literature to the unique mediating needs of special populations of children: whether they are those who are mentally gifted or those who have learning and behavioral disabilities. There is evidence to suggest, for example, that children with emotional disorders, learning disabilities, and mental difficulties are potentially more sensitive to the influences of television and thus need more direct parental involvement and mediation, as they do in other realms of their lives. In comparison to children without such special needs, they usually watch more television, prefer more violent programs and characters, demonstrate stronger identification with television characters, tend to concentrate more on the salient aspects of programs, have difficulty understanding television content, and assign high levels of realism to television content.[11] However, these are limited findings and much more attention should be devoted to both research and development of appropriate educational interventions for this population of viewers.

Television-Related Conversations

Conversation is one of the main means that parents employ in their attempts to be involved with their children's television viewing and its consequences. Just as understanding viewing requires contextualizing it, so research of television-related conversation must be studied within the social and physical surroundings: the room setting, the presence of other family members and their composition, social norms of behavior and the like. Naturally, individual characteristics influence the nature of interaction too: the degree of a parent's or child's fatigue or alertness, involvement and excitement from over-viewing, as well as personal tendency for talkativeness. Finally, the nature of the program viewed affects the interactions as well – some programs are better facilitators of talk than others. As with other issues that we will be discussing, a comprehensive account of any aspect of television viewing has to take into consideration characteristics of the context, the viewer, and the medium.

Conversation types

Television-related conversations can be divided into two main categories: those oriented to information and those to behaviors. Often the two types are intertwined in the natural flow of talk.

Information-oriented conversations develop due to the fact that television presents children a world with which they are unfamiliar, one that raises many questions and stimulates children to seek more information. For example, an excerpt from a study in the USA, relates a conversation between an 8-year-old boy and his mother over the issue of the death penalty, while viewing an action-adventure drama:[12]

Son: Is there still an electric chair?

Mother: In some states. They want to vote on it.

Son: What is it?

Mother: It's a chair where they strap you down like this. [She demonstrates.] And then they pass an electric current through you so you die. It's not good.

Conversations such as this expose several additional dimensions of conversation to the informative, such as the moral and the political. Parents' comments can expand the child's informative world and/or reinforce knowledge gained from other sources, including the school system. This is demonstrated for example, when a 12-year-old girl in the above study asked for information about England's King George III, following a viewing of a theater production (*Masterpiece Theater*), her mother explained to her that he was the king of England during the American revolution, to which the child responded that indeed, she had learned about it in class. Thus, verbal intervention of parents has a very important role in reinforcing direct and intended learning from television content, as is often the case with educational and informative content. Further, it was found that children remember information presented on the news much better when their parents elaborate on that information.

Simply watching a program with children and making limited comments can advance learning. Mothers watching the pre-school educational program *Sesame Street* with their children encouraged better attention to the program, more efficient learning from it, as well as much more fun watching it! Interestingly enough, often even the mere presence of adults during viewing, even without any form of intervention, is very valuable for young viewers. An adult viewing together with a child conveys a message of interest in and respect for the program, as well as, the pleasure gained from a social sense of "togetherness." Thus, even "passive" adult participation encourages the child to pay more close attention to the program, thus increasing the chances for better learning.

For example, in Israel, it was found that the mere presence of mothers during the child's viewing not only increased viewing time, but encouraged and stimulated the child to be actively involved with it. In the USA, children demonstrated better learning of letters and numbers following viewing with mediating adults who called their attention to these messages and gave them feedback during viewing. Adults' verbal interventions, such as – "this letter is called B;" "let's read this word together;" or "look, the Giraffe is a vegetarian, he only eats plants" – have very positive influences on children's learning from television, just as they would when parents engage children about other stimuli in their environment. Clarification points regarding television content made by parents during viewing times such as "what she means is that …" or "he was referring to …" improved children's ability to understand and make inferences from television content, and thus complement young viewers' lack of knowledge and experience. Similarly, parental verbal intervention contributed to children's abilities to make better comparisons between television reality and their understanding of everyday life.[13]

As we can see, a lot of information, some trivial, is acquired through viewing and discussion. Occasionally, joint viewing can also induce conversations on very fundamental and sensitive topics, such as sexual relationships, death, suicide, prejudice, religious beliefs and the like, and create opportunities to elaborate on ideologies and value systems that do not come up naturally during everyday family routines or that otherwise make family members uncomfortable in discussing. "Let's talk today about homosexuality" does not sound like a natural conversation opener around the dinner table. It could, however, come up naturally following viewing a comic stereotype or a news item discussing the debate over gay-marriage. Like their children, parents differ greatly in their capabilities to cope with such queries; from complete inability to respond all the way to seizing nearly every opportunity to engage the child in deep and serious conversation.

The second type of conversations, the behavioral, refers to those where family members discuss behaviors observed on television as related to their own or to others' real-life experiences. For example, when a parent tells a child "in our family we don't hit each other like that;" or a child says to a parent "See! Why can't I have that too?" In conversations such as these, the content viewed on television provides a basis for comparison with the child's real-life experiences, often presenting the latter as much preferable. An illustration of this was related to me in a focus group of pre-adolescent girls in Israel: "Let's say we are watching *Beverly Hills*. My mother immediately will go: 'see how she has no shame at all!' My parents really like to teach me a lesson from movies. For example: 'see how she behaves; how would you have been in that situation'? those kind of questions".[14] A similar exchange in a study in the USA was observed while a 5-year-old boy and his mother were watching a soap opera with a divorced mother as a character. In responding to her son's inquiry about divorce, the mother reinforced her faith in their family's loving relationship and remarked on the pain involved in divorce.[15]

In addition, television-related conversations can also serve a significant role in helping children understand the constructed nature of the television world and to distinguish it from life in their own social environment. Parents comment to their children about the reality of television in a variety of ways: "This is (or is not) how things happen in the real world;" "This is (or is not) real." A particular case in point is reference to "television families," such as those depicted in situation comedies and dramas, since often they deal with a realm of life relevant to children who are members of any sort of family. How much do children perceive these families to be similar to families with which they are familiar, including their own family? How do parents' comments facilitate children's ability to be critical consumers of portrayals of family life on television?

As we will see in Chapter 2, understanding the nature of "real" on television is a very complicated developmental task, one that is dependent to a great degree on the child's cognitive development as well as on his or her accumulated experience with everyday life inside and outside of the television world. Parents' comments can greatly facilitate development of their children's critical abilities by reinforcing, expanding on, as well as negating television content; by exposing the unique audio-visual means by which television represents the world; as well as, by providing additional sources of information and knowledge as the basis for comparisons.

Television as a talking book[16]

Even babies and toddlers at the stage of initial language acquisition were found to be able to benefit greatly from active, joint viewing with a caring adult. For example, we know that while viewing educational programs geared to their needs, such as *Sesame Street*, they learn vocabulary and concepts (e.g., geometrical shapes, colors) and are better able to identify letters and numbers. This process can be aided, as one North American mother of a 15 months-old baby-girl reported: "She learned to count from *Sesame Street* and we reinforced it. I say: 'one,' and she would say: 'two-three-four' and then I say 'five' and she would say 'six'."

Parents of babies and toddlers are more active in employing television content as "a talking book," perhaps because this age group requires both closer supervision and more intensive investment in language development. Participant observation studies of parents caring for their young ones revealed at least three types of inter-related verbal exchanges: Designating, questioning, and responding.

- *Designating:* the practice of naming of objects and characters appearing on television helps both language acquisition as well as conceptual development. "What is this?" a 2-year-old toddler asked her mother. "Look, it's a flashlight. You see, it gives light," responded the mother. Mothers corrected their children's vocabulary: a 20 month-old toddler watching a cartoon pointed and said: "Dog!" "No," responded the mother, "it's a rabbit, and also a cat." Parents encourage their children to practice new vocabulary. For example, during viewing of *Sesame Street,* a father asked his 15 month-old baby daughter: "What is this?" "A frog," responded the baby. "And what's that?" continues the father in calling her attention to the screen, "hop, hop, hop" responded the baby. "What is it?" The mother continues to challenge the baby. "Ball" she responds. "Ball," mirrors the mother, "Three balls. One, two, three."

- *Questioning*: Parents direct questions to their children for a variety of reasons, including trying to direct their attention to the set, to express their own involvement in the viewing, or as a rhetorical question, one to which they are not really expecting an answer. For example, they commonly say: "Do you want to watch ...?" as they place the child in front of the television set and turn it on. Often the questions were not really intended to start a conversation, as they are behavioral directives, a form of viewing supervision and mediation.

- *Responding*: Parents respond to their children's viewing behaviors, as they may be mirroring back their verbal utterances, expanding and/or correcting them. Here is an example of an exchange between a 25 month-old toddler-girl and her mother while they were viewing *Sesame Street. Girl*: "Boy." *Mother*: "Boy." *Girl*: "Yellow boy." *Mother*: "Yellow boy." *Girl*: "Boy." *Mother*: "Another boy. What kind of a boy is this?" *Girl*: "Brown boy." *Mother*: "Brown boy. And what is this?" *Girl*: "Girl." Parents also respond to children's behaviors in a directive manner: "No, turn this on again!" or "Here is your song! Do you want to dance?" as well as answering direct questions. For example, in response to a 23 month-old toddler-girl's question: "Is she going to pre-school?" the mother said: "No she is not, although she wished she could." Girl continued: "Am I going back to pre-school?" "We just got home," answers the mother.

The above illustrations demonstrate the unique contribution of studies collecting observational data within the natural environment of viewing television, as complementing other studies that are based on parental reporting of their children's behaviors. They provide us with unique insights into the dynamics of interactions occurring around an operating television set. What is the meaning of this kind of conversations for parents and their children? How are they being integrated within the patterns of behavioral norms prevalent in their families?

How consistent are the parents in their reactions to behaviors on television? How prevalent are such interactions in cultural contexts outside of the North American ones observed? Those questions are of great importance in evaluating the influence such conversations may have on children's behaviors.

From what we know, however, about children's viewing of television around the world, it seems that joint viewing is the rare occasion. Parents are usually over-committed, overly tired, and if they happen to be at home, they may well use children's viewing as a quiet time to get something done or to re-charge their own batteries. If so, then the most common type of parental intervention is an incidental comment by a parent walking in and out of the room, mostly of a negative nature: "turn the volume down," or "what is this nonsense you are watching, don't you have anything better to do?" Even if these comments may be appropriate, they do little to encourage critical viewing of television and rather convey a general negative message toward the medium that may inhibit potentially positive learning experiences, when such are available. We can, therefore, conclude that while parents can potentially play many important roles in mediating television viewing, they differ greatly in their aptitude, motivation, skills, and circumstances that facilitate doing so.

Conversations and fear

A much debated public concern is the important issue of parents' ability to mediate frightening television images, particularly those dealing with the negative sides of human existence – wars, disasters, poverty, evil actions, and famine. Children today are exposed increasingly to such phenomena due to their high media presence, even in homes where parents actively try to shield them from such events. In an increasingly global world, even crises and catastrophes that take place in countries thousands of miles away become relevant issues for children's daily lives. Children must cope with these frightening, worrying events that were once the preserve of adults alone. They have to endeavor to assimilate the fragments of information they receive from the media and try to make sense of them. They have to deal emotionally with the suffering of others and with gruesome portrayals of atrocities.[17] Clearly the picture they develop of such events is a function of their developmental stage, life experiences, and the media offerings available to them. However, adult mediation at home and in their educational systems was found to be of particular importance.

Clearly, frightening television content can be fictitious, based on real events or even a direct broadcast of events happening in real time. What is "scary" or "non-scary" content is not an absolute concept, as children may react very differently to these contents, depending on their age, experiences, context of viewing, how relevant is the threat to their own lives, and the like. For example, a pre-school-age child may be very threatened by make-believe monsters, sudden noises, close-ups shots of snakes, or even dark scenes, but will be completely indifferent to a video footage or news discussion of weapons of mass destruction. A child living in Palestine, Chechnya, and Iraq may react completely differently to a scene depicting tanks and soldiers, than one living in New Zealand, Italy, and Uruguay. North American children may react very differently to news about terrorism following the events of 9/11 than before them and South African children may be particularly sensitive to discussion of AIDS, high rates of mortality, and the large number of children living in orphanages in their country, in comparison to those growing up in the Nordic countries.

Similarly, parental strategies necessary for handling fear reactions are very different too. Younger children can be more easily comforted by physical strategies such as holding them, hugging a security object (e.g., favorite blanket or stuffed toy), or snacking than by any verbal strategy. They have a hard time understanding the concepts of "rarely," "very low chance" often used in attempting to distance children from threatening messages: "earthquakes rarely happen;" "the chance of an airplane crash is very low;" "these kinds of catastrophes usually take place in other parts of the world" and the like are not very efficient with children below school age. It is very difficult to verbally convince young children that something that looks scary may not really be dangerous at all, while something that looks very appealing, is indeed dangerous. As children grow older, however, they need to be gradually approached cognitively in order to learn to recognize real threats, while reinforcing their sense that things are "under control," and that the adults in their lives and in their society are working hard to protect them.[18]

Studies conducted following traumatic events that effected children in many countries of the world in various manners, such as Gulf War in 1993, the September 11 2002 events in the New York, or the war in Iraq that began in 2003 (and that continues as these lines are being written) reveal to us that an "ostrich" strategy that assumes that children are not aware and are not concerned is simply wrong. Research of children's reactions suggests that their television-related questions need to be attended to and answered honestly when appropriate and, as well, their fears and concerns respected and legitimized. They need to know that their feelings and fears are being taken seriously and not dismissed by statements, such as "you're still too young to understand," or "you shouldn't be watching this." If the child has already begun to watch a program, it is too late to tell him or her that "there is nothing to worry about." What they need in such a situation is to be offered means to express their anxiety and to share their thoughts about what to do about the situation, as minor as it may seem.[19]

Disturbing news that related to the emotional well-being of children has been a focus of research and educational concern and has elicited attempts to find ways to help children cope with fearful elements of the television world. However, little attention has been directed to the role such portrayals on television serve in developing in children a sense of social responsibility, civic awareness, empathy, compassion and ethical issues related to the pain and suffering of others. Parents all over the globe who are raising their children within such perspectives can find television to be an immensely important resource for discussing social issues and developing a humanitarian understanding by their children.

Conversations with siblings and peers

Very little attention in research has been directed to date to the joint viewing of children with their siblings and friends as well as to the television-related conversations they hold. This is quite surprising given that this is the most common viewing situation among children who grow up in the same household and should be expected to have an important role in their social, emotional, and cognitive development. From the little we know, children enjoy talking while viewing, as do many adults. They talk about the program, they talk about the logistics involved in the viewing, and they often embark on conversations stimulated by the viewing, but may meander a long way away from it.

Here too, data collected during a few observational studies in the USA provide us with some insights as to how this process operates in its natural habitat. For example, children were found to ask older siblings for explanations and clarifications: "What is it?" "Why is he doing it?" "What does she mean?" are typical of such questions. Other questions they might ask relate to understanding the codes and conventions of the audio-visual language. For example, typical questions relate to trying to understand the use of the "flashback" ("how come he is back there?"), "re-runs" ("how did she do it again?"), "slow-motion" ("how can they run so slowly?"). Similarly, children can facilitate younger siblings' understanding of the structural characteristics of the broadcast schedule. For example, here is an interaction between 9- and 6-year-old brothers concerning the concept of a television "promo" following viewing for one for a *Pacman* cartoon.[20] The younger boy asked: "Can I see something for a second? (changes channel for a few seconds) not yet." *Observer*: "What do you want to see?" *Child*:

"They're showing *Pacman.*" The older brother shouted: "They said this Fall ... Tell me, is it Fall yet?" The exchange between the two brothers clearly served to help the younger one learn the meaning of a "promo" for a program that is intended for broadcast at a later time.

Other "why?" "how?" and "what will happen now?" types of questions relate directly to understanding the narrative. Older children provided explanations and expressed their viewing tastes and preferences during the viewing and, in doing so, may have shaped those developing in their younger siblings. For example, while viewing a new series, the older of three brothers declared: "No way are we watching this goofy show – it's for dummies." The two younger brothers agreed and the channel was switched.

Older children's responses during the viewing can facilitate understanding, allow the young child to keep up with the narrative and to acquire some basic television-literacy skills, as well as to help shape more general attitudes toward television, just as adults do. Similarly, when children watch with other children, be they siblings and/or friends, they are socially attentive and influenced by their behaviors, attention level and interactions. Joint viewing is sometimes just that – a fun way to spend time together.[21]

Concluding Remarks

The discussion of viewing television within the home environment highlighted the centrality of understanding this everyday behavior as contextualized within family patterns and, in turn, how those are shaped by a host of more general social processes. Television is an important force in family life due to its central place in a family's daily routines and the many social and personal roles it serves for all members of the family. The concept of mediation allowed us to replace the commonly asked question of how television affects children with a very different one: how family life and the reciprocal relationships within it shape the experiences different family members have with the medium. This approach emphasizes the important role of understanding everyday life and routine behaviors, including those related to television viewing.

We have pointed out that such phenomena require a kind of research methodology that can investigate and problematize both the depth and the nuances of children's television viewing in everyday life. To do so requires a shift from functionalist theories of human behavior, including the sole application of quantitative measures to study them, through surveys and experimental designs. What it requires is inclusion of theories that posit that an active negotiation process is used by children as viewers and consider the contents of their viewing as a form of meaning making grounded in specific contexts. Consequently, it also calls for different methods of inquiry: Qualitative approaches that employ participant observation and in-depth interviews were found extremely valuable in documenting and analyzing the dynamics of the very act of television viewing.

We have also argued that discussion of families and everyday life needs to be rooted in an understanding of the complexity of cross-cultural differences including the different values attached to viewing television and diverse practices of its use. The way television fits in family routines is shaped by the wider culture, its values, traditions, and history. The concept "family" itself, as the social context of viewing, has a wide variety of meanings in different societies, as does the term "domestic" and its relationship to the "public." Different societies change over time, social norms allow flexibility, growth, and accommodation to change, including to the significant changes that have taken place in home entertainment technologies such as television and its accessories.

This is why it is so important to study the meaning of television in the family longitudinally, as it changes over time, going through some typical milestones of development. What is the role of television in family life during the early years of child rearing? When children grow up? When they leave the home? When the parents are in retirement? Changes in the structure of both traditional and modern families, which are taking place rapidly in recent times, allow for many forms of family arrangements. At the same time, the medium of television has changed dramatically too – with the growing viewing options, cable subscriptions, satellite technologies, interactive computerized viewing, and cellular viewing. All of these define the study of television in the family today as a dynamic, meaningful, and fascinating field of inquiry. Children, too, are a diverse and complicated group of people who undergo significant changes as they grow up. How do children of various ages understand television content? What is the relationship between their development and the meanings they acquire from their viewing? We will turn now to the next chapter to explore these questions.

Notes

1   Livingstone and Bovill (2001).
2   Lemish (1998a).
3   Jordan (1992).

4 Andreason (2001).

5 Lull (1980a; 1980b).

6 Gray (1987), Livingstone (1992), Morley (1986), Walker and Bellamy (2001).

7 For Pakistan–Denmark comparison see Lull (1988). For discussion of European countries see Pasquier (2001). For comparison of Asia and USA see Shanahan and Morgan (1992).

8 Chaffee and McLeod (1972), Chafee, McLeod, and Wackman (1973).

9 Buerkel-Rothfuss and Buerkel (2001), Tidhar and Levinson (1997), Valkenburg, Krcmar, Peetrs, and Marseille (1999), Warren (2003).

10 Based on a series of studies at the Center for Research on the Influences of Television on Children (CRITC) headed at the time by Aletha Huston and John Wright.

11 Abelman (1995), Sprafkin, Gadow, and Abelman (1992).

12 Quotes taken from Messaris (1983, pp. 295–6).

13 See for example: Collins, Sobol, and Westby (1981), Lemish (1987), Reiser, Tessmer and Phelps (1984), Salomon (1977), Vandewater, Park, and Wartella (2005). For a review see Fisch (2004, chapter 9).

14 Lemish (1998b).

15 Messaris (1983).

16 Based on Lemish and Rice (1986). All quotes in this section are taken from this study.

17 Smith and Moyer-Guse (in press); Smith and Wilson (2002), Walma van der Molen (2004), Walma van der Molen, Valkenburg, and Peeters (2002).

18 Cantor (1996), Cantor (2002), Smith, Moyer, Boyson, and Pieper (2002).

19 See for example a collection of articles in Lemish and Götz (forthcoming).

20 All quotes from Alexander, Sallayanne Rayan, and Munoz (1984, p. 358). See also Haeffner and Wartella (1987).

21 Jenkins (1990).

2

Television and Individual Development

Developmental Theories

Television viewing is portrayed as a mindless activity by some critics. According to this populist notion, children sit in front of the medium and expect to be entertained. No one challenges them to remember what they view, to analyze it critically, or even to pay full attention to it. However, as we will demonstrate in this chapter, children are not the passive viewers claimed in the populist notion. Rather, research confirms that they chose to engage with the medium and its content in a variety of active ways, including managing their attention to it; making meanings out of its messages; analyzing and criticizing; and selectively remembering it.

"Reading" the television text, a concept borrowed from the Cultural Studies approach to media, refers to the process of making meaning of television messages and relating them to various other meaning systems available in everyday life. This activity requires viewers to use a variety of cognitive strategies related to thought and perception. Thus, we can ask questions such as: What attracts children to television? What do they understand? How do they make sense of information? What do they remember? How do they relate these experiences to their everyday knowledge?

The underlying premise of various approaches that focus on the interaction of the individual child with the medium of television is that children's cognitive, emotional, and social skills develop over time. This is based on the assumption adopted from developmental psychological theories: Children make meaning out of television programs with the skills and tools that they acquire with age and experience.[1] As children grow and mature, their viewing tastes as well as interactions with television change dramatically, and so does what they take with them from the experience. Accordingly, the "meaning" of television content can be understood as residing neither in the particular television program nor as an independent creation in the child's head, but rather it is produced in the interaction between the child and the program.

What does change over time mean for children's development and how can it be studied appropriately? Age differences in and of themselves are but a descriptive variable: Surely we can notice that 10-year-olds have a much better understanding of a televised narrative than 5-year-olds, but why is this so? What are the psychological, physiological, social, environmental, and other processes that explain the meaning of age differences?

Various psychological theories that deal with human development are based on the concept of "stage." The key to stage theories is the understanding of "stage" as a unique period of development, with each stage typified by its own special behavioral and cognitive characteristics. According to psychological research, all individuals progress through the same stages in a fixed chronological order, although genetic and/or environmental factors can accelerate or slow down the speed of transition from one stage to another. The stages are also perceived to be both hierarchical, as well as, integrative. What this means is that more advanced stages are based on earlier ones and advancement results in a "re-organizing" of the various cognitive skills. Furthermore, these stages are also perceived as universal: though children grow up in very different cultures and environments and possess very different genetic maps, they seem to proceed through the same stages in the same order. In other words, such a development process has been found to hold true, at least in general terms, for Charudet who is watching television in his houseboat on the Chao Phraya river in Thailand, for Manual who is watching it in a community center in the Cordillera mountains of Peru, and Dominique who is watching TV in a small apartment in Paris France. In summary, the concept of "stage" is a theoretical means of organizing in an integrative manner the various characteristics of children's thinking and behaviors within particular age groups, above and beyond individual differences between them.

The psychological stage theory that has been applied widely in studies of television and children is that of Jean Piaget and it focuses on cognitive development.[2] Piaget demarcated four major developmental stages, each of which is characterized by development of different mental structures called "schemas." Let us examine how this theory been applied to television by his followers. During the first two years, the baby-toddler passes through the "sensory-motor" stage, where mental schemas are shaped by the infant's senses and actions. When applying this stage theory to television, for example, we suggest that a baby may learn about the unique world of television by such actions as touching the screen when a favorite puppet appears, clapping hands to the music, or by playing with the power button. These sensory-motor experiences are gradually integrated within the child's developing understanding of television and social reality. Thus, the child understands that puppets on television feel very differently when "touched" on the TV screen than does a favorite stuffed animal cuddled in the crib; that television can be turned on and off at will; but, a care-giver who went away to work does not return at the press of a button.

The "pre-operational" stage between 2 and 7 years of age is characterized mainly by the acquisition of language. This frees the youngster from the sensory-motor experiences of the "here and now" and allows for the development of representational thought. Thus, for example, the child is able to think and talk about television experiences outside of the viewing situation. During the "concrete operational" stage, around 7 to 12 years, schemas develop so that the child is able to engage in mental transformations in interactions with the concrete world. For example, a child at the concrete operations stage is able to see, mentally, an object from the perspective of another person and to understand that the amount of liquid does not change when placed in containers of a different shape and size. Such mental transformations are crucial for understanding many of television's codes and conventions that require filling in gaps in story lines (e.g., what happens after seeing the driver lose control of the car and the quick camera "cut" to the next scene when the driver is lying unconscious in a hospital bed); or to understand the meaning of "close-ups" (e.g., the ability to understand that the quivering mouth on the screen is part of the face of the driver's daughter sitting by his hospital bed).

Finally, according to Piaget and his followers, from about the age of 12, the soon-to-be adolescent functions in the stage of formal operations developing capabilities of abstract, logical thought that is not restricted by mental operations related to the concrete world alone. From this age on, youths are assumed to be able to understand television-content from a mature cognitive point of view, in a manner similar to adults, although clearly their life experience, interests, and emotional world continue to differ greatly from those of adults.

The cognitive skills that develop through these stages are applied by children to the world of television just as they are to any other aspects of their lives. These skills shape in significant ways the meanings that children make of the content and the forms of television programs. In turn, viewing television becomes an opportunity, once again, as other experiences in the child's everyday life, to develop and to practice a variety of cognitive skills, some of which are specific to the medium of television, though many are applicable to all realms of life. Several of these specific skills have been the focus of the research to which we now turn.

Attention to and Comprehension of Television Content

What do children attend to on television and how is this attention related to what they comprehend of the content? Clearly, the child needs to demonstrate some form of attention to television as a necessary condition for the initiation of any related thought processes. However, understanding this process is complicated, as "attention" to television is not easily defined. Is attention to television measured by the visual orientation of the child's eyes towards the operating screen, even if he or she may be daydreaming or otherwise disengaged? Does it require a visual fixation on a particular element on the screen to indicate active interest? And, what about the pre-schooler who is playing with building-blocks on the rug in front of the television and who glances occasionally at it following an audio cue, such as a loud siren, a familiar commercial, or a child's giggle?

One commonly applied research approach argues that attention to television is fundamentally reactive; that is, attention is controlled by external elements of the medium to which the child reacts. According to this research approach, the younger the viewer the more attracted the child is to television's formal features, such as visual elements (camera movements, sharp cuts from one angle to another, slow or fast motion, and the like) as well as audio ones (such as unusual noises, music, sound-effects, and the like). Accordingly, this approach assumes two central characteristics: First, the direction of influence is from the television to the child; and second, the motivation for viewing the programs themselves and the viewing experience of the children are of minimal interest as children are perceived as passive viewers attracted to the TV set due to the nature of its appealing audio-visual language.

While there is very little empirical evidence for this approach, it was whole-heartedly adopted by many anti-television advocates and is cited extensively in popular publications given provocative titles.[3] Such writers see television viewing as a terribly dangerous, addictive "drug" that should be eliminated from children's lives, a passive reactive behavior devoid of active cognitive processes.

In contrast, other researchers applied an alternative approach – *active attention* – that assumes that attention to television is an active form of behavior undertaken by children.[4] Instead of viewing attention as a passive reaction to the screen, they argue that children's attention to television can be understood as an active cognitive integration between the viewer, the television content, and the environment within which it is viewed. It is shaped by existing cognitive schemas that are based on past experiences in the world, including television. Thus, attention to television involves at any given moment strategies applied to comprehend television content as well as processing that leads to understanding such content.

This active-attention approach can best be summarized by the following four theoretical assumptions that attempt to explain moments when the child is visually oriented to the screen:[5]

1 *Alternative activities:* Attention to television is dependent to a large degree on whether the viewing context encourages alternative activities. Such activities could take place simultaneously with viewing (e.g., snacking, cuddling a stuffed animal); interchangeably with viewing (e.g., drawing a picture on the coffee table during the talk-show but watching during the commercial break); or completely independent from the television (e.g., reading a book on the couch while the rest of the family is viewing a drama series). Here it is useful to recall, in this regard, the discussion in the first chapter that viewing television is located within a social context.

2 *Maintenance of visual attention:* Continuing to attend to a television program is dependent also on the child's ability to respond to the challenges posed by the content. For example, the child is likely to lose attention if the information provided in the program does not present anything new, as in the case of an over-simplistic and predictable narrative or when the program is intended for a much younger audience. The same is true for the other extreme; that is, the child is likely to lose attention if the program presents overly complicated and/or unfamiliar content that the child is incapable of comprehending by means of existing mental schemas. For example, a girl watching a program on TV with her parents, which is a political discussion between opponents with varying positions in regard to economic issues, may be able to operate a mental schema that enables her to understand that this is "a program for adults," but it is quite likely that she lacks the knowledge and cognitive schemas to pose questions that would enable her to close the comprehension gap. Hence, it is likely that she will lose interest in the program.

3 *Elicitation of visual attention:* While busy with alternative activities, a child may be regularly and subconsciously scanning the audio

portions of the operating television set to detect sounds that indicate content changes. Here children use audio cues to orient themselves back to the screen (such as an opening tune of a favorite program, sudden noise, familiar voice) or behavioral cues from people around them to shift their attention levels.

4 *Attentional inertia*: Attention to television is also directed by a process of what researchers refer to as "viewing inertia." This concept refers to the process that takes place when viewing may overcome moments of comprehension "breakups" or confusing transitions in content. It has been found that the longer a viewer continues to view television, the greater the chance that this behavior will continue regardless of viewing difficulties. This process works in the opposite direction as well: The longer visual orientation is away from the screen, the lower the chance that the child will return to it. This process has been found to exist regardless of content viewed and age of the viewers.

While inertia may seem to support a reactive approach to television viewing, it is important to emphasize that researchers understand that it indicates quite the opposite: While young viewers may lose attention when content becomes non-comprehensible, the process of inertia facilitates continued viewing that seems to enable them to temporarily overcome comprehension difficulties and exposes them to new cognitive assignments. While such attention may be brief, as our second theoretical assumption outlined above suggests, alternatively, it may facilitate a growing experience by overcoming the cognitive challenge.

The development of attention to television

Attention to television develops from birth. Newborns of a few weeks have been observed reacting to sounds coming from the TV set by stopping their feeding and turning their heads towards it. Babies continue to be dependent mostly on audio cues in directing their attention to television for few seconds at a time during their first few months of life. However, particularly attractive contents, such as commercials, peppy musical openings of programs, and programs designed for the very young are capable of holding their attention for much longer stretches of time. This fact has not escaped the "eye" of entrepreneurs and, consequently, there is a recent growth of programs and videotapes designed for viewing by this very, very young audience. Home observation of babies, as well as reports from care-givers, suggest that from the age of a few months babies will often stop their activities, move to the music, clap their hands, make happy gurgling sounds, toddle toward the television set, and point at objects and characters on it. Preference for familiar content viewed with pleasure over and over again intensifies during the second year of life.

Here, researchers distinguish between "foreground television," television-content to which young viewers attend closely, and "background television" that may operate as background noise in a room where the young child is engaged in other activities. As they mature, "foreground" viewing by young viewers becomes more dominant, particularly in regard to television programs and videotapes designed especially for the younger audience (e.g., *Teletubbies*, the *Baby Einstein* videotapes series, and the like) that are clearly more comprehensible to them.[6]

Toddlers' attention to television is greatly influenced by the behaviors of people around them. For example, placing a baby on one's lap or cuddling together in front of the television will significantly lengthen the baby's attention period. Food, too, seems to ensure longer periods of satisfied concentration. Babies offered a bottle or a snack while viewing continued to be relaxed, attentive viewers. By the end of their second year, toddlers' viewing sessions gradually lengthen with signs of growing interest in the animation genre. While accurate measurement of attention to television in babies and toddlers is a complicated matter, researchers claim that around the average age of $2\frac{1}{2}$ years many youngsters are capable and willing to stay tuned to a program that they find to be of interest for a full half hour or even more. This age coincides with the transition into the language oriented pre-operational stage of cognitive development, as well as, with all the physiological and social changes typical of this age group. Thus, in contrast to populist views that claim that toddlers as well as children from older age groups are "hypnotized" by the screen, they clearly demonstrate very frequent changes in orientation from the screen to the surrounding environment and back.

From this age on attention to television continues to grow as a function of the child's development, personality, and environment. The ability to sustain interest in the television program for longer stretches of time and to manage attention to television as well as competing activities is gradually strengthened and modified. By the age of six, attention to television can be sustained for longer periods of time and remains so until adolescence, when a decline in television viewing occurs as part of the many changes taking place in youth's physical, social, emotional, cognitive, and environmental realms of life. As a result, most research on attention to television has centered on children younger than 6 years of age.[7]

Relationships between attention to television and comprehension

The reactive approach to television assumes that attention to television is an antecedent condition to any process of comprehension of its content; that is, attending to television leads to its comprehension. Critics of television argue that attention to the fast tempo of television is mostly reflexive and immediate; it does not allow children the necessary conditions to reflect over the content or to organize their mental processes. Thus, comprehension and memory of television content is understood to be superficial in nature, according to this approach.

In contrast, the active approach to children's attention to television understands the relationships between attention and comprehension quite differently. Children are assumed to be active viewers whose attention to television is motivated by attempts to understand it. Researchers have found that children are able to devote selective attention to television, inquire about the content viewed, decode new information with the assistance of the cognitive skills available to them at the time, and use television content to refine and develop new skills. This approach assumes that television content contributes to children's developmental processes defined by Piaget as assimilation and accommodation: they assimilate comprehensible television knowledge into existing mental skills and accommodate them by refining those skills according to knowledge newly acquired via television. The active approach sees the relationships between children and television as reciprocal. Attention does not necessarily cause comprehension, but comprehension can shape to a large degree the attention directed to television. While television conveys particular messages, understanding them (or ignoring them) is dependent to a large degree on the particular social, cognitive, and emotional needs of the individual child's personality and personal development.

The more viewing and social experience the child has the greater the chances that the child will be attentive and gain more from viewing TV. This interactive process between child and television content has been conceptualized through the acronym - AIME (Amount of Invested Mental Effort).[8] AIME portrays a process through which the child evaluates television content as easy or difficult for understanding, as familiar or novel, as important or negligible. In assessment of this process, the child determines the amount of mental effort needed to process the information. For example, if the child perceives a particular behavior or situation to be very familiar to him or her, the amount of AIME as well as attention to television will be lowered. However, if it is perceived as new and intriguing, the amount of AIME will increase. Furthermore, when children are offered challenging and appealing television contents to view, they demonstrate active involvement and a higher degree of AIME.

As children grow older they learn to associate particular formal features of television with specific genres and their viewing expectations develop according to their interest in a particular genre. They learn to distinguish between programs directed to adults and those aimed at children; between commercials and programs; between comedies and action-adventure programs. And, they learn to allocate their attention according to their interests and to activate those thinking schemas that are more appropriate to the particular genre.

Further, children develop clear distinctions between "boys" commercials and "girls" commercials, based on formal features alone, regardless of the product advertised, and attach clear gender meanings to them. They understand that commercials that are aimed specifically and stereotypically at boys are typically characterized by loud music, sharp "cuts" from one camera shot to the other, special audio effects, intensive activity level, and the like. While commercials aimed at girls have soft background music, female voices, pastel colors, photographic features such as "fade outs" (pictures fading out into blackness) and "dissolves" (pictures dissolving into other pictures), gradual changes between camera shots rather than sharp "cuts," and the like.

Individual children differ in attention and comprehension, but such differences also exist within each child's varying viewing experiences, in different social contexts due to the availability of alternative activities, and their internal motivations at different points in time. Clearly then, attention to television programs is not a mechanistic, casual process dictated by a mesmerizing television set that is received by a passive manipulated child-viewer. Rather, viewing by children is a much more complex, active, reciprocal process.

The Development of Viewing Preferences

The availability of particular television program genres worldwide, on the one hand, and the generally universal course of development of children, on the other, results in quite predictable viewing preferences of children that change as they move from one stage of development to the next. As beginning-viewers, babies and toddlers seem to attend more closely to programs that are designed for them. Design features include peppy music, sound effects, animation, lively pacing that is not overwhelming, humor and noises of laughter, as well as, female and children's voices. They seem to react, too, to content that looks and makes sense to them: short verbal outputs, smiling faces, loveable animals, pleasing colors and shapes. *The Teletubbies* is a good example. Produced by the BBC and first broadcast in 1997, the program quickly became a hit among young viewers and has been marketed in over 60 countries around the world. The four colorful, cheerful, and energetic figures move and behave like toddlers using minimalist language and repetitive behaviors and utterances. They are situated in a world that combines open green natural spaces and a modernistic dwelling. Research conducted in Australia, Germany, Israel, Norway, the UK, and the USA found the evidence of the program's popularity among babies and toddlers that included high levels of attention and active viewing including singing, dancing, pointing, imitating behaviors, speaking back to the television, and generally reacting enthusiastically with great joy.[9]

As toddlers grow into pre-schoolers, they gradually become more interested in comprehensible narratives and in diverse magazine-like formats. Produced originally by the Children's Television Workshop in New York (later to be re-named Sesame Workshop), *Sesame Street* is by far the most proclaimed and researched exemplar of programming for this age group worldwide. We will discuss this television phenomenon in depth in Chapter 5, however, for now, it is appropriate to note here that the program's "quilted" magazine format combines segments of animation, puppets, documentaries, and drama designed with the understanding that pre-schoolers' attention and viewing preferences develop gradually. Such a format allows each child the opportunity to interact with the program in accordance with individual needs and abilities. Many countries have developed special locally produced programs targeted for this age group with similar consider-ations in mind.

From about age 5 or 6, children start developing preferences for more fast-paced programs, more complicated content, and accordingly start gradually to disassociate themselves from clearly educational and "safe" pre-school programs. Individual preferences start to emerge and take shape for a specific animation series, a favorite Disney movie, "family" type comedies, or soap operas (or telenovela, as they are named in many parts of the world that import them from Latin America). In addition to watching specific channels targeted for children, they gradually move to what has been coined by the television industry as the "family" fare – comedies, dramas, quiz shows, reality TV, sports, music channels, movies and the like, that are aimed at a wide and diverse audience, who share interest in a common denominator.

Here, it should be noted that the range of program options varies greatly between different regions in the world, due particularly to economic reasons.

The most pronounced differences in taste already very evident at this young age are associated with gender. The development of "gender-appropriate" behavior, typical of socialization processes that take place in most societies, results in behavioral compatibility in relation to viewing choices, as well. Here, boys seem to outgrow the more quiet educational programs at a much younger age than do girls and to demonstrate a growing preference for action-oriented animations (produced mainly in the USA and Japan) that so strongly dominate the screens of children's television around the world. They seem to be attracted more than girls to action, aggressive, and dangerous fantasies, and sports as well as to programs featuring male heroic characters. Girls, for their part, continue to prefer programs with story lines about human relationships, friendships, and feelings that take place in non-aggressive settings. Thus, they continue to watch and enjoy many of the educational programs for a much longer period than the boys.

This clear gendered division of preferences continues throughout the school years and seems to be resilient to major changes taking place around the world in regard to gender equality and socialization processes of gender roles. We will continue to discuss aspects of gender throughout this book as it interacts with several aspects of children's television viewing.

As children move through the elementary and middle school years, they gradually experiment with the entire range of television genres, including those specifically not intended for them – such as violent movies and pornographic material. Many remain generally disinterested in programs that are based predominantly on "talking heads;" that is, programs that feature adults talking about issues framed as solely of concern to adults that are conducted in a language that is mostly inaccessible and unappealing to children – such as current events, political or cultural discussions, and most news programs (with the exception of particularly attractive news items that include violent or otherwise unusual and stimulating scenes).

As in many other areas of their lives, children develop individual tastes based on the variety of programs available to them and are capable of expressing their preferences as well as articulating their reasoning for selecting particular programs. On the other hand, we, the adults in their lives, may not always approve of their selections and taste or even understand the reasons for their attraction to such programs or contents.[10]

Development of Fantasy–Reality Distinction

The ability to distinguish between fantasy and reality on television is one of the primary differences between children's and adults' thought processes. While "television reality" is a complex and multidimensional concept, we refer here specifically to the degree of factuality of the mediated reality: When are children able to determine that people and events presented on television exist beyond the screen? Are they real people representing themselves or are these actors playing a role? Do the events depicted on the screen happen in the outside world or are they created according to a script? When do children understand that television is not a "magic window" to the real world? Studies of social realism focus on children's answers to these questions as well as: Are the people, places, and events on television similar to the ones familiar to us from the real world? Are they believable? Is it probable that events depicted in fictional programs will take place? Is knowledge acquired through viewing television applicable in real life?

In most cases, children are not systematically instructed in developing such distinctions, but rather they develop them on their own as they mature, as they gain experience and come to understand the real world, and as their knowledge of television expands. As children grow older, their perception of television as a "magic window" is gradually replaced by a growing understanding that television reality is not quite like the everyday life reality in which they live. The age of 8 (the beginning of the concrete-operational stage, according to cognitive development theories) has been pin-pointed by researchers as an important turning point in the development of such understanding.

Research suggests that children gradually develop the ability to make distinctions along five reality–fantasy criteria:

1   *Constructedness*: The degree to which children understand that the television world is a product of some sort of construction and that all television content, including news and documentaries, are a fabrication, to some degree, in comparison to reality outside it.
2   *Physical actuality*: The degree to which children evaluate the reality of television based on their perceptions of the person or event actually existing outside of the television world.
3   *Possibility*: The degree to which children evaluate the reality of television based on their perception of whether events portrayed are possible in the reality familiar to them beyond the screen.
4   *Probability*: The degree to which children evaluate the reality of television based on their perception of whether it is probable that it

represents something that could happen beyond the screen, even if it is possible. For example, it is possible that one family will experience all the intensive events happening in the life of one television-family and solve them in similar ways, however, our life-experience suggests that it is not very probable that this would be the case.

5   *Formal features*: The degree to which children understand the formal features of television as "cues" to what may be real or fictitious. For example, older child viewers come to understand that a live, unedited series of pictures of a war scene followed by a medium range camera shot of an adult who seems to be talking seriously and who is seated in a studio behind a desk indicates a "real" news report, while a colorful, animated scene of talking animals in children's voice with background music is "unreal."

We can organize the above criteria in a complementary manner: external cues enable viewers to make comparisons between their knowledge of the world and experience in it in regard to the television content. Internal cues within the medium itself direct their evaluation of its realism. Generally speaking we can argue that younger children are more heavily dependent on the internal criteria (e.g., animation is "imaginary" because it is drawn and does not use live actors). However, as they mature, children learn to incorporate external criteria as their knowledge of the world expands (e.g., a specific animation series can be much more realistic in content then many programs employing live actors). No wonder then, that by the age of 12, much like adults, respondents to research questions will answer: "What do you mean by 'real'?" or, "real in what sense?"[11]

The development of genre distinction

As we have seen, the ability to distinguish between television fantasy and reality involves the ability to identify and to distinguish between different television genres. Television programs are designed according to well-defined formulas. Each formula has its own production codes and conventions of typified story lines (such as characters, locations, photographic-techniques, pace, sound tracks, and the like). Such molds are "filled in" with content from diverse cultures and with diverse qualities. Furthermore, beyond being an aggregate of common characteristics, genres can also be understood as an aggregate of viewers' expectations. For example, when a program is identified as "news," the viewer will apply a very different set of expectations towards the degree of its realism in comparison to expectations applied to a program identified as "fantasy," such as science fiction.

Children learn to associate program characteristics with genres along a continuum from those perceived as the most "real" to the most "unreal:" "Real" programs deal with what is happening in the world – such as news and documentaries; "realistic" programs, a median category, are narratives and characters that potentially could take place but are being played by actors, such as situation comedies and soap operas; and "unreal" genres are mainly narratives with characters that are not taking place in the world and – to the best of the child's current knowledge – could not happen, such as science fiction, fantasy movies, animal animation, and the like. As children grow older, they learn the formal features associated with each particular genre and develop specific expectations in regard to the degree of realism the program will represent.

Kindergarten age children are already capable of defining the two ends of the continuum: news is "real" and animation is "imaginary." An excerpt from an interview I had with Amy, a 6-year-old North American girl, in relation to a situation comedy illustrates this developing ability. The series, *Full House*, deals with three girls who lost their mother and who are being raised by their father, his best friend, and their uncle. Amy attempted to explain to me why the news is different from *Full House*, her favorite situation comedy:

Amy:	Because *Full House* comes with real people and they make it up, and the *Full House* is very silly.
Interviewer:	They make it up?
Amy:	Uh, huh.
Interviewer:	So *Full House* are like real people on television?
Amy:	Yeah, yeah. They're like real people, but they are silly. It is almost like the news, but it is not.
Interviewer:	It is almost, but it's not? I see. So the real people are silly and the news are real people and they are not silly? I see. That's interesting.
Amy:	and cartoons are pretend stuff.

According to this young girl, animation programs are at the imaginary end of a continuum of programs. Comedies are located in the center of the continuum, as they include real people who are acting "silly," while the news is about serious real people.

Children in the concrete operational stage come up with alternative ways of dividing programs. For example, there are "good" versus "bad," or programs that are "for children" versus those that are "for grown-ups." Or, they may organize them according to their perceived content: for example, a situation, family comedy could be grouped with an educational program, because both convey messages of concern and love for family members. An action-adventure program and an animation program could be understood to be of a similar genre, because both have shooting in them. A commercial for a food product, a news program, and a math instructional program were all perceived as educational, because they all "teach things."

In this regard, commercials are a very difficult genre for children to understand, since they intentionally blur distinctions between real and imaginary and, as well, employ a range of audio-visual means to sell children products. Studies on children growing up in an environment with commercial television (conducted in the USA, Europe, and Israel) suggest that they can already identify commercial breaks as a separate genre at a very young age, often as early as 3 years old. They learn to identify those cues that indicate a transition between a program and a commercial (e.g., a logo, sign, or sound effect that are repeated regularly). However, their ability to explain this genre develops much more gradually, as does their ability to distinguish between their attitude towards the product in comparison with their attitude towards the commercial for that product (i.e., a commercially literate person may like a product, but not the commercial advertising it, and vice versa; that is, enjoying a commercial is not necessarily an indication that the product is enjoyable as well). Their ability to explain this genre develops much more gradually. As they start elementary school, they may understand that the commercial's intention is to sell products, but not its tactics of manipulation. They continue to trust commercial statements as being "real;" have difficulty identifying the indirect advertising present in much of commercial television programs, and do not understand the economic processes that drive the television industry.[12] However, there is evidence that suggests that it is doubtful if most adults understand these complicated issues either.

The importance of distinguishing between televised fantasy and reality

Clearly, then, distinguishing between various forms of fantasy and reality on television and sorting television programs into genres is not a simple, objective, or clear-cut task. Indeed, children continue to be confused by realistic genres, as do many adults, as they continue to mature as viewers.

Increasingly, it is the case that the television environment changes and poses new challenges to viewers around the world. Realistic movies incorporate segments of animation or documentaries. News reports include reconstructions of past events and employ dramatization features. Docu-dramas combine use of real places and people together with actors and fictitious dialogue. Commercials incorporate scientific information to create "infomercials;" news and entertainment are combined to create "infotainment;" and educational programs integrate entertainment features to form "edutainment." "Reality shows," such as *Big Brother, Survivor,* police investigations, and matchmaking programs, purposefully blur genres through the use of "reality" formal features (e.g., rough camera moves, no editing, no music or sound tracks). In such cases, viewers have the feeling that they are watching events that take place in reality within unreal situations (e.g., directed script, characters selected for particular roles, unnatural context). All these genres continue to challenge the ability of young, as well as older and more experienced, viewers to define and understand television's "reality." Therefore, such a development requires re-examination of the criteria we use to evaluate television reality.

Finally, there is the important role that cultural experience plays in socialization to attaining a particular perspective on reality. Thus, we realize that a seemingly independent cognitive skill is very much culturally dependent. Since the development of the distinction between fantasy and reality on television is shaped by experiences with life on and outside the television set, the nature of such experiences is bound to shape this skill. For example, while "animals portrayed with a human soul" may be perceived as an imaginary feature of an animation program by Paola who is raised in the catholic culture of Italy, it may seem perfectly reasonable to Kumar from a Hindi faith in India who believes in the reincarnation of human souls in animals. Similarly, a dramatic series on the Jewish Holocaust may be understood as imaginary fiction by José in Mexico, but is very real and relevant to Dana raised in Israel, whose grandparents are holocaust survivors. Yuji in Japan may think that life in outer-space seems completely in the realm of fantasy, while for Marina in Russia, whose parents are scientists, it may be perceived as quite real. And, dramas describing the lives of the very rich (e.g., the youth series *Beverly Hills 90210*) make complete sense to Kevin from upper class USA, but it may seem to be completely fictional to Tomaselli from the poor classes of Botswana. Such examples about the role of cultural context in perception of television reality as similar to or different from actual reality are abundant. The important role of culture too, as in gender, will be taken up throughout the book.

The Development of Understanding of Television Narrative

Viewing television is a demanding and challenging form of information processing that requires tackling diverse content that opens up many layers of interpretation. In order to understand the plot of a television program, the viewer has to distinguish between central and incidental information and to pay selective attention accordingly. In addition, the viewer needs to organize the central events in the program in their chronological order and to be able to make sense of causal relationships where one event leads to another. This has to be accomplished even when the events are separated by different scenes, presented in different time frames, or embedded in incidental information. For example, in a particular action-adventure show, understanding the reason for the arrest at the end of the program is dependent on understanding the opening scene that introduced the crime. In order to understand that the criminal has been dutifully punished, the viewer has to be able to connect between the two scenes. Given such a challenging process, we can ask if young viewers are capable of such cognitive challenges.

Pre-school-age children understand television content in quite a different manner than adults. For example, they are capable of reconstructing individual episodes or scenes of programs, but have difficulty connecting them into a coherent story. Most of their thinking centers on the present, thus they also have difficulty following a chronological development. They assess whether information is central or incidental in a manner different from adults and, thus, they may pay less attention to what adults consider to be primary information and may not be able to remember it as adults do. Similarly, in terms of prognostication, that is when their viewing is interrupted and they are asked to project future developments in the program, they may propose quite different suggestions than those of an average adult-viewer.

Children gradually develop a better mastery of language, an ability to assume others' points of views, and to create meanings relevant to the plot line during elementary school. Their thinking skills become more flexible as they expand from the limits of "here and now" thinking processes. They are better able to focus on central content, to reconstruct a television story, and they often interweave in it their own personal interpretation, in a manner similar to older viewers. Developing a personal perspective facilitates meaning-making processes as well as memory of the program. These and other skills continue to develop gradually and thus the differences in viewing TV of 7- and 12-year-olds are dramatic[13].

Some of the difficulties that young viewers experience in understanding television narratives are a result of the complexity and abstract nature of content that is not produced with them in mind, but rather intended for an older, very diverse adult audience. Further, the content of the program may be removed from children's experiences and thus more difficult to understand. In this regard, it is particularly interesting to study children's understandings of television programs that center around family life, in its various forms, as this is the most familiar social setting for most children. Indeed, children are very much attracted to programs that they perceive as relevant to their own lives. As in other areas, the older children become and the more relevant knowledge about family life they acquire, the more capable they are of judging the realistic nature of families portrayed on television and to understand the meaning of implications of events in those families' lives. It is important to remind ourselves, once again, that here, too, the personal circumstances of the individual child play an important role. Children apply their own life knowledge and attitudes to the televised content and thus may experience difficulties understanding television families that are structured or composed of members different from their own. For example, children raised in a single-maternal-parent family expressed more negative attitudes towards television-fathers than those raised in two-parent families. Following this same logic, it is easy to predict that children raised in more hierarchical families with authoritarian fathers and traditional mothers may have difficulty understanding as well as judging the realistic and moral nature of programs presenting rebellious teenagers who speak their minds to their parents and disobey them.[14]

An additional contributor to the complexity of children's understanding of television programs is the type of formal features employed; in particular, visual techniques that manipulate time (such as flashbacks and slow motions) or mark transitions (such as different editing styles) require considerable viewing experience. We can conclude, therefore, that a reciprocal process operates here: children's life experience, television experience, as well as age-related development shape their understanding of television narratives. But, at the same time, accumulated experiences with television content assist children to perceive their own reality, and vice versa. This leads to the intriguing concern with the relationship between television viewing and the construction of reality that will be discussed in Chapter 4.

The Development of Understanding of Television Characters

Imagine the social world of a child in your own neighborhood. What kind of people and professions does he or she meet on an everyday basis? It is safe to assume that most children around the world have first hand encounters with family members, teachers, salespeople, perhaps medical professionals, bus or taxi drivers. They may have an occasional encounter with other professions, depending on their personal life circumstances. But most of the adult professional world is quite inaccessible to them (as it is to most adults too). Television thus becomes a "peek hole" to roles beyond their everyday reach, particularly to those highly prioritized and stereotyped in dramatic genres: eloquent lawyers, tough law-enforcers, brilliant surgeons, glorious celebrities, slimy Mafia leaders, promiscuous students, etc. Meeting these varied characters on television confronts children with many value-related issues as they compare themselves with: Who am I? Am I similar or different from them? Do I want to be like them? Are they good or bad? Am I good or bad in comparison? How can I change my behavior or appearance to be more like them? Answers to such questions become part of the process of self-definition and learning about one's place in society. Television characters thus become role models for identification and imitation as well as a resource for learning about the world. If so, how do children perceive television characters and their behaviors?

From an earlier discussion, we recall that a cognitive schema is a structure for organizing knowledge related to a particular idea or term (e.g., "criminal," "singer"). A schema may be shaped by knowledge acquired through first hand experience as well as through mediating sources, such as other people, the media, and more specifically in our case – television. In turn, schemas have implications for understanding how new information is processed. For example, schema regarding gender differences shape the way we attend differently to content that involves female and male characters, the way we process and remember content, the way we perceive it to be relevant to us, and our evaluation and preferences of the characters themselves. As a general rule, children tend to pay more attention and remember more accurately characters that conform to their expectations of traditional sex-roles (e.g., male doctor and female nurse) than those who rupture these traditions (e.g., female doctor and male nurse).[15] We will return to this issue in Chapter 4.

Following what we already know about cognitive development, we can surmise that as children mature their understanding of television characters changes dramatically. Younger children are more dependent on external appearance in evaluating characters. Accordingly, they tend to equate the unfamiliar look of a foreigner as well as unattractive body and facial characteristics with negative personality qualities, thus perceiving an "ugly" person as "mean." However, as they mature, they gradually assign more importance to internal personality traits as well as circumstantial explanations to characters' motivations and behaviors. But, like adults, they remain highly influenced by social expectations and stereotypes engrained deeply in different societies that are emphasized all too frequently in commercial television.[16] Many persons continue throughout their lifetime to be wary of characters – on television as well as real life – who look very different from them (e.g., persons of a different race, disabled people, who wear a non-conforming clothing style, etc.), as well as, those perceived to diverge greatly from cultural beauty standards (e.g., overweight people or those with non-proportionate facial features).

While very helpful in understanding general trends in the development of human thinking, developmental theories alone are often unable to provide us with satisfactory and comprehensive understanding of thinking, behaviors, and emotions. Clearly, many of the issues involved with children's supposed "deficient" cognitive abilities are not even resolved during adult years. So how large is the gap between adults and children, and are children really as "deficient" as some persons assume? A good example of an additional body of theory needed to understand children is the adaptation of developmental theory to the realm of moral judgment, in general, and its particular application to children's viewing of television. A discussion to which we now turn.

The development of moral judgment

Television is a central source for learning moral judgment as it presents many tales about human conduct. For example, understanding the motivations for violent behaviors and their implications for the victims is crucial in application of moral judgment by viewers. Adults will usually apply moral criteria differently in regard to a person who purposefully aims to hurt others for some personal gain as opposed to a person who is forced to behave violently in order to save a loved one. That is, we apply different criteria to acts of violence that seem to us to be random and unjustified in comparison to those that individual societies might perceive as justified or even sacred (e.g., acts of violence by military forces in some countries or those committed under the guise of preserving "family honor" in others). Do children apply the same processes and criteria?

The way children judge television characters and their behaviors is central in development of their understanding. Researchers argue that children's moral and cognitive development are similar, as each progresses through specific stages in a fixed order, with each stage being fundamentally different from its previous one. Similarly, moral judgment, too, is understood to develop through combined development of skills, cognitive schemas, and experience.[17] Children are socialized within their families from an early age and learn by imitation as well as by a desire to please their caregivers and respond to their expectations. As very young children have yet to internalize cognitive standards that define what is "right, good" or "wrong, bad", they are highly dependent on external reinforcements that teach them what their society perceives as "right" or "wrong." And, as they view television, they will often seek such guidance when they ask questions, such as: "those green characters – are they good or bad?" in attempting to understand the world in clear "good–bad" terms.

As they move to the concrete-operational stage, around the age of 7, children gradually become more able to exercise moral judgment autonomously and to use it as a tool to evaluate human behaviors. They start applying their understanding of behavioral motivation to their judgment: the same behavior will be evaluated as good or bad according to the motivation behind it or the circumstances in which it occurs. Gradually they also learn to experience the world in less dichotomous terms. So, television characters, much like real-life ones, are neither good nor bad – but complicated beings that can behave in appropriate or inappropriate ways in different situations and within complex cultural norms.

Let us examine an example of moral development based on the following study: imagine presenting children with a program depicting a person pre-meditating a crime. Children over 10 years old will probably be able to perceive the person as a "wrong-doer" when his immoral intentions become clear (i.e., understanding motivations). The 7–8-year-olds will probably identify him as such when he is about to actually perform the crime (i.e., dependent on actual behavioral cues), and younger children will probably recognize the criminal when he is arrested by the police since "obviously," a handcuffed person being held by a policeman must be a criminal (i.e., morality is defined by external sanctions and cues).

Identification with television characters

Why is it at all important to dwell on how children evaluate and understand television characters? Two related answers come to mind: First, television characters are the focus of identification, imitation, and idolization. Second, because television characters serve as behavioral role models for children to imitate.

Many viewers, both children and adults, develop emotional relationships with television characters. We care about them, we want to get closer to them, we are curious about their lives. Identification with television characters can take various forms.[18] Viewers (particularly the younger ones) may feel a similarity between themselves and the character – perhaps they share the same gender, ethnic origin, age, or appearance. The character may be perceived to be of same class and educational level or to hold dear the same values and worldview.

Younger children may identify with children or with animals that are smaller or in subordinate positions, representing their own powerless position. Often the child-viewer shares the same perspective as the TV character and lives "through" the same experiences with the character. In this way the television character serves to reaffirm the child's own self-worth, beliefs, attitudes, and worldview and as a role model for possible suitable (or unsuitable) behaviors in situations relevant to his or her life.

The child may also be involved in a form of "wishful" identification – when he or she seeks to be "like" or to "behave like" the television character. The child may imagine exchanging places with the subject of identification and feel during the viewing that things that are happening to the character are happening to him, too. In this way the child exchanges her role as a viewer with the role of the character in the program, thus becoming someone else for a short and intense period of time.

Related to identification – yet not quite the same – is "para-social interaction" according to which viewers feel that they know the television characters quiet closely and engage in imaginary interpersonal relationships with them. Para-social interactions may be formed following a long period of viewing (e.g., a drama series; a leading-role in a magazine TV format; a singer on MTV), when the child grows to feel that he knows the character's personality, behaviors, tastes, relationships with others, and the like and cares about the character as if he was a close friend. The child may seek advice from the character's role, wish to be part of his social world, and to engage in close friendly relationship with him. Para-social relationship may provide a deep sense of personal and social satisfaction and encourage loyalty to the program. One possible implication of such a "relationship" is that children (as well as adults!) may treat the actress and the character they play as one and the same person. Thus, it is not uncommon for actors to receive comments, gifts, admonishments, requests, etc, directed to the character they portray.

In studies conducted in several countries, the most predictable characteristic of identification – both similar and wishful – as well as of para-social interaction with television characters among children was found to be that of gender. Boys of all ages almost exclusively identify with male figures, while girls identify mostly with females, but with males as well, particularly during their earlier years. It is possible to propose at least two complementary explanations for this finding: First, to date, television continues to purvey a much wider range of male roles for children to identify with than female roles. The latter are still restricted both in absolute numbers as well as in diversity of personalities, roles, settings, plot lines, and the like. This holds true for television all over the world. Second, as a general rule, our societies are much more tolerant towards girls who adopt a more typical "male" style of behavior and appearance than of boys who adopt a typical "girly" style. Thus, the general rule of thumb supported by research evidence is that there is a better chance of girls watching television programs designed for boys and featuring male protagonists than vice versa. This conclusion is well known – and indeed utilized – in the commercial domain of the children's television industry, where there is a clear desire to invest resources in developing "boys" genres. However, recent successful productions with global appeal (for example, *Dora the Explorer* by Nickelodeon) featuring independent child-female protagonists have started to challenged these assumptions.

The personality traits that determine the degree of attractiveness of children to television characters reflect, to a large degree, the cultural norms and expectations from males and females. For example, research has found that children of all ages wish to identify with "winners," even when their behaviors were evaluated as negative. For boys, this is expressed mainly through characters that excel physically and are very active. Both boys and girls value intelligence as a central characteristic that singles out male characters that they identify with. However, quite unsurprisingly, this is not true when it comes to girls pointing out their favorite female characters: Those are mainly valued for their attractive appearances. It seems that girls growing up today in many societies still internalize, quite well, the value that society-at-large assigns to female appearance, while ambitious and intelligent women are often sanctioned in television programs. Similarly, boys still grow up to believe that manhood is defined by action, physical force, and intelligence superiority. We will return to this central issue in Chapter 4.

Based on our discussion so far, it is easy to see how identification with television characters may be related to imitation of their behaviors. The underlining assumption is that the viewer enters the character's shoes – so to speak – that is, plays the character's role, and even internalizes unknowingly the value system that the character represents. This raises many important questions: Are there any particular personality characteristics that might predict imitation of negative behaviors (e.g., violence, lying) and others that predict imitation of positive behaviors (e.g., mutual aid, sharing)? Do specific personality characteristics lead to particular kinds of behavior patterns (e.g., physical force and violent behavior; physical attraction and sexual behavior)? We will discuss these and other questions related to imitation of behaviors portrayed on television at length in Chapter 3.

Children's Fear Reactions to Television Content

Another form of emotional involvement of children with television is that of fear reactions, already discussed in relationship to parental mediation in Chapter 1. Much television content, of all genres, can instigate fear and anxiety in viewers of all ages. Investigation into children's processing and reactions to such experiences raises many ethical issues. Clearly, we should not intervene in children's viewing habits by intentionally presenting them with scary material in order to study their reactions to it. Rather, we need to find ways to study these influences when they occur as a result of children's own viewing – by choice or coincidence.

There are many television elements that create fearful emotions: dangerous situations, injuries, bodily distortions, characters' own fearful reactions, and many more. Children may express their fear not only during the viewing situation, but also way beyond it – in nightmares, in situations that are associated with the televised scene, and the like. Some traumatizing television moments stay with them for many years and may affect their understandings and behavior in the real world.

As in other phenomena discussed so far, children's development is central to understanding their fear reactions. Contrary to what might be expected, children do not become less easily frightened as they mature. Instead, what seems to happen is that some stimuli that bothered them in the past produce less fear, but other stimuli that never elicited reactions in the past come to be problematic. For example, pre-operational children up to the age of 7 to 8 are scared of animals, the dark, super-natural forces (such as ghosts, witches and monsters); things that look anomalous or move unexpectedly. In the concrete-operational stage, these anxieties are largely replaced by fear of personal injury, as well as fear of injury or death of loved ones. Adolescents continue to worry about themselves, but also develop fear reactions in regards to political, economical and global issues. Concrete television stimuli (what we see and hear on television) decreasingly evokes fear as children mature with more abstract concepts gradually taking their place, such as the ability to understand the meaning and implications of dangers.

For example, pre-school children might be more afraid of something that looks dangerous, physically, but in fact is not threatening, rather than something that does not look dangerous, but may in fact be so. Such reactions are reversed during school-age years. No wonder, then, that young children react more fearfully to imaginary programs (e.g., cartoons, monsters) than to real dangers (e.g., news reports about an anticipated natural disaster). Such behavior, too, can be explained by applying lessons from developmental psychology: In order to develop anxiety over certain kinds of complicated threats presented on television, children require life experience, capabilities to distinguish between what is real and imaginary as well as to think in abstract terms, and knowledge about actual events such as the spread of a new plague, threats of nuclear disaster, or global warming.[19]

However, here too, we cannot ignore the relevancy of children's social context to their fear reactions to television content. A particular case in point is reactions to news reports about wars and terrorist events. Unfortunately, recent events have provided many opportunities to study this aspect more closely. Reactions to news of the Gulf War in 1991 among children in Europe and the USA who felt quite removed from the situation were quite mixed. However, reactions to the bombing of the Twin Towers in New York in 2001, the war in Iraq since 2003, as well as terrorist attacks by the suicide bombers in Israel were much more dramatic. The growing intensity of live news coverage of the events, particularly when the coverage "drives it home" by presenting the danger as more relevant and immediate, seems to result in an increase in fear reactions among children, as well as in a host of additional emotional reactions, such as anger, frustration, sense of helplessness and despair.[20] Producers of television for children at a time of war need to attend to both their cognitive needs for information and interpretation, as well as to their affective needs by recognizing their fears and concerns, and assisting them in emotion management.

In a study of Israeli children's reactions to news coverage of the Iraq war in 2003, Shirley, a 9-year-old girl explained these needs when she suggested what she would have done if she was a television producer for children: "I would have made a special program for children, because adults know what war is and children don't. I would have explained what is war, how they build missiles, and what will happen to us. I would have also made fun of them, and imitate George Bush or Sadam so the children will calm down."[21] Clearly children, much like adults, need appropriate outlets to express their emotions and to learn to channel them constructively. We will discuss other aspects of televised war coverage and children's political notions of the world in Chapter 4.

Television, Imagination, and Creativity

Television has been accused of "killing" children's imagination by imposing on them a limited range of narratives, characters, and ideas about the world. What are indeed the effects of television viewing on children's fantasy worlds? Several early studies found negative relationships between television viewing to children's scores on a variety of creative tasks such as thinking, problem solving, and writing abilities, thus concurring with the popular belief that heavy television use, particularly of a violent nature, indeed impedes the development of children's creative abilities. A series of studies found that children raised in communities without television rated higher on tests of creativity in comparison with children of similar background and life circumstances that were raised with it. These studies were conducted during a period of time when researchers were still able to find non-television societies that do not differ from the general population (e.g., those refraining from television for ideological or religious reasons; or the very poor and homeless). Today, however, it is difficult to find such societies and nearly impossible to reconstruct them. Thus, though these findings remain unverified, they continue to fuel and inspire a lively debate about the possibility that there does exist a causal negative relationship between television viewing and creativity and imagination, i.e., that television viewing impedes the development of creativity in children.[22]

Another line of investigation focused on how television stories differ in comparison to other forms of stories as stimuli of children's creativity and imagination. For example, one hypothesis claims that a televised version of a story stimulates less creative ideas, story lines, and problem-solving solutions than the same story told verbally (as in audio or print forms). Here the assumption is that the attractiveness of the visual aspects of television – what has been coined "the visual superiority effect" – is confounded by the advantages of auditory-verbal track for comprehension. Put simply, listening to a story on the radio may better stimulate the ability to create new story lines, characters, and events than viewing it on television.[23] Since these studies have been conducted primarily in the USA and Europe – this finding begs the question of universality: For example, will children growing up in a more orally oriented culture (e.g., traditional societies, orthodox-religious groups, homes that refrain from watching television for ideological reasons) as opposed to visually oriented cultures (e.g., heavily dependent on screen culture) perform differently on these tasks, simply because they have been raised to prioritize particular sets of mental skills over others?

The role of television as a stimulant of fantasy play (interchangeably termed "pretend," "make-believe," or "imaginative" play) is another area of research. Many of these studies are based upon the premise that television viewing may displace free play, particularly among young children who normally are expected to engage in such play. The accumulated research in this area suggests that ultimately the types of content children watch are more important in determining outcomes of fantasy and imaginative play than the quantity of time spent viewing. For example, viewing fantasy-violence on television content may inhibit or take the place of imaginative play, while educational programming that encourages pro-social behaviors designed to stimulate fantasy play may actually encourage it. Critics of commercial television argue that most of the programs appearing on commercial stations encourage passive viewing rather than active thinking and imagination, and rarely provide opportunities for young children to engage in creative imaginative play, presumed to be essential for their development.[24]

In contrast, there are many rich descriptions in ethnographic case-studies and anecdotal reports that illustrate the potential connections between media texts as stimuli for children's imagination and play: Embracing Ernie from *Sesame Street* as an imaginary companion in the USA; playing *Batman* or *Dragon Ball Z* games in Germany; imitating *Power Rangers* or playing out the roles of friends in *Neighbors* in the UK; aspiring to be like a member of the *Spice Girls* pop group or a *Pokémon Master* in Israel; imagining meeting friends from the *Mongol* television series in South Korea; to name just a few.[25] All of the aforementioned forms of television content were found to be used by children to construct their make-believe worlds and in doing so to express their desires through imagined play within those worlds. Further, children were found to borrow from settings seen on TV (e.g., a space station, a jungle, even a television studio), objects (e.g., a vehicle, a piece of furniture, a building), characters (e.g., an animated super hero, a celebrity, a protagonist), customs (e.g., a cape, a mask, an accessory), narratives (e.g., action-adventure, soap-opera, situation comedy), and specific information (e.g., name of places, characters, events, scientific inventions, medical treatments) and integrate them in their imagined and/or wish for stories for themselves. Take, for example, this story told by Omer, a 9-year-old Israeli boy, in an interview setting. Omer is describing a drawing he has made of his make-believe world:

> This world is only mine … here I am the ruler. I can do whatever I want. Everything is allowed. I am wearing a suit. The red-cloak is like Superman's. The green are my hands so that I can climb on everything like Spiderman, those blue things in my hands are my fire laser-ray weapons. The red is a belt like Pokémon's. The purple are my flying boots, and the horns I took from Batman's mask. I am the master and I also have a sword, like in Star Wars."

He continues with his story, combining a host of media sources, unrelated to the original superpowers, including books – new and old classics:

There is a carpet and a bed and lots of things for training ... like in the Olympics. Also Pokémon figures, a huge Pikachu ... In this world there are good people and bad people, and also a school in a castle, like Hogwart's school in Harry Potter, that I have already graduated from ... In the middle of my world there is a mystery island like Jules Verne's, with lots of whales, like Moby Dick. When I am asleep I dream about the powers of television heroes, and I added a bit from my own imagination ...

Omer "slips" on the various super-powers as one slips on a dress, including the special skills he possesses as the master (*Star Wars*) and those he has learnt at the school of magic (*Harry Potter*). He goes out armed for adventures in a world where the good and the bad co-exist, as on the famous *Treasure Island* or in the fight with *Moby Dick*. Omer adopts the status of the media character, on one hand (i.e., being a graduate of the school of magic and being the master), as well as the special skills and weapons of superheroes, on the other hand.[26]

Omer's story is but one illustration of the intense inter-relationship between media culture and children's fantasy world as expressed in their everyday lives. However, while recognizing that children do use television content in their fantasy play, many questions remain unanswered: for example: What is the frequency of television's contribution to fantasy play? Is play induced from a non-television-related source more or less imaginative (e.g., a book, a story told by an adult, a theater play)? Does it make sense to deliberate, as researchers, about whether one kind of imaginative play is of higher quality and more desired than the other?

A Conceptual and Methodological Reflection

This is a very good point to stop our review and reflect over some of the conceptual and methodological issues involved in studying children and television as they have been discussed so far in the first two chapters. We will use the latter discussion of television, imagination and creativity as an illustration of a much wider debate. The accumulating body of knowledge that suggests that overall negative effects of media on children's creativity, imagination and fantasy play are stronger than its positive effects has largely emerged from the research tradition of media effects. These studies of children and television embrace developmental theories in cognitive psychology that center on the individual child. Accordingly, this approach sees children as in the process of "becoming" an adult. Their abilities and skills are tested and measured in comparison to the ideal model of the adult thinker. This approach has been named "the deficiency model" as it assumes that the child is "deficient" in comparison with the adult. It is a research paradigm with roots in various stimulus-response models whose goal is to find correlations between television content and fantasy activity. Research applying this approach has been conducted primarily through experimental designs, where children are brought into a study-setting and presented with various tasks. In most cases, such studies quantify pre-defined fantasy activities. Thus, the researcher counts the number of times the child behaves in specific manner; for example, says something aloud, sings a song, dresses up, re-arranges furniture, and the like. The major strength of studies conducted in such a manner is that they can isolate and control the issues selected for study and place each child in a comparable situation. For example, they can control the kind of television material to which the child is exposed during the experiment, the skills tested, the toys available in the room, and the like. Researchers assume that such a context has a greater chance of attaining more specific as well as causal explanations. For example, they can determine that a specific educational program elicits a certain activity while a violent program does not. Many questions can be raised regarding the type of activities selected for coding and the researcher's value judgments attached to them (e.g., is it "good" when the child dresses up as Princess after having been read a story, but "not good" if she dresses up like a Princess she saw on television?). Reservations can also be made regarding the suitability of the unnatural experimental setting for eliciting and observing fantasy-related activities.

In correlational studies, another often applied research format, home-viewing behaviors are measured through responses to questionnaires and correlated with other cognitive skills. The major strength of this research method is its ability to examine long-term, accumulative influences of viewing television on a very large number of subjects and thus it can offer insights that can be generalized to other situations.

In contrast to the approaches mentioned above, naturalistic or ethnographic studies observe children in their own familiar settings as they express or articulate their inner worlds in play, drawing, and/or talk. Such studies are of a smaller scale, but take place in more natural environments such as the children's homes and schools, where children engage in and reveal fantasy and creative behaviors more spontaneously. Researchers who apply the ethnographic approach do not test the children, rather they observe as well as talk to them, and try to make sense of what they do and say. Rather than seeing children as in the process of "becoming" adults, they focus on seeing children as a "being" in their own right, at each individual stage of their development. Rather than perceiving children as "deficient" in comparison to adults, they treat them simply as being different.

Ethnographic studies have emerged from a very different research tradition than the positivist-based approach summarized earlier in this section. Here children are presumed to act subjectively in meaningful ways that express their own perspectives, worldviews, and self-image. This approach argues that children are often underestimated by experimental research that is psychologically oriented, and more specifically, that the significance that television has for children's fantasy world can hardly be encapsulated in studies conducted through experiments in unfamiliar settings. Rather, they approach children as autonomous individuals, socially competent, who actively make sense of, indeed construct and express meanings as they interact with the world around them. What is perceived as central or important in a television program for adults is not necessarily so for children, thus the comparison with adults as a central criterion to evaluating children's comprehension or creativity is perceived as misleading. Known as the qualitative method, such studies concentrate on "the meaning television has for children" and "what children do with television," rather than on "how children's comprehension is deficient in comparison to adults" and "what television does to children."

Furthermore, this alternative approach argues that adopting an approach that assumes that a television story has one clear, true, deep structure and that grasping it is crucial for mature comprehension of the story prevents the possibility of exposing alternative interpretations of it. Evaluating characters, judging their morality, or identifying with them is deeply ground in the social context of the child. If we pursue this criticism further, we can appreciate its possible epistemological implications: understanding television is by definition, a contextualized experience. Any attempt to enforce one "correct" interpretation, one possible "meaning," for example, an imagined adult view, is misleading. Adults too, just like children, have a gender, a race, a social class, a religion, a culture, a political view. Adults, too, live in very diverse cultures all over the worlds. Accordingly, there is not, nor can there be one ideal adult-comprehension model.

Could we possibly see these two approaches as complementary rather than competitive? Can we integrate the knowledge gained from both traditions into a fuller and more comprehensible understanding of the role of television in children's lives? Can we accept that children lack the skills and knowledge that adults have developed as they mature and at the same time respect the meaning children produce from television in their own right? Can we consider each child's individual development and at the same time integrate our understanding of this development as embedded in complicated social contexts? Can we employ experimental, correlational, as well as ethnographic methods as appropriate to our research questions, and combine the results of all approaches to create a more comprehensive understanding of children? We need to keep these questions in the back of our minds as we assess other studies and discuss other issues in this book.

Notes

1 Valkenburg (2004), Van Evra (2004).
2 Piaget (1969), Piaget and Inhelder (1969).
3 Mander (1978), Winn (1977).
4 Anderson and Field (1986), Anderson and Lorch (1983), Bickham, Wright, and Huston (2001).
5 Anderson and Lorch (1983).
6 Anderson, and Pempek (2005).
7 Anderson and Lorch (1983), Lemish (1987), Valkenburg and Vroone (2004).
8 Salomon (1981).
9 See issue 12(2) of TelevIZIon (1999), devoted to research on the *Teletubbies*.
10 See also Valkenburg and Cantor (2000). For discussion of gendered preferences, see Lemish, Liebes, and Seidmann (2001).
11 The discussion in this section has been informed by Chandler (1997), Dorr (1983), Fitch, Huston, and Wright (1993), Hawkins (1977), and Messenger Davies (1997).
12 Hansen, Rasmussen, Martensen, and Tufte (2002), Lemish (1997), Valkenburg and Cantor (2002).
13 See in particular the work by Collins (1981, 1983) and Collins and Wellman (1982).
14 See, for example, Dorr, Kovaric, and Doubleday (1990), Heintz-Knowles (1992), Newcomb and Collins (1979).
15 Calvert and Huston (1987), Signorielli (2001).
16 Hoffner and Cantor (1991), Reeves (1979), Wartella and Alexander (1978).
17 Theories of moral development are heavily influenced by Kohlberg, see for example Kohlberg (1984) as well on the feminist critic of his work, originally voiced by Gilligan (1982). As applied to television, see Collins (1983) and Rosenkoetter (2001).
18 Hoffner (1996), Hoffner and Cantor (1991), Raviv, Bar-Tal, Raviv, and Ben-Horin (1996).
19 See particularly Cantor's work: Cantor (1994, 1996, 2001).

20 See in regards to the Gulf War of 1991, Cantor, Mares, and Oliver (1993). Hoffner and Haefner (1993), and Wober and Young (1993). In regards to the Twin Towers, see Smith (forthcoming) and Walma van der Molen (forthcoming); in regards to everyday news reporting, see Smith and Wilson (2000, 2002).
21 Lemish (forthcoming).
22 MacBeth (1996). Most notable opponents of television in this area are the Singers, see for example, Singer (1993), Singer and Singer (1976, 1981, 1983, and 1990).
23 Greenfield and Beagles-Roos (1988), Greenfield, Farrer, and Beagles-Roos (1986), Rolandelli (1989).
24 Valkenburg (2001), Valkenberg and Van der Voort (1994), Van der Voort and Valkenburg (1994).
25 Quoted in Götz, Lemish, Aidman, and Moon (2005, pp. 5–6).
26 Ibid., pp. 93–5.

3

Television and the Behavior of Children

The concern that television may effect children's behavior, primarily in negative ways, has been the center of much of the public and academic debate over the role of television's in children's lives. While early studies of television's effects on children were ground in a variety of theoretical traditions, they gradually adopted much of the discourse of the "strong effects" theories of mass communication that focus on studies of public opinion and political campaigns. Dominant in mid-twentieth-century North American research, the basic premise of studies of effects is that viewing television results in related behaviors: television violence instigates violent behavior; commercials lead to purchase of products advertised; sex on television leads to sexual permissiveness, and the like.

This accusatory assumption has fueled public debate about television's effects on children and has been the cause advanced by researchers seeking funding from governmental institutions for study of these effects. A milestone case in point, is the US Surgeon General's Report of 1972; a five volume report of government sponsored academic studies that focused solely on the issue of television violence, a source of much public anxiety at the time.

What exactly is meant by the term "effect?" As is often the case, the question asked determines to a large degree what has been studied and the methodology applied. There are two particular sets of questions that have dominated studies of children and the effects of television: First, does television re-enforce existing behavioral tendencies and/or create new ones? Second, what are the immediate and long-term effects? Each set of questions asked in regards to television effects has significance in regard to the methodology to be applied in order to pursue them.

The first set of questions assumes that television has a powerful role in influencing people's lives and that it has significant implications in regard to the degree of responsibility that can be ascribed to those in charge of its production. Let us take, for example, the aforementioned concern over the effects of televised violence on children. The position that television reinforces existing behaviors will have us predict that, on the one hand, aggressive children will be affected by television violence, while on the other hand, non-aggressive ones will not be so effected. This will place much of the responsibility for children's behavior on other factors – the child's personality, family background, earlier violent experiences, and the like, all external to television. However, an approach that suggests that children may learn aggressive behaviors from television, even those without a predisposition to violence (i.e., without a prior record of having aggressive tendencies), assigns a much more powerful role to television messages. According to this approach, children are exposed to and learn a host of influences via television, be they negative or positive. Consequently, the responsibility for such behaviors lies directly with the creators of television messages as well as with parents who allow such viewing.

The set of second questions focuses on the temporal dimensions of effects: Are the behavioral effects immediate (e.g., a "copy cat" imitation of a soldier firing a rifle on the TV screen; asking for an advertised candy) or are there long-term behaviors that develop over time and that involve a change in the behavioral repertoire of the child (e.g., become more aggressive in non-television, but related situations; changing eating habits). While sometimes short-term effects are isolated events that have no lasting influence, perhaps they can be indicators of the beginning of a trend toward long terms effects?

Despite interest in different sets of questions, there does seem to be an agreement that in all societies around the world children are perceived to be the most vulnerable members: they are smaller and physically weaker; they need protection, care, feeding, fostering, and socialization to the adult world; they lack life experience and knowledge; they think differently than do adults; and they lack social and economical resources. If, indeed, television has the potential for short- or long-term effects upon behavior, feelings, or thought, whether it be in reinforcing them or creating them, then children are the most prone to it.

In contrast to the effects' school of research, the cultural studies alternative grew out of European theoretical traditions. While this approach, too, recognizes the fact that children are different from adults, as noted in the previous paragraph, it does not view them as "deficient" in comparison to adults, but focuses its attention on how their unique characteristics mediate the effects. The central premise of this approach is that what children bring with them to the encounter with television determines in large degree what they take from the experience. Here, children are not assumed to be passive, defenseless, receptors, the proverbial tabula rasa, on which television "writes" freely. Rather, they bring with them and apply in the viewing encounter their own accumulated knowledge and experience, needs and sensitivities, meanings acquired in complicated socialization processes, tastes and preferences. Accordingly, the active viewer cultural studies approach assumes that the meanings (rather than effects) of television for children are a result of complicated processes of negotiation that develop over a multitude of viewing encounters, over an extended period of time, and in given social circumstances.

The differences between the two approaches to television effects is embedded in a fundamental theoretical controversy within the field of mass communication and have significant methodological implications, as we have already discussed at the end of the previous chapter. Furthermore, it should be noted that in certain academic circles even the term "effects" itself has been ostracized as being old fashioned and misleading and its study as superfluous. This having been noted, most of the research discussed in this chapter is embedded in the more traditional "effects" approaches that apply psychological and sociological approaches to the study of human behavior.

Television and Violent Behavior

Of all topics related to children and television, violent behavior is the one that has attracted the most attention. The media in particular are keen to report cases that stimulate this concern: In Israel, a 7-year-old boy who broke his spine was reported to have shouted – "Look how Superman flies!" – before jumping out of a window. In Norway, a 5-year-old girl was severely harassed by her friends following the viewing of a particular television series. In the USA, the viewing of the Oliver Stone's movie *Natural Born Killers* (portraying a series of murders) was blamed for a 15-year-old youth's murder of his parents. In Thailand, a 9-year-old boy hung himself in imitation of a scene from a popular series that had depicted a killing by the hanging of a victim. Each of us can probably remember similar cases reported in our own media. Often, such reports dramatize the news event and target television as its sole cause. Among the best-known cases at the time was that of a teenager from Miami Florida who murdered his elderly neighbor, arguing in defense that he was imitating a specific episode from the then popular *Kojak* detective series. The trial of this case in the mid-1970s was reported widely and aroused significant public interest. The boy, however, was found responsible for his criminal act and television was cleared of guilt.

The predominance of violence in many commercial television programs is hardly a debated fact. Violence on TV is exciting, easily
understood regardless of language and cultural barriers, and thus
"travels well" in the global market of television programs. If we choose
to define violence as a purposeful hurting of another being or property
(and some may extend the definition to include also un-intentional
injury, such as accidents, as well as violence located in the animal
world), we find that there are many violent elements, salient or overt,
in most television genres: war movies, westerns, crime detectives,
dramas, news, documentaries, sports, cartoons, music-clips, and commercials. If we include verbal violence (a form of intended harm
performed through words rather than physical force), we will find
that many comedies, talk as well as entertainment shows can also be
included in the long list of violent broadcasts. Studies that measured
the frequency and types of various forms of violence on television in
various countries have re-affirmed the international scope of this phenomenon.

A second, undisputed fact is that, at the risk of over-generalizing, we
can state that most children, from a very young age, watch many of
these genres and thus are exposed to a variety of violent expressions on
a regular basis over the entire life cycle. While it is virtually impossible
to actually count how many acts of violence a child may view over time,
let alone to suggest an "average" number that can hold true for the
"average" child, it has been suggested that by the age of 12 children
viewing commercial television will have been exposed to about 20,000
murders and about 100,000 other acts of violence. Putting aside the
validity and accuracy of such numbers, there is little disagreement that
children all over the world watch a lot more violence on television on a
regular basis then they would ever come close to witnessing in real life.[1]

But it is not only the mere volume of violence on television that is of
concern for the potential of children to develop a healthy social life, but
also the types of violent acts and the circumstances in which they occur.
Consider the following example: A comprehensive study that analyzed
US television programs (to which people in many societies all over the
world are exposed) revealed that three-quarters of the violent characters go unpunished for their acts; about half of the representations of
acts of violence did not show injury to or suffering of the victims; only
about one-sixth presented the long-term implications of violence, such
as those of an emotional or economic nature; and only a fraction of the
programs (4%) that presented violence used the opportunity to be
critical of it or to discuss non-violent options for resolving problems.[2]

Different genres, of course, present violence differently. For example,
movies tend to show violence in more realistic terms and to include

more gory scenes than other television genres. Children's programs, on the whole, hardly ever present the long-term effects of violence and often contextualize violent scenes in humorous situations.

Do children learn moral as well as practical lessons about a "mean world" through such viewing? About the role of violence in our society? About certain violent acts that can be committed without punishment? These are just a few of the questions that have been investigated in the research on children and the media reviewed in the following pages. We will examine what we can learn from the accumulated research on the effect of viewing television violence on children's behavior on two levels: first, the immediate influence of learning specific violent behaviors; and, second, the long-term effects of viewing television violence. The effects of such viewing on children's mental world will be discussed in Chapter 4.

Learning violent behaviors

Do children tend to imitate violent behaviors viewed on television? We may want to dismiss the cases cited above as extremely exceptional, ones where television might serve as a catalyst for a child who possessed an already fertile ground of aggressive tendencies, for a failure to distinguish reality from fantasy, and the like. This not withstanding, the question remains – do most children who could be described as possessing the "normal" range of behaviors, the ones we see around us everyday, learn violent behaviors from television? In order to establish a causal relationship between television viewing and imitation of violent behavior, researchers have presented children with different versions of violent television stimuli in experimental settings and measured their reactions to it. For example, in doing so they sought to understand the conditions under which a child would imitate an aggressive act of hitting following a similar scene on television.

Ground in social learning theory, one approach to this question argues that children learn a repertoire of behaviors imitating the actions of role models that are, in turn, positively reinforced. Television is a rich resource for such learning, in general, and of violent behaviors, more specifically. Violent programs supply children with many ideas for specific acts of violence. They also teach viewers the functionality of violent behaviors: those that receive positive reinforcement (e.g., praise, a reward) versus those that are rejected (e.g., scolding, punishment). Justification of violent behavior is important as it increases the chances of children's imitation while positive reinforcement provides added value by suggesting to children what society values. Furthermore, it is argued that viewing violence may serve to remove inhibitions in performing violent acts through a process of desensitization to their implications, as well as, a process of legitimization of such behaviors as being normal and acceptable in society.

Indeed, studies performed in this widely accepted tradition in psychology found that children imitated televised violent behavior, performed newly acquired behavior even after a lapse of time, and were more prone to behave violently during a play session following the viewing.[3]

A different interpretation for the effect mechanism is offered by arousal theory. According to this approach, viewing violence on television generally arouses children and stimulates them to behave violently, though not necessarily through the imitation of the same specific behaviors. Arousal theory may also complement social learning theory, as arousal may prepare the ground for learning more specific behaviors.[4]

Here, too, it is important to note that caution is required given the many ethical as well as methodological critiques posed in regard to studies that have attempted to document direct causal effects of television violence. Is it moral to expose children in research settings to violent content knowing that this exposure may be harmful to them? Is it ethical to create research circumstances that allow children to behave aggressively? Is it at all possible to isolate the many variables that may affect the relationship between viewing violence and the violent behavior (e.g., characteristics of the viewer, of the program, of the violent act, of the circumstances)? How similar are the television segments viewed in the experiments with those children view at home on a daily basis? How similar are the viewing circumstances in the unnatural research setting in comparison to those at home? In summary, as in all studies examining human behavior in research settings, these studies, too, are open to the central criticism leveled against studies that attempt to generalize from children's behaviors under artificial experimental circumstances to their everyday reality and behavior.

Cumulative effect of television violence

An even more complicated issue is the question of the nature of the relationship between long-term viewing of television violence and aggressive behavior. Put simply, do children who watch a lot of violent television tend to be more violent than the average, reasonable child? Or, perhaps, is it the other way around: children who watch more violence are much less violent because they have more opportunities to relieve their aggression through a process of catharsis? And, a third possibility, perhaps there is no relationship between viewing television and violent behavior? In statistical terms, such correlations will be termed positive, when viewing television violence is associated with violent behaviors; negative, when heavy viewing is associated with lower violent behaviors; and zero, when there is no clear relationship between the two. Researchers have applied two major research strategies in their attempts to confront these questions: Field experiments and correlational studies.

Field experiments are a form of methodological "compromise" that attempts to study the phenomenon in more natural settings, while controlling for some variables (similar to attempts made in many experimental designs). Schools, daycare centers, and summer camps are settings that are best suited for this kind of research, since it is possible to control to a large degree the kind of television programs children view there. A typical study assigns children to different viewing "diets" (i.e., research "treatments"). For example, one group might view typical children's programs with violence on a daily basis (e.g., action-adventure cartoons); a second group views programs that promote socially acceptable behaviors and non-violent resolution of inter-personal or social problems; and a third views programs perceived to be "neutral" - they do not promote any kind of behavior (e.g., nature programs). We can describe this research design in a general graphic form, as follows (see Figure 3.1).[5]

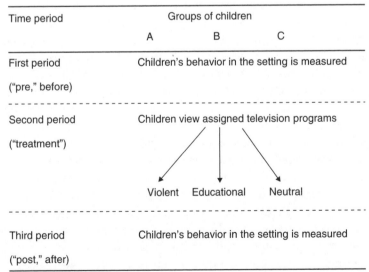

Figure 3.1   Field study design

Children's behaviors are rated in such studies according to the degree of its aggressiveness, sociability (e.g., cooperation, mutual aid, verbal expression of feelings), and self-control (persistence, obedience, ability to handle frustration). Comparisons between these measures of behavior of children in the two periods before and after the exposure to the programs are expected to provide an indication of the cumulative effect of watching television: Would children in group A become more violent? Would children in group B become less violent and more involved in socially accepted behaviors? Would children in group C show any behavioral change?

Interestingly, studies that applied this design have not been able to arrive at unified conclusions. Some found that viewing violent programs made a significant difference for children who originally rated higher on measures of aggressive behavior. Others concluded that their findings do not allow them to indicate such an effect. Increasingly, researchers have been searching for alternative methods that will not involve the ethical problem of exposing children intentionally to violent programs and that will be less obtrusive in children's everyday lives.

The alternative approach, *correlational studies*, does not attempt to look for direct effects, but rather searches for long-term correlations between viewing television violence and violent behavior. The amount of violent television content a child is exposed to is calculated based on detailed reports of viewing habits (for example, via questionnaires or weekly viewing diaries). The level of child aggressiveness is usually evaluated by others – reports of parents, teachers, or peers. These kinds of studies are characterized by participation of very large numbers of a wide age range of children. A few such studies have been conducted over the span of a number of years and even returned to the same children following extended lapses of time to investigate changes that developed over time. One such study also attempted a cross-cultural comparison and was conducted in Australia, Finland, Israel, Poland, and the USA.[6] Overall, correlational studies have found that children who were rated as more violent by their friends were also those who were heavy viewers of violent television. Furthermore, the more a child watched violent television in a given year, the more likely it was that the child would be rated as aggressive in the following years.[7]

One way to interpret such findings is to perceive them as a vicious circle; viewing of violent television stimulates aggression and this aggression stimulates more viewing of violent television, and vice versa. Several critiques of these studies have focused on the social context within which the children involved in the studies are located. For example, would children growing up in a more violent society be more prone to accept television violence as justified and normative and thus be more prone to be effected by it? Would children raised in a peaceful environment where violent behavior is uncommon and is strongly sanctioned be more resilient to such an influence?

In summary, many academics conclude that despite the methodological diversity employed by researchers and the differences in specific findings produced, there seems to be common agreement that is reinforced with each new study. Most studies conclude that there are positive correlations, although low, between violent behavior and exposure to television violence. That is, viewing television violence is related more to the aggressive behavior of an individual child. Further, the more accurate the measure of television violence, the greater the positive correlation (for example, a calculation of the child's actual viewing with the level of violence in the specific programs viewed).[8]

These conclusions reinforce claims made by experimental researchers, who argue that there is a positive correlation between viewing violence and behaving violently. However, though this correlation has been found repeatedly within a relatively constant range, its level is not very high. Furthermore, it should be noted that a correlation does not necessarily indicate a causal relationship: that is, the positive correlation found does not offer a clear explanation regarding the nature of the relationships between the two measures. Is viewing violent television the cause of violent behavior or is it the case that violent children are more attracted to violence on television? Or, perhaps, both viewing violence and behaving violently are related to an external, unrelated variable (e.g., learning disabilities, attention deficits)?

It seems reasonable to conclude that the relationship between viewing violence on television and violent behavior is not one directional, but circular. There is very little doubt that children with aggressive tendencies tend to watch more violent television. However, at the same time, there is substantial evidence that viewing violent television encourages aggressive behavior even in children without such a previous record. This conclusion reinforces the view presented earlier that children are not merely passive victims of television violence, but active initiators who search for content that appeals to their tastes.[9]

Our discussion of this issue would not be complete without mentioning the popular "catharsis hypothesis." Since Ancient Greece, drama in all its forms has been perceived as a means of emotional outlet for fears, tensions, sorrow, and the like. Here the assumption is that physical and mental energies can be relieved in a variety of ways, including through fictitious violence. For example, frustration caused by failure or an insult may cause intensification of violent urges. Since this urge creates internal discomfort, the frustrated person searches for ways to dispose of it. Viewing television violence is perceived as one accessible and acceptable way of reducing violent urges and for creating a feeling of "purification" or "cleansing," otherwise known as "catharsis." Following this line of argument, television violence may serve as a substitute for violent behavior in the real world.

While this hypothesis may appeal to many, it has been often exploited by interested bodies (such as commercial broadcasters) who cite it as "proof" of the social benefits of viewing violent programs. Yet, researchers agree, in general, that there is no evidence to support such a process, certainly not among children. If catharsis was in operation, we could have expected to find negative correlations: children viewing violent programs should have had many more opportunities to relieve their aggressive urges and therefore to be less violent than those not watching such programs. The general research evidence presented earlier is quite unequivocal that that this is not the case.[10]

Intervening variables

Who, then, among the children are more prone to be effected by television violence? What are the intervening variables that differentiate between children and the process mediating these effects?

We have seen that many of the studies of effects repeatedly suggest that there is evidence of correlations between viewing violent programs and children's pre-disposition to violence, their social and adjustment difficulties, and the like. First hand data gathered in a unique, small case study of 8 juvenile delinquents in Sweden found that they were inspired by aggressive film heroes and learned specific acts of violence from them.[11] One underlying assumption associated with these findings is that children with a variety of behavioral, social, cognitive, and emotional difficulties may turn to television as a substitute for the need to cope with real social situations and, thus, they are much more prone to its negative effects. For example, cognitive difficulties may intensify television's influence, since children may turn to viewing television as a substitute for other more cognitively challenging activities (such as school work, reading, Internet surfing). In addition, they may have more difficulty comprehending television content and tend to accept more readily violent problem-solving behaviors viewed on television as relevant to their own reality.

The general level of the child's arousal during the viewing situation, too, may be related to the aforementioned personal characteristics. The more aroused the child (e.g., tensed, frustrated, angry, hungry) the more likely is the chance that his or her temper may flare. As a result, the same level of violence in a particular program may affect even the same child differently, given different emotional states during the viewing.

Research also suggests that there are quite consistent gender differences in regards to attraction to violent programs as well as related behavior. For example, UNESCO sponsored a global study of media violence of 5,000 12-year-old children in 23 countries reflecting a representative range of human and technological variables. The study found that boys were fascinated by aggressive media heroes. Among participants, 88 percent knew about Arnold Schwarzeneger's film representation of the *Terminator*, a popular icon at the time of the study (1996–7).[12] This and other studies suggest that on the whole girls enjoy violence much less than boys, they are much more critical of it, and perceive it as less realistic. They also tend to react more emotionally to violence and to demonstrate signs of fear. These differences become more distinct from around the age of 10, perhaps as a result of the growing consolidation of gender identity and growing awareness of social expectations of "masculine" and "feminine" appropriate behaviors.

Recently, there seems to be evidence of a trace of a tendency of a closing of the gender gap, according to which it seems that more girls are starting to show an interest in violent programs and characters that have been traditionally perceived as "masculine." Here we need to remember that while men still perform most of the violent acts on television (as in life) and women are presented much more often as victims than as aggressors (again, true to reality), there is a growing number of women, in both children's and adults' programs, appearing in active roles, in general, as characters in the powerful world of police, crime, and science fiction, as well as a new trend to present "sexy-tough" women as aggressors. Notice, too, in this regard that this trend does not seem to be working the other way around. That is, we have yet to see a trend of more boys distancing themselves from violent "masculine" role models or a growing interest in non-violent modes of "feminine" conflict resolution.

The child's family background, too, plays a major role in mediating the potential effects of television's violence. The educational and value system guiding each family, in general, and attitudes toward violence, in particular, characterize the child's home environment. We expect children raised in non-violent homes will watch less violent television and that they will be affected by it to a lesser degree. Similarly, it has been argued that children who come from a home that employs physical punishments, where television is the sole source of leisure, and where there is no parental control of amount and content of television viewing will be more prone to such effects. Research studies on the role of the home in mediating the effects of viewing violence are few and far between and the findings are not clear cut, leaving many parents with the concern that the task of holding one's own in a world dominated by television is difficult.

Finally, a special note of caution regarding cultural diversity, too, is required. Most of the research about television violence reviewed here was undertaken in television-rich countries, primarily in Northern America and Europe. In contrast, research from other countries suggests cultural variance. For example, an argument has been put forth by a Japanese researcher that violence on Japanese television is represented quite differently from that portrayed in typical American television, including the showing of the after-effects of violence on victims and their suffering. Could this difference serve as a mediating variable that weakens the relationships between viewing violence by Japanese children in comparison to their American counterparts? Could the fact that Israeli children glorify wrestlers of the *World Wrestling Federation* as American heroes be due to their living with an omnipresent threat of conflict and thus viewing the *WWF* intensifies their vulnerability to such portrayals of violence? Additional evidence comes from the UNESCO global study cited above in which it was found that 51 percent of the children from high-aggression environments (such as areas of recent-war zones and refugee camps in some African countries in the sample, as well as some crime-stricken economically poor environments) wanted to be like their admired aggressive, televised role model, in comparison to 37 percent of the children in low-aggression neighborhoods.[13]

By way of further reservation, some researchers have questioned charges that television has any contribution whatsoever to social violence these days. Their critique of specific studies suggests that it may be possible to ask serious questions about these findings and arguments. Others raise ideological arguments to refute the effect argument – both over the social assumptions underlying the studies as well as the search for causal explanations for human behavior. Television, it is argued, did not invent violence, but serves only as a means of presenting it, as did other media before its invention. Further, it is important to remember that the majority of these studies were undertaken in the USA and thus contain an inherent cultural bias. Some would argue that both US society and television is more violent than many places in the world. In any event, we cannot discuss television violence in a vacuum: it is necessary to contextualize it within the dominant forms of violence in each society, its consequences, and the societal norms associated with it.

Finally, it has been argued that coping with violence is part of childhood as it is in all periods of human existence. Viewing violence allows children to experiment with different feelings, such as fears and anxieties, to internalize definitions of good and bad, the permitted and the forbidden. Indeed, part of growing up includes the development of defense mechanisms against the unpleasant aspects of life, and those include, unfortunately, violence.[14]

In summary, it appears that a rebuttal can be made for each position on this issue. However, one claim that all can agree upon is that to date no one has been able to question the accumulative, general finding produced in hundreds of research projects undertaken through a variety of research methods by many different researchers in many countries all over the world that suggest the existence of at least some effect of television violence on children's behavior.

So, does viewing television violence influence aggressive behaviors among children? The answer seems to be yes, with reservations. Clearly, television is but one factor, but certainly not the sole nor an isolated one in stimulating a-social behaviors. That is, the influence of television is confounded by a host of other factors and embedded in specific cultural contexts.

Further, all agree that this is a complicated issue with meaningful implications for children's broadcasting policy, as well as, an undisputed need to develop critical viewing skills in children. These are dimensions that we will return to in Chapter 6. Finally, irrespective of whether or not there is an agreed upon academic verdict on the effects of television violence, some families prefer to limit its presence in their home, as they find it unbefitting the culture in which they wish to raise their children.

Television and Pro-Social Behavior

The same principles and methods that characterize studies of television's effects on anti-social behaviors are also applicable to studying other types of behavior. If indeed it is possible to learn negative behaviors from television, would it not follow that it will be also possible to learn positive, pro-social behaviors as well? Indeed, this is an important question, as it reminds us that television is a multifaceted medium and certainly cannot be cast in negative terms alone.

Pro-social behaviors are those that are perceived to be desirable by society at large. For example, the following television contents have been evaluated as pro-social: contents that promote cooperation and mutual aid; expressions of regret for harm doing; sympathy and empathy with another person's situation or emotions; learning to persist in a task and to delay satisfaction; seeing things from another person's point of view; controlling violent urges; expressing feelings; resisting temptations; and the like.

For example, educational programs for young viewers often emphasize the value and uniqueness of each person, including the child-
viewer, in order to encourage a positive self-image as well as respect
for others. Such programs focus on learning to cope with problems,
issues, and situations typical of children's lives; for example, "the first
day of school;" "moving;" "arrival of a new baby;" "wearing glasses;" as
well as having tolerance and accepting diversity (minorities, disabilities,
foreigners), and so on. Many of the situations and issues posed are
common to all societies, but others vary from one society to the other.
Thus, in many Western societies we might find a segment dedicated to
"divorce," while other cultures promote their own social concerns: for
example, in South Africa an educational program for pre-school children focuses on the emotions of a child orphaned by AIDS; in Israel
children learn about how to wear a gas mask in preparation for war; in
Thailand children learn the value of helping parents in the field; in
Brazil boys are encouraged to engage in traditional female household
chores.[15] Programs for older children present topics appropriate to
their stage of development: conflicts with parents, issue of self-identity,
sexuality, professional career aspirations, peer pressure, rejection by
friends, and many more.

Here, too, the topics and their means of presentation may vary
greatly from one society to the other. For example, while Nordic
educational programs typically handle issues of sexuality openly and
with no inhibitions, most other societies are much more reserved in
dealing with these issues on the airwaves, and, indeed, some would find
it completely inappropriate to even attempt to do so at all. Even within
each society, there are many disagreements regarding what constitutes
pro-social behavior (e.g., is using contraceptives a pro-social behavior?
does volunteering for military service constitute pro-social behavior?)
In pluralistic societies, in particular, there is no one unequivocal code of
ethics regarding the kind of values and behaviors that television needs
to promote, and thus producers often find themselves dealing with a
public debate of issues presented.

All television genres, not only educational and public ones, include
pro-social role models among their many characters. A situation comedy, a sports program, a commercial, and indeed even a program with
violence often include pro-social behaviors as well. Many of these are
embedded in the program intentionally, as a result of social pressure by
various lobbying groups following negotiations with commercial
broadcasters: for example, including non-smoking behaviors, wearing
a seatbelt, eating nutritious food, saving money in the bank, learning to
read and write, refraining from driving under the influence of alcohol,
applying non-violent solutions to family conflicts, and so on. The logic

of including such strategies is that incidental learning of behaviors while viewing entertainment genres can be particularly effective as the viewer chooses to view the program, is emotionally engaged with the content, identifies with the characters, and perceives the message as a legitimate and natural form of behavior in the social setting depicted in the program.

Similar to the violence studies, here too, researchers have applied both experimental as well as correlational methodologies in order to investigate the effectiveness of pro-social television messages. Actually a limited number of studies have been devoted to such inquiry, as clearly the fear of violent effects of some television programs has been deemed to be much more central to the agenda of most societies than the exploration of the positive potential of television. However, from the knowledge that has already been gained in this area, it is clear that children are capable of learning positive behaviors from television in the same manner as they are able to learn negative behaviors.

For example, several studies were conducted in the USA on *Mr Rogers' Neighborhood*, a pre-school program broadcast for over 30 years. The program featured a father/grandfather type character, Mr Rogers, who invites the young viewers into his television home and neighborhood. Together they visit some concrete places relevant to children growing up in that culture (e.g., a post-office, bakery, school). He introduces viewers to many professionals as well as shares with them emotional experiences. Mr Rogers himself talks to the children at "eye-level" in a relaxed manner, full of respect and affection without any form of condescension. Each program also includes "the neighborhood of make-believe," a puppet show with a clear transition marked by a trolley ride. Studies found that ongoing viewing of this program improved over time children's ability to persist on tasks, to be more cooperative, to have learned skills involved in assisting others, to delay satisfaction, and to participate in creative games.[16]

Studies of other programs have found that viewing television can encourage generosity, cooperation, and delay of satisfaction, social integration of shy children, and many other pro-social behaviors. It can contribute to modifying many different kinds of specific behaviors, such as reducing young children's fears of dogs or dentists; wearing helmets while riding bikes; using sunscreen lotions; or wearing seat belts. These findings were found not only in regards to segments designed specifically for research purposes and educational programs (such as *Sesame Street* that will be discussed in length in chapter 5), but also as a result of viewing dramatic programs.[17]

Also evident from much of this research is that most of the documented behavioral learning is short term and that significant long-term changes require integration with educational and public campaigns that reinforce the televised message over a period of time. The question also remains of whether children are able to apply these newly acquired behaviors in novel and unfamiliar situations.

Can we generalize from the accumulated body of research about whether television's potential is greater for teaching negative or positive behaviors? One meta-analysis that reviewed this broad field of study suggested that the negative effect of television violence is double that of the pro-social. While pro-social behavior is highly regarded by adults, it is not necessarily perceived as valuable by children. Furthermore, anti-social behaviors, such as violence, seem much more attractive and the latter are often very simple, physical, and direct acts, both on television and in real life. As a general rule, then, it is much easier to imitate a specific violent act and to release aggressive urges than to control them and commit an act of generosity or patience.[18] As in other broad conclusions presented earlier, it is important to note that not all researchers accept this view. More specifically, a more recent meta-analysis disagrees with the above interpretation and suggests that children will model explicit behavior seen on television – negative or positive to the same degree – given that they find it to be realistic and applicable to their own situation.[19] Thus, in conclusion, we have seen how complicated it is to answer questions regarding television's effects on children and how difficult it is to achieve and to agree upon on clear cut conclusions acceptable to all, at least to date.

Television and Advertising

Having become the dominant form of broadcasting, commercial television perceives of children mainly as a market for advertising goods. The growth of advertising has led to intensification in the increasing variety of the forms of advertising – commercials, sponsorships, covert advertising, and program-related merchandizing – as well as in the spread of such phenomena all over the world. But this trend has also been growing in terms of defining the potential child-consumer: The targeted age of children has been lowered systematically – to the point that no age is now protected from commercial forces, not even baby-viewers of several months of age for whom television programs serve to entice parents to purchase goods for them. As a result, the effects of television advertising on children are a very important area of concern in many places in the world.

The trend in the growth of advertising is also affected by different interactions with various local cultural changes. For example, middle- and higher-class children in many Western societies have gradually become active consumers in their own right: they have their own money to spend (from gifts, allowances, work) and they influence many family purchase decisions, particularly in the areas of entertainment, leisure, and food. Furthermore, they are the present as well as the future's big spenders. As a result, advertisers highly value this "market segment" (as they are called). In lower-class societies, as well as most developing countries, most children do not have funds available to them and their families live on a limited budget. Therefore, advertising raises a host of very different concerns: growing frustrations from unfulfilled expectations, family conflicts over purchasing decisions, and pressure to adopt a lifestyle that may be unattainable or socially inappropriate.

From a research perspective, the issue of advertising is of particular interest, as this is the clearest content area of television where specific and more readily measured behavioral change – purchase of a product or adoption of a particular life-style or habit – is the goal. Many resources are invested in well-planned, detailed efforts to achieve this goal. Talented persons, enormous amounts of funds, and the most advanced forms of technology are recruited for this purpose. This is television's ultimate "test:" to what degree can television actually change our behavior?

As with studies of television violence, here too, it is impossible to estimate the volume of exposure to television commercials. Clearly, it is virtually impossible to offer accurate estimates of exposure to advertising of children worldwide.[20] However, a number often quoted in the USA estimates that the average child in the 1990s was watching about 130 commercials per day, 900 a week, or 45,000 a year. Added together, this amounts to about 7.5 hours of viewing commercials per week. While these numbers are constantly changing and should not be taken at face value, they should serve to impress upon us of the range of the phenomenon.

The discussion of advertising and its effect on children's developing consumer behavior is a fascinating illustration of the value-driven ambivalence involved in the discussion of television effects: Is advertising exploiting children's trust and naiveté as well as their limited cognitive capacities in order to sell products, at least some of which are superfluous, wasteful, and even harmful to their health? Is intensification of consumerism among children necessarily negative? From whose point of view? And what about advertising's contribution to the development of consumer-skills and to the availability of relevant information? Is advertising entangled – and in what ways – with more wider ideological issues, such as modernization, consumer society, and capitalism? Here, too, public pressure has served to contribute to both academic research and the formation of policy decisions.

Advertising for children

Obviously, companies must believe that advertising is effective to continue investing so much money in it. Some argue that they cannot afford not to advertise, as it is not the effectiveness of the advertising sought, per se, but rather the desire to avoid a situation of non-visibility that will result from not advertising. Stated succinctly, one needs to advertise simply because everyone else does. So what does research tell us about advertising effectiveness?

In Chapter 2 we learned that as children grow older they gain the capability to distinguish between commercials and programs, to remember them for a longer period of time, and gradually come to recognize their persuasive intent. As they mature, children also gain first hand experience, both in "nagging" their parents to buy them advertised products, as well as, with the products themselves. They learn from those interactions to restrain themselves, to repeat their requests in spite of parental refusal, and to become more realistic regarding those situations when there are greater chances of their requests being fulfilled. Experiences with the products enable children to be more critical of commercials, as they learn to compare the image with the actual product. Their developing cognitive abilities facilitate their understanding of advertising tactics and manipulations. In societies where children experience them daily, signs of distrust of commercials have been found to be quite common from the age of 10. While initially they are more critical of the lack of realism of the product in comparison to its image on television, gradually they learn to focus on the persuasive nature of advertising and the possible tactics of manipulation employed.[21]

Perhaps, as a result of these developments, several studies suggest that beyond the first few exposures to a particular commercial, there is no increased intensification of the product's attractiveness. That is, the original impression of the product usually remains constant. Watching commercials over time does not seem to have the same cumulative effect as does watching violent television. However, the development of the ability to be critical of television commercials does not necessarily reduce the effectiveness of commercials in arousing desires in children for new products or in reinforcing existing purchasing habits. It seems that children's attitudes (perhaps like those of many adults) are not necessarily predictive of their actual purchasing behaviors.

Several specific advertising tactics have been proven to be particularly effective with children. Offering prizes and gifts with the product (e.g., a toy within a cereal box) seems to be particularly effective in enticing children to prefer one product over its competitors. Similarly, employing celebrities (such as actors, singers, athletes) in commercials impresses children's evaluation of the product even when the celebrity's "expertise" is non-related to the product advertised. "Program-length" commercials, such as programs that present characters and accessories that are also offered for sale in the market for children (e.g., toys, clothing, accessories, school products, decorations, computer games, magazines, cards), seem to be particularly effective, as is evident from the growing trend to saturate the market with merchandise with the promotion of each new television series.[22]

Advertising, nutrition, and alcohol

Of the many products advertised on television, special concern has been directed to those deemed inherently harmful to children. Unhealthy food is one such domain, particularly those containing high levels of sugar (sweets, cereals, soft drinks) and unhealthy fats. Advertising such unhealthy products constitutes a significant part of advertising directed at children in the USA, for example, and the current concern needs to be understood in light of the growing awareness in wealthy societies of the relationship between unhealthy nutrition and many of modern medical problems. The few studies that actually examined this issue indicated the effectiveness of such commercials on influencing children's food choices, particularly, when they are reinforced by a variety of promotional strategies (including prizes, Internet links, cross-selling) and when they are not presented with counter-messages (for example, advertising for healthy fruit). Even brief exposures to televised food commercials were found to be effective, and many argue that the intensive efforts of food marketing to target children and youth have produced a detrimental influence on their overall eating habits. At the same time, this type of study has been criticized for remaining quite narrow in its conception of direct and immediate effects, as well as, for its being disassociated from other factors in children's lives, as will be further discussed in this chapter in relation to television and leisure.[23]

Similarly, there has been a growing concern over the effect on children of television's advertisements for alcohol. In contrast to sugary foods, alcohol is not advertised during children's hours, but does appear at times when children may be watching television with parents or older siblings. Alcohol advertisements are associated with growing up and being "in," with providing a wide range of physical and psychological pleasures, including intimate relationships. Yet, alcohol abuse has become a great concern in societies all over the world as it is associated with car accidents, violence, sexual crimes, and domestic violence. Once again, there are not enough studies to tackle the complexities of the many issues involved here. However, the few studies that have been conducted with young people do present some evidence that advertising can encourage non-drinkers to hold positive attitudes toward drinking and to express an interest in drinking when they grow up. They seem to be impressed by the positive advertising message that associates alcohol with "the good life." Youth who are already drinking were influenced to change preferences to particular beer brands. There is also an indication that television commercials are particularly effective when other socializing agents and social pressures – such as parents, educators, religious upbringing, peers – are non-committal, and specifically at the beginning of adolescent years. These findings, however, need to be treated with caution, due to the under-developed nature of this body of knowledge.[24]

Advertising, social and emotional well-being

Finally, a somewhat different concern regarding harmful effects of advertising relates to indirect types of effects on parent–child relationships; for example, advertising can serve as a stimulant of conflict and in doing so affect the general sense of both parents' and children's well-being and happiness. The cycle that leads to such unpleasant feelings includes the fact that television commercials do seem to stimulate young children's requests of their parents to purchase a particular item. According to parents' and children's self-reports, frequent "buy me" demands often lead to arguments, quarrels, and even temper tantrums. Researchers' observations of children's behaviors in supermarkets attest to such exchanges, as well. Children exert direct influence over their parents purchasing habits by requesting products, as well as indirectly, as parents internalize their children's tastes and make purchases that will please them even without the latter making explicit requests or even being present when purchases are made. Clearly, commercials have become a central force in socializing children into consumer culture and different families respond to this force and handle this process in different ways; some, perhaps many accede to children's requests to purchase an advertised product, while others help their children acquire skills, knowledge, and attitudes to evaluate commercials and the products advertised.

As a socialization process, advertising is entangled with another indirect effect – the degree to which it contributes to the child's general sense of satisfaction or dissatisfaction with his or her life, in general, and materialistic conditions, in particular. This feeling can be stimulated by the ability or inability to purchase everything advertised that children have been lead to believe is "a must," as well as with the disappointments from products they have been motivated to purchase that do not fulfill their advertised promises (e.g., to make them happy, thrilled, popular, pretty, successful). Children denied a product of their choice or disappointed with it may react by expressing strong feelings of disappointment, anger, frustration, and sadness. Furthermore, the world of advertising as a whole is designed to make all of us – including children – feel dissatisfied with whom we are and what we have, in order to sustain the motivation to purchase new products that promise to improve our lives. Advertising results in making children feel "not good enough" and in need of constant improvement in at least three complementary ways: first, by presenting social, physical, materialistic or mental achievements that no one, including children, is capable of achieving (no matter how much money they will spend for products and services); second, by presenting children who are similar to them, but who have been placed in subordinate roles (e.g., girls in comparison to boys, children in comparison to adults, a member of a minority group in comparison to a member of a majority group); and third, when characters similar to the viewer are presented as having a much better life socially and economically.[25] We will discuss these and other issues in depth in Chapter 5.

Is advertising working?

We have seen in this chapter that the influences of advertising on children's behavior is not as taken for granted as we might have thought or as advertisers might have hoped. The overarching research finding, once again, seems to be related to the developmental process: As children grow older, they develop more awareness and critical attitudes toward the world of advertising, even when such attitudes do not necessarily express themselves in their purchasing choices or habits. Younger children are more vulnerable to the prominence and attractiveness of commercials and less able, cognitively, to view them critically. They have more difficulty understanding the purpose of advertising and they watch it less discriminately in comparison to older children. However, studying the direct effectiveness of commercials is complicated, as the actual behavior is ground in complicated sets of intervening variables, including those related to personality, family background, society, and culture. Reconstructions by adults in the USA of the role advertising had in their past as children (through the employment of a method called "life history") reveals that it was a source of entertainment and family conversation and had a central role in development of their consumer habits as well as critical skills. However, they

were aware of the fact that knowledge and understanding of the advertising world does not necessarily protect against the effects it has on
them.[26]

So does advertising for children sell goods? The answer according to
researchers seems to be, probably, affirmative, though under certain
conditions. The answer according to companies seeking to sell their
products as well as advertising agencies seems to be much more de-
cisive, otherwise how can we understand their costly and extensive
efforts? However, here we need to ask ourselves whether this is the
only relevant research question to be pursued? For example, studies of
the role of commercials in the everyday life of children re-iterate that
their contribution is in other realms of life in addition to purchasing
products: emotional responses such as enthusiasm and joy, aesthetic
pleasure, dramatic imitation, singing and dancing along with the ads,
and the like. Thus, commercials seem to have a wide variety of functions for children and their role cannot be measured in terms of sales
alone.[27] Here, too, we can conclude that the search for causal effects of
television on children has produced valuable, but limited results
of narrow scope. Furthermore, there is a need not only for more
research, but for extending such investigations to a more holistic
study of the complexity of children's behaviors.

Television and Sexual Behaviors

Sex is the third domain at the heart of public moral and educational
debate about television's effects on children. However, while violence,
as we have discussed, has been the focus of sustained research attention,
the study of the contribution of television to the sexual behavior of
children and youth is still quite marginal. This is quite surprising given
the growing sexual permissiveness in some countries, as well as, concerns over teen pregnancies and spread of HIV-AIDS. In contrast to the
general consensus over the undesired nature of violence, attitudes
towards human sexuality vary enormously: They are deeply conflated
in mythologies, taboos, inhibitions, moral and religious beliefs, and
cultural practices that formalize intimate relationships. Contrary to
what we might believe, sexuality is hardly limited to bodily functions
– it involves many more aspects of our lives, is socially constructed, and
varies immensely within and across cultures and periods. Studying sex
and sexuality, in particular in relation to minors, is a very sensitive issue
in most societies that often raise many objections and in many cases is
even an unthinkable taboo.

Is there reason to believe that sexual behavior on television may affect viewers' behaviors, too? We have already established that television has a potential for a greater effect when real-life experiences with the phenomenon are limited and there is restricted involvement of other socializing agents. Sexuality is an excellent illustration of this line of argument: Most children are exposed to sexual behavior for the first time through the media, often on television, years before they attain the physical, social, and emotional maturity needed to be sexually active. They also lack opportunities to examine television images in comparison to real life around them, as most sexual behaviors are conducted in the private sphere. In addition, the dominant socializing agents of family, school, or religious institutions generally repress activity or discussion of sex, or deal with it very minimally.

In contrast, sex and sexuality are central themes of the content of many television programs, either explicitly (as in particular films broadcast on movie channels or off prime time, or on rented videos, rated in many societies as films for adults only) or implicitly in a wide variety of programs. The content addressed or alluded to includes not only erotic behavior, but also references to sex-roles, intimacy and care, marriage, and family life. Analyses of sex-oriented themes on television suggest that the content and images divert greatly from reality. For example, most televised sex takes place outside normal marital or otherwise committed relationships, or involves some kind of financial engagement. Often sexual behaviors are entangled with violence, and intimate relationships on the whole are not necessarily presented as part of a warm emotional relationship. Sex is often portrayed as something that happens "spontaneously," in the heat of the moment, without much planning. Attractive actors and actresses are depicted as also being more sexually active, but do not necessarily do so in a responsible manner. The potential negative implications of sexual relationships, such as undesired pregnancy, sexually transmitted diseases, or emotional distress are hardly ever presented. More than anything else, however, the argument has been made that television engages young viewers with heavy exposure to conversations about sexual desires and practices. Indeed, many television programs seem to be preoccupied with discussion of sex, thus arousing young people's naturally developing interest in it even more, and priming them to over-emphasize its centrality in human life.[28]

There is little doubt that children growing up in Western as well as many other societies around the world have access to a variety of sexually oriented content on television. The evidence of such exposure comes from a variety of sources, including commercial rating systems, as well as parental and children's self-reports. Here, the same mechanisms explored in relation to television violence can be applied. In this regard, researchers have argued that television portrayals may affect behavior by inducing learning of new behaviors, reinforcing old ones, or converting existing behaviors to new ones. These kinds of changes can happen in various ways: a change in expectations regarding the possible consequences of the sexual behavior; identification with the characters; removal of behavioral inhibitions; assigning particular meaning to specific behavioral cues; and the like. As a result, it makes sense to assume that intensified viewing of sexual content may increase the chances of similar behavior, either through imitation, and/or sexual arousal, and/or removal of inhibitions.

Several survey-type studies conducted in the USA that investigated possible correlations between viewing sexual programs and sexual practices found conflicting evidence. No consistent causal relationships could be established between amount of viewing sex on television and initial age of sexual activity (i.e., there is no substantial evidence that heavy viewers start being active sexually at a younger age); nor was there a systematic relationship between the types of favorite television programs and sexual experience (i.e., no evidence that those preferring more sexual programs are also more active sexually). However, the adolescents themselves reported that they were affected by what they view on television and that the higher the proportion of sexual content, out of all content viewed on television, the higher the chances of being involved in sexual relationships.

Here, too, the direction of the sexual behavior–television viewing relationship is not clear-cut. Are adolescents who are sexually active attracted more to sex on television or are those watching more sex on television more sexually active? As with violence, there is agreement that both directions are in operation: as youth mature physically, the sexual content on television become more relevant, they seek such content more actively, devote more time and attention to watching it, and thus become more influenced by it.[29]

Attending to what children and young adults themselves have to say about sex on television reveals many additional complexities. A lot of what youngsters report attending to on television is not necessarily sexual activities as much as conversations about sexual experiences that offer rich content for fantasy and social learning, but also leave much for the imagination. Clearly then, it is not only graphic depictions of sex that are of interest to both young viewers and their researchers. In addition, children value this source of information about sex in a social context that offers them little and mostly unsatisfactory alternatives. It also seems that they do not absorb it all uncritically, but bring to these encounters their existing worldviews and critical skills. Here too, we find that the meaning made of sexual content on television is shaped by the context of its consumption. Clearly, viewing sexual content with peers, for example, allows for an experience that is quite different from that created in a family situation or in an intimate one.[30]

Not surprisingly, the various studies suggest differences between boys and girls – as girls find fewer sexually active role models with which to identify and seem less effected by television sex than boys. This finding can be explained by the double standard that most societies still uphold regarding gender and sexuality: Clearly, sexual activity is still much more risky and costly for girls (e.g., losing virginity, chance of undesired pregnancy, lower self-image, social sanctions, even capital punishment in some societies). While these views may be gradually changing, young males in Western societies associate sex more often with pleasure, fun, and physical gratification; whereas young females associate it more often with emotions, romantic love, and commitment. While young males' engagement in sex may be reinforced on television by gaining prestige and peer popularity, it is often negatively sanctioned when it is the young female's sexual exploits. These normative pressures on and off the television screen appear to be much stronger than any television portrayals in influencing actual behavior.

It is also important to consider the indirect, positive or negative contributions television may be making to sexual development when it serves as the dominant source of social scripts of possible attitudes and behaviors, language and forms of talking about sexual issues, as well as opportunities to bring such discussion into the open. Indeed, it is possible that sexual content "appearing" on the screen in the family's living room on a daily basis can provide an opportunity for social learning and, perhaps, open up discussion of topics that otherwise involve discomfort.

Finally, once again, we need to remind ourselves that the types of content to which most youth in the Western world are exposed, from a relatively young age, may be completely unavailable or even banned in other parts of the world, thus making the entire discussion above superfluous in those societies.

Pornography and teenage sexuality

A particular case of interest and concern related to the foregoing discussion is the study of pornography, a genre devoted entirely to the depiction of sexually explicit behavior intended to sexually arouse its audience. Pornography also differs from most sexual content on television because of its use of photographic conventions of genres dealing with the real world. In doing so, it creates the illusion that one is viewing a "documentary" of real people performing their regular sexual behaviors.

Although the definition of pornography is the subject of intense ideological and methodological debate, there is agreement that a distinction may be made between "soft" pornography (depicting all kinds of sexual relationships perceived as consensual and non-harmful in a given culture) and "hardcore" pornography (depicting extraordinary and non-consensual sexual behaviors such as those involving violence, children, animals, and objects). Pornographic material of both kinds is now easily accessible to children in many countries via special television channels, video stores, downloading from the Internet, as well as the traditional forms of pornography published in print format.

The nature of the debate over the effects of viewing pornography on children and youth is cast in terms very similar to those applied to discussion of violence – Do youth imitate sexual behaviors depicted in pornographic materials? Do they learn to expect their sexual partners to perform acts that they perceive to be legitimate and enjoyable? Do they become less sensitive and caring for their partners' sexual needs and expect them to enjoy pain and humiliation as depicted in the pornographic material? Do viewers of pornography become more sexually active and from a younger age? Or is it the other way around; do sexually active youngsters turn to pornography in search of relevant content, role models, and arousal? And what about intervening variables – are there particular youth that are more prone to viewing pornography and to being influenced by it?

In addition, researchers from several feminist schools of thought perceive pornography to be a form of racist content that is degrading women as sex objects and is aimed at maintaining women's subordinate status in all human societies. Pornography is assumed to feed the exploitation of women in the sex industry, including the enslavement and trafficking of girls and women around the world. Does indeed pornography contribute to the sexual exploitation of women and to gender inequality in society?

Research conducted on the effect of pornography has been limited and indeed restricted to young adults (imagine the methodological and ethical issues involved in attempting to study the effects of pornography on school-age children!). As a result, the questions listed above that continue to enflame the anxiety of many segments of society (e.g., sex education specialists, parents, religious groups, feminists) remain un-answered.[31] However, based on what we have already learnt about other behavioral effects of television that have been explored with children, we can feel safe in assuming that viewing pornography may well add to our concerns regarding the issues raised above.

We have seen that the debate over the role of television in shaping human sexuality is embedded in many central ideological issues that are valued differently in different societies, for different age groups, and for different periods: sex-roles; the nature of male and female sexualities; the role of sexuality in human relationships; the interrelationships between sex and violence, sex and emotions, sex and commitment, sex and family, sex and childbearing, sex and homosexuality; and the like. Furthermore, the role of television in shaping human sexuality also needs to be viewed in light of theories on the changing nature of childhood, including those that perceive all humans, including young children, as sexual in nature. We will return to these issues in Chapter 5, when we discuss the role of viewing television in the construction of social reality.

Television and Children's Leisure

In the 1950s, when television entered the lives of those who were children in many Western societies and gradually spread from there, it demanded much of children's time. This intervention in children's leisure culture aroused public and academic debate over the question related to television's "displacement effect:" Does watching television displace other important activities such as reading, doing homework, or playing outdoors? Indeed, at the time, this and associated questions were primarily stated in negative terms: Does watching television take away important time that should be better devoted to activities that foster cognitive development (e.g., reading, homework); physical development (e.g., outdoors activity, sports); and social development (playing with other children, participating in social events)?

Today, it is almost impossible to study the possibility of such "displacement effect," as television has become a fact of life and an integral part of the lives of most children. Those who are not raised with it probably differ greatly from children exposed to television either ideologically (e.g., being raised in very religious or anti-television families) or in their social-economic conditions of poverty and homelessness. Indeed, several comprehensive studies that concentrated on the introduction of television in its initial days (in Canada, USA, and UK) as well as under special conditions (such as during major television strikes, or voluntarily giving up television for a while) arrived at similar conclusions.[32]

Television was found to have lead to significant changes in children's allocation of time and organization of activities outside of the home. However, following a short period of a "novelty effect" of television, most of the recorded changes in children's daily schedule where not related to time devoted to homework, playing with friends, reading, or sleeping, but to use of other media. Why were some media-related activities affected more than others? This question can be answered by the following principles of the "displacement effect"[33] :

1 *Functional similarity:* According to this principle, children only give up activities that basically fulfill similar but less effective functions than does television. For example, for younger children, viewing cartoons replaced to a large degree reading comic books and going to the movies. This was not the case for older children, as going to the movies gratifies many social needs that television cannot fulfill for them. Similarly, those activities that are perceived to have functions that differ from television were not affected by its introduction. For example, most of the children studied preferred playing with other children instead of watching television (a finding that was repeated 40 years later in another comprehensive study of 12 European countries).[34] And, reading newspapers did not diminish among older children, as it was perceived by them to be a source of information, while television mainly served entertainment needs.

2 *Marginal fringe activities:* Activities perceived as marginal and unstructured are replaced by organized and structured activities. This principle assumes that children clear time to watch television at the expense of activities that have no set time boundaries and that are perceived by them to be incidental, such as "hanging out" or "going out" for no particular planned reason. In short, television seems to replace "idle" time, when one does "nothing." On the other hand, free playtime was not replaced by television; perhaps because it was perceived by children to be central and meaningful in their lives.

3 *Transformation:* The use of other mass media is transformed into more specific, goal-oriented uses with much less overlap with television. This principle assumes that instead of competing with television, media that preceded it needed to readjust in order to survive. In turn, succeeding in development of a newly adopted specific purpose provided them a new independent right to exist. Thus, radio found new ways to satisfy listeners' audio needs in ways that differ from those provided by television: for example, an emphasis on music and news, interactive call-in programs, and more specialized programming directed to different audiences. Central in children's lives before the advent of television, radio became secondary for some, as it faded into the background. Yet, in doing so radio became a more personal medium, allowing the

pre-teenage girl or the teenage boy a source of comforting solitude with personal thoughts and moods. Similarly, the print media changed significantly for children. Many books printed, even imitated, stories that appeared on popular television programs; there was a growth in the consumption of non-fiction books; and new magazines designed for specific audiences with specific interests came into being.

4   *Physical and psychological proximity:* Activities are more likely to be displaced if they occupy the same physical space (e.g., living room) as television, but provide less satisfaction than viewing does (e.g., doing homework). This principle is probably the weakest of the four, as it is based on very little empirical evidence or theoretical foundations.

Of particular interest is the question of why there is no substantial evidence that television has displaced reading books, contrary to expectations and common belief? One line of reasoning proposed is that books fulfill a wide variety of functions for children beyond the content and the process of decoding the written text; for example, a different context of use that allows privacy, personal pacing, and lingering, and that provides a very different mental and emotional experience than watching television. Furthermore, it has also been argued that children really did not read a lot before the age of television and they continue not to read a lot today, as well ... Some children read more than others, girls as a whole read more than boys, and neither of these trends seem to be related to television. We will return to this issue in Chapter 5.

Above and beyond these conclusions, it seems that more than anything else television replaced feelings of "boredom" and idleness. In a house with a working television set that allows zapping between various channels and viewing this or another program, there is little need to work through feelings of being bored. Are children today more impatient with boredom? And if so, is this state of mind affecting their behavior? These are interesting questions that have not been studied to date.

Children's enjoyment of television viewing is perhaps taken for granted, but it remains a source of anxiety for many parents. Are they watching too much of it? Are they watching harmful content? Are they wasting their time? Television has been pejoratively referred to with such provocative names as "gum for the eyes," "talking wall paper," "electronic babysitter," and "boob tube," among others. Similarly, viewers are often described as "addicted" to television. The metaphor of addiction is employed to describe some of the common characteristics of children's viewing: they use viewing as a way to reduce tension, pain or anxiety; viewing encourages more viewing; they loose sense of self-control and sense of time while viewing; they arrange their daily schedule around viewing; and they miss it when they are away. As much as this viewing metaphor seems to encapsulate the essence of the populist argument, there is no research evidence to support it, particularly none that presents any of the physical consequences of addiction to substances or habits. As with other psychological and behavioral addictions (e.g., gambling, shopping), addiction to television is a rare phenomenon. As a metaphor, the term "addiction" refers to heavy viewing. However, even heavy viewing is not necessarily addictive, particularly not according to approaches that understand children's viewing of television as an active process motivated by needs and interpreted according to personal abilities and capacities.[35]

The correlations between television viewing and obesity is a relatively new and growing concern that has been supported by documentation from the medical literature of increased prevalence of childhood obesity worldwide, its many physical and emotional health risks, and the national costs involved in its treatment. Children's weight gain is determined by a host of biological, social, and environmental factors. The argument made by medical researchers that television viewing may be one such important factor is advanced through four claims: First, television replaces physical activity. Second, this effect is multiplied when viewing is accompanied by over-eating (snacking, disordered-family eating habits of unbalanced meals). Third, viewing commercial television increases exposure to the advertising of unhealthy and highly caloric foods (discussed above, under advertising). Finally, much commercial television has been criticized for promoting hedonistic life styles with a heavy preoccupation with eating in an unhealthy manner.

Indeed, being overweight has been found to be associated with heavy television viewing (more than 4–5 hours per day). While these findings hold true for all children, they were found to be particularly the case for those generally less active – particularly girls and several minority groups. Programs that succeeded in reducing children's viewing time, among other interventions, were successful in reducing body weight in children.[36] While the accumulated evidence is quite convincing, it is also possible that a vicious circle is in operation here: overweight children prefer non-demanding physical activities, such as viewing television (and perhaps also eating during viewing), and thus television viewing reinforces their weight problems.

In addition, the medical literature is also contributing to a highly contested debate over a recent study that suggested the potential contribution of television viewing at an early age to attention related problems (such as attention deficit/hyperactivity disorder, known as ADHD) in later years.[37] This line of research will no doubt continue in the coming years with the growing interest in the special place of media in the lives of infants and toddlers, and has particular relevance to the implications for learning, discussed in Chapter 5.

Concluding Remarks

In summary, we can suggest that television has an important role in children's behavior in everyday life. As in other areas of study in the social sciences, significant difficulties are encountered when seeking to discover or to prove the existence of causal relationships between viewing television and specific behaviors. However, there is plenty of evidence that television contributes to reinforcing existing behaviors and that it sometimes creates or converts behaviors.

Discussion of behavioral effects is deeply entangled in other areas of children's lives: it involves children's individual development, their viewing abilities, parental mediation, and the like, as discussed in the previous chapters. It is also strongly related to the complex value systems involved in the processes of socialization and construction of reality, to which we turn in Chapter 4. Finally it also has important implications for the development of policy for broadcasting to children, as well as to education for television literacy, issues that will be discussed in Chapter 6.

Notes

1 Berryand Asamen (1993), Van Evra (2004).
2 National Television Violence Study (1996).
3 This line of research is mostly associated with Bandura, see for example, Bandura (1965), Bandura, Ross, and Ross (1963).
4 See for example Liebert and Sprafkin (1988).
5 Based on the prototype offered by Stein and Freidrich (1972).
6 Huesmann and Eron (1986).
7 Lefkowitz, Eron, Walder, and Huesmann (1977).
8 Comstock (1991).
9 Jones (2002), Tobin (2000), Van der Voort (1986).
10 For an extensive review see Bushman and Huesmann (2001).
11 Uddén (n.d.).
12 Groebel (1998).
13 For discussion of these examples, see a collection of essays in Carlsson and von Feilitzen (1998).

14 Buckingham (1993), Messenger Davies (1989).

15 Based on interviews with producers of quality television for children who participated in the *Prix Jeunesse*, June 2004, Munich (Lemish, work in progress).

16 See Fisch (2004), Stein and Freidrich (1972).

17 For reviews of this literature see Mares and Woodard (2005), Van Evra (2004).

18 Paik and Comstock (1994).

19 See Hearold (1986). For a more recent meta-analysis see Mares and Woodard (2005).

20 Kunkel (2001), Valkenburg (2004), Van Evra (2004).

21 Valkenburg and Cantor (2002).

22 Macklin and Carlson (1999), Valkenburg (2004), Van Evra (2004).

23 Adler, Friedlander, Lesser et al. (1980), Borzekowski and Robinson (2001), Gorn and Goldberg (1982), Story and French (2004). For an integrative evaluation and critique, see Livingstone (2005).

24 Aitken, Aitken, Eadie, Leathar, McNeill, and Scott (1988), Atkin (1990), Atkin, Hocking, and Block (1984), Gobod and Pfau (2000), Grube and Wallack (1994), Thomsen and Rekve (2003).

25 Atkin (1980), Comstock (1991), Ward, Wackman, and Wartella (1977).

26 Heintz, Shively, Wartella, and Oliverez (1995).

27 Buckingham (1993).

28 Greenberg, Brown, and Buerkel-Rothfuss (1993), Gunter (2002), Kunkel, Cope, and Biely (1999).

29 Brown and Newcomber (1991), Peterson, Moore, and Furstenberg (1991), Wartella, Scantlin, Kotler, Huston, and Donnerstein (2000).

30 Buckingham and Bragg (2004).

31 Cline (1994), Gunter (2002), Weaver (1994).

32 In the UK: Himmelweit, Oppenheim, and Vince (1958); in the USA: Schramm, Lyle, and Parker (1961), and in Canada: Williams (1986).

33 Offered by Neuman (1991).

34 Livingstone and Bovill (2001).

35 Messenger Davies (1989), Smith (1986).

36 See for example: Anderson, Crespo, Barlett, Cheskin, and Pratt (1998), Coon, Goldberg, Rogers and Tucker (2001), Deitz (1990), Gortmaker, Cheung, Peterson et al. (1999), Gortmaker, Must, Sobol, Peterson, Colditz, and Deitz (1996), Robinson (1999), Shannon, Peacock, and Brown (2001).

37 Christakis, Zimmerman, DiGiuseppe, and McCarthy (2004).

4

Television and the Social Construction of Reality

Previous chapters repeatedly referred to television as a major socializing agent in children's lives, one that complements and often competes with other more traditional socializing agents such as family, school, peer group, community and religious institutions. The popular view of successful socialization is that it enables children and youth to fit into the society in which they live because they have learned what is considered to be socially appropriate behaviors. Specifically, through socialization the child learns about his/her culture and internalizes its values, belief systems, perceptions of itself, and of "others."

Passive notions portray socialization as unidirectional – from socializing agent to the child, yet the process is much more complex and seems to include an important, activist process referred to as the social construction of reality. First learned in childhood but applied throughout our life, this process involves using mental capacities to understand and to construct meaning as we interact with the world and society.

Television viewing involves both socialization and the social construction of reality. On the one hand, it introduces us to the world outside our immediate "here" and "now." It expands, interprets, highlights, judges, legitimizes, or excludes social phenomena that the viewer encounters in reality or in the other media. Often television functions as the first, sometimes the only, encounter with varied and unfamiliar social situations. Some researchers go so far as to argue that television has replaced religious institutions: It constantly reinforces certain ideological, mythological, and factual patterns of thought and so functions to define the world and to legitimize the existing social order.

Yet, on the other hand, children all over the world have been found to be active, selective viewers who use television to learn about the world, a process that helps them to define their own place within it. Be it telenovelas in Latin America, the South Korean wave of popular television dramas in Asia, European reality TV in Africa, or US sitcoms in the Middle East, children find many genres to be informative in addition to entertaining. Viewing is also considered to be used by viewers in the process of identity formation – be it of gender, sexuality, social, or political in nature.

Given these multiple processes, we can ask such general questions as – what is television's contribution to children's emerging social definitions of good and bad, right and wrong, true and false? How does it share our collective identity definitions and excludes those deemed to be different and foreign? How does it shape gender perceptions, sexual expectations, social and later professional knowledge? These and other questions that have been studied in regard to young audiences have assumed the concept of "schema" borrowed from psychology (see Chapter 2). Again, schema is a cognitive structure that organizes the knowledge of given phenomenon. It functions to direct the way we perceive, remember, process, and relate to information. For example, a gender schema is a framework that organizes the knowledge and expectations we have regarding masculinity and femininity. In doing so, it guides interpretation of encounters with male and female TV characters. Similarly, schemas of minorities, professions, places, and the like, are enforced, even challenged, via the viewing of television and so enrich our understanding and experiencing of the world. Interestingly, in an encounter with unfamiliar stimuli or information, a child or an adult will attempt to assimilate it into existing cognitive schemas or to change the schema in a way that it will be able to accommodate itself to the new information. Through the processes of assimilation and accommodation, schema multiply, expand, and become more complex as the child matures, so adding to the experience, understandings, and skills accumulated.[1]

Schema, therefore, are structures that assist in organizing social knowledge. They are formed through experience and include representations of the world gathered through first hand encounters or mediated experiences, for example with the media. To follow up on the example presented in an earlier chapter, gender schema develop in encounters with men and women in real life, as well as, those viewed on television, found on the toy shelf, or seen in magazines. This is a dynamic process involving constant learning in which television has a central role.

Exposing attitudes and social perspectives involves a complicated if not problematic research process. First, it is deeply value-laden and therefore reflects to a large degree the ideological departure point of the researcher. For example, a researcher such as myself who advocates the necessity of achieving full gender equality may study television's role in facilitating or preventing such a change in judgmental ways.

Furthermore, the social views of researchers are not easily detected or measured. They, too, develop over time in complicated and salient ways. Therefore, in order to study the relationships between viewing particular television content and the construction of social reality, a sophisticated methodology must be applied that includes forthright reflexivity about the researcher's own values and processes of constructing reality, as well as, grounding the findings in deep understandings of specific social–cultural contexts.

As reviewed in Chapter 2, as a result of their cognitive development and experience in the world, children and adults use different structures of comprehension. Therefore, social meanings, as children understand them, can be very different than those of adults. Developmental researchers often evaluate children's understandings as "less" – less complete, accurate, or relevant than those held by adults. Researchers from the cultural studies' perspective, on the other hand, may define them not as "less" but as fundamentally different. Furthermore, as explained in Chapter 1, children's television viewing is embedded in family life and does not operate in a social void, therefore, its role as a socializing agent, is a function of its interaction with other agents. It is here, at the pivotal point of interaction that the study of young viewers' social perceptions and the role of television in their lives must focus. Further, to do so, researchers must listen as they express themselves in their own voices and present their own perspectives. With this proviso in mind, we will examine a number of central issues in social science research that have been addressed in the research literature by focusing on selected social phenomena – gender, sex and sexuality, violence, relations with others, politics, and social values.

Construction of Gender and Gender Roles

Based upon the intellectual contributions of feminist theories, there is a growing recognition in the social sciences that gender differences (in contrast to biological differences in the reproduction organs) are socially constructed, learned sets of behaviors and perceptions. For example, while it is a biological fact that women can give birth, it is a social construction that women should be expected to be the dominant caregiver of children. Thus, learning the characteristics and behaviors that are "accepted" as masculine and feminine in a given society is a process that starts at birth.

The role of television in such a construction of gender schemas is particularly important, as most of the content of television present characters that can be assigned to one of the two gender categories, be they humans, cartoon figures, animals, or science fiction characters. Such characters supply a varied pool of models for identification and imitation, as we have discussed in Chapter 3. They define for the young viewers what is "normal" and accepted in their society, and, therefore, win positive reinforcement, as well as what is deemed exceptional, even deviant, and therefore negatively sanctioned.

The many studies that have examined the portrayals of women and men on television point to a social world that differentiates between the two quite systematically. On the whole, men are identified with "doing" in the public sphere and associated with characteristics such as activity, rationality, forcefulness, independence, ambitiousness, competitiveness, achievement, higher social status, and the like. Women are associated with "being" in the private sphere and are characterized, generally, as passive, emotional, care-giving, childish, sexy, subordinate to men, of lower social status, and the like. Television, as a general rule (there are many exceptions, and these are growing gradually in number and scope), defines men by their action, and in contrast, women by their appearance. The external appearance of women is still perceived as the most central characteristic of a woman's essence. This emphasis is most commonly expressed through glorification of a particular beauty model, the "beauty myth," that is highly European in orientation and practically unattainable. External appearance is directly related to television's over-emphasis in portrayal of women as sexual beings whose central function is relegated to being objects of male sexual desire and pursuit. Thus, such dominant media messages continue to promote restrictive ideologies of femininity, glorify heterosexual romance as a central goal for girls, encourage male domination in relationships, and stress the importance of beautification through consumption, while dismissing the validity of girls' own sexual feelings and desires apart from masculine desire; and say nothing about all the many other aspects of women's essence, capabilities, and potential contributions.[2]

Even children's television offers a significant under-representation of female main characters and under-development of female characters. Males – both younger and older – are the main heroes of children's programs. They succeed in overcoming everyday problems, deal successfully with all sorts of dangers, and have lots of adventures. Even non-gendered imaginary characters – such as creatures and animals – are considered "naturally" to be male, unless they are specifically marked as female through processes of sexualizing their appearance (e.g., hair ribbons, long eyelashes, colored lips, short skirts). In this way, female characters continue to symbolize a deviation from the dominant male-norm and remain the "second sex" in the classical sense, as portrayed by Simone de Beauvoir.[3]

Female characters in most media texts for children are there to be saved and protected by the males and provide the background for the adventure. Above all, their position is defined by their meaning for the male heroes. Certain symbols, such as horses, dolphins jumping in front of a sunset, bunnies, and flowers are gendered in our societies and reinforced by the market forces as "girlish." Other areas, such as technology, action, or fighting are almost always framed as male themes and pre-interpreted as masculine. Television advertising for children applies gendered clichés excessively in presenting goods for consumption by signaling gender intention via glittery or pastel colors for girls and action-packed dark hues for boys. Even educational programs were found to have an under representation of female as well as employment of traditional stereotypes.[4]

Following this brief introduction, we turn now to consider questions such as: Do such portrayals shape young viewers perceptions of gender roles? Do they contribute to young people's emerging self-image and perceptions of sex, sexuality, and sexual orientation?

Construction of gender roles

Overall, research on television's role in developing gender stereotypes among children is not unequivocal. One possible explanation is the difficulty in separating the specific contribution television makes from those of other socializing agents. In addition, traditional perceptions regarding gender roles are so deeply embedded in all societies and cultures that children have ample first hand opportunities to internalize them.

Consider, for example, the stereotypical gender division in the workforce. Research suggests that pre-school-age boys and girls already have different professional aspirations. Does television contribute to development of these aspirations? First, according to school-age children who participated in several studies, television serves as an important resource for learning about the existence of a variety of professions. For example, children completed a questionnaire that included questions about different occupations, their sources of information about them, the status of these professions, whether they perceive them to be "female" or "male," and whether they were willing to consider them for themselves. The respondents also provided information about the programs they watch on a regular basis. The results suggest that children did gather a lot of occupational-related information from television, even when they did not have first-hand acquaintance with certain jobs. They tended to rate them according to social expectations – assigning higher status to professions that were perceived as masculine (police officer, detective, surgeon, lawyer) and were wary of accepting breaks in stereotypes (e.g., a female police-officer or a man in a care-giving role). Some evidence was found that connected the type of programs viewed and these attitudes, suggesting, for example, that girls who were heavier viewers of programs that present traditional female roles tended to prefer those kinds of roles for themselves.

Taken as a whole, this type of study and others that experimented with alternative methods suggest that there is a relationship between viewing television and holding stereotypical views regarding the various roles that men and women in our societies hold, but this relationship is conflated with many other variables.[5] Most of these studies were conducted in the USA quite some time ago and are quite dated. In addition, most did not refer to viewing of particular programs and their characteristics, but to the mere exposure to television in general terms. The logic behind such a general measure was that viewing a lot of television by definition exposes children to a large quantity of stereotypical content.[6] However, many questions remain unanswered. For example, is the quantity of viewing per se the best predictor of the influence television has on attitudes? Would there be a difference between children who watch a lot of educational or public television programs versus those who mainly watch commercial television? And what about differences between children who regularly watch different television genres? Is it possible that studies that measure only the amount of viewing television are actually measuring different kinds of effects, some that may even cancel out one another?

Correlation studies that attempted to find a relationship between viewing habits and gender-related attitudes assume that stereotypical attitudes are indeed absorbed from television en large, but have not considered the ways in which children comprehend and process the content viewed. The social location of children – in their families, peer groups, schools, too, has great relevancy in the examination of these relationships. According to research findings that applied this methodology, television's influence is stronger when it provides complementary and consistent information with knowledge already obtained, while influences dim when television presents a contradictory or deviant world from that with which the child is familiar. Since children do possess gender-related schema, they apply them in processing television information. Therefore, it seems that television may serve more to reinforce existing attitudes towards gender roles learned in other social contexts, than to create new ones.

It is also important to emphasize that no necessary relationship has been found between attitudes, including those shaped by television, and actual behavior. For example, in one study children who were heavy viewers of television, were found to rate various types of house-work as stereotypically something that "girls do" or "boys do," but no necessary relationship was found to exist between viewing television and actually doing housework chores associated with the other gender (for example, boys washing dishes and girls mowing the lawn).[7] It seems that in this matter, too, the behaviors of other family members and significant others mediate viewing television and actual behavior. Furthermore, we need to remind ourselves that stereotypical gender roles are in of themselves controversial, with very deep cultural differences and motivations for and against change.

Interestingly, the same principles are upheld when we examine the few studies that have been conducted on TV programs that tried intentionally to rupture gender stereotypes. The rationale applied in such programs, as well as in the studies, is that if television contributes, even in a small degree, to the construction of gender reality, then we could expect that exposure to socially challenging television content will contribute to the development of counter-stereotypical attitudes. Here, the view held argues that television can be a socializing agent that facilitates social change, and not just an agent that preserves and reinforces the existing social order. It is reasonable to assume that portrayals that are contradictory to normative expectations will arouse a variety of responses from viewers. On one hand, their innovative and unpredictable nature makes them very conspicuous, but on the other hand, their rarity might make it difficult to remember amidst a sea of more traditional portrayals.

Not surprisingly, correlation studies reveal here, too, that adolescents who regularly view programs with counter-traditional gender roles hold more positive attitudes and aspirations for non-traditional occupations. The same was true for pre-school children who were regular viewers of American educational television (where extensive efforts have been made in recent years to break gender stereotypes), rather than commercial programs.[8] Once again, we can pose the question relevant to all studies of this type: Is it the viewing of particular kind of messages that shape children's attitudes regarding gender roles or is it the case that the children attracted to these kinds of programs in the first place are more receptive to non-traditional gender-roles due to family background, personality, etc.? Is the source of such openness with parents who are more highly educated, hold liberal views regarding gender roles, and who encourage their children to view more educational or other programs that advance non-traditional gender roles? Overall then, the direction of the primary effect remains an open, yet central question to be clarified in further studies in this research tradition.

Findings from several experimental studies investigated this phenomenon by means of controlled situations (for example, children
were presented with specific portrayals and measurements were taken
that revealed if there were changes in their attitudes in comparison to
control groups of children not exposed to such portrayals). The
findings suggest that children can learn new gender roles from television characters, particularly those related to their own gender. As we
have discussed in regards to identification with television characters,
girls seem to be more open to accepting roles that are traditionally
associated with men in comparison to boys who are more reluctant to
accept roles that are traditionally associated with women. However,
here too, there is no evidence that such changes are internalized, have
a lasting effect, or are transferred from attitudes to actual behavior.[9]
Clearly, deep social change requires on-going presentation of non-
stereotypical portrayals along with other environmental stimuli that
reinforce and encourage such values. This is as true for gender
portrayals as it is for any other types of portrayals, as we continue to
re-iterate: Television's role in children's lives can only be understood in
their social context.

An interesting case in point is the restrictive role that television
might be playing in constructing the notions of "love" and "romance"
for children. One such innovative study asked children and adolescents
in the USA to chose, from a pool of typical advertising pictures, those
that best depict "the couple most in love," the scene that is "the most
romantic," and the "most romantic dinner." Analysis of the findings
suggests that children framed romance in consumer terms. Hence,
when these young people imagined ideal love stories, they incorporated
in them elements of leisure and consumer culture. For example, eating
in a restaurant and going out to the movies constitute a typical date. A
more romantic relationship is expressed in a higher status restaurant
atmosphere. Expressing romantic commitment involves purchasing
luxury goods. And, when young participants in the research described
courting relationships, they reconstructed typical television story
lines.[10] Given such findings, it may be necessary for young adults to
reconcile the popular and exciting model of "love at first sight,"
embedded in consumer culture and stories of luxurious romance,
with the much less exciting reality in which relationships are build up
gradually through the routine of everyday life. Here we can only
speculate, but it may be the case that televised portrayals shape fantasies
and expectations from partners that lead to possible disappointments.
Furthermore, we can ask if such TV-based fantasies of romantic love are
shared by children in other societies. Is the cultural effect strong enough
to become the fantasy of children growing up in poor countries? Do

they, too, yearn for the capitalist model of romantic love? How do the forces of reality interact with the irrelevancy of television messages? These and other questions remain open for further inquiry.

Construction of gender identity

One central issue regarding gender socialization that has developed primarily through feminist theories and research is the role that popular culture, including television, plays in the processes of constructing personal gender identity. Here researchers have asked questions, such as: what is the meaning of masculinity and femininity these days? Does media content reinforce hegemonic notions of patriarchy (i.e., the overriding structure of society is controlled by men and masculine values and worldviews) or serve to accelerate social change in gendered dimensions of social structures and power? How do young viewers negotiate meaning in their interactions with media content, in general, and in relation to their personal gender identity?

Research of such questions has been advanced via the mass communication tradition of reception studies that inquire into the ways audiences "receive" media content (i.e., make meaning, interpret, relate it to their own lives). Such studies usually search for methodological ways of allowing people to express their inner worlds through in-depth interviews, individually or in focus groups, or through creative means, such as personal compositions, diaries, and art-work. Many of these studies have centered on women and girls in the context of media content traditionally associated with them (e.g., soap operas, women's magazines, romance novels, pop music, advertising) and uncovered the dynamics of how female viewers gain pleasure, sometimes even a sense of empowerment and control, from content that is seemingly oppressive to women.[11]

Research on pre-adolescence and adolescence is particularly interesting as identity development and dealing with social pressures that dominate perceptions of femininity and masculinity are important tasks in this period. Researchers working through approaches such as feminism and/or cultural studies view media texts as "sites of struggle" between conflicting social forces such as: traditional patriarchal forces versus female resistance; capitalist value systems versus alternatives such as socialism, Marxism, or religious moralities; uncritical acceptance of the adults' way of life and worldviews versus the cynical, critical visions of the younger generation.[12] In-depth analysis of case studies is usually applied in this line of research. In order to understand better the contribution of the structural approach to our understanding of the dynamics of the relationships between media and children, we will be benefited by a momentary departure from the more general discussion and examine an illustrative case study – the role of the pop group, the *Spice Girls*, in the lives of pre-adolescent, middle-class, Jewish girls in Israel.[13]

During the mid-1990s when the case study of the *Spice Girls* was conducted, this British group was enjoying record breaking sales world-wide of their music and extensive fare of related merchandising. At the time, the group included five "Spices": "Baby" Emma; "Sexy" Jerry; "Scary" Melanie B.; "Sporty" Melanie C.; and "Posh" Victoria. Girls all over the world listened to their music, watched their video-clips on MTV and on television specials, read and memorized details published about their idols in the gossip columns in the press, hung posters in their rooms, wore T-shirts and head bands decorated with their images, collected memorabilia of the group, covered their schoolbooks with *Spice Girls* bookpaper, and talked endlessly about the group.

What the research sought to understand were the meanings found in the *Spice Girls* by pre-adolescent girls' culture in Israel. How was it involved in the development of female identity? Based on focus group interviews with a total of 39 girls, aged 9 to 14.5 years old, the study provided detailed evidence about the importance attached to the pop group in these girls' lives. In particular, they described their enjoyment from the *Spice Girls'* television appearances, their idolization of the singers, the interviewees' own attempts to imitate their performances, singing, and behavior.

The analysis of the data gathered in focus group discussions elicited several central themes related to the role of the media in the meaning making process of pre-adolescent girls. The group's slogan – "Girl Power" – was interpreted by the interviewees as a sign of independence, power, success, and a feeling of self-worth. Some of the girls understood it to mean those female qualities that oppose boys' culture. For example, many of the girls cited what they perceived to be the independent, free behaviors of members of the pop group as the types of response that should be adopted in response to their own daily experiences of inequality and gender discrimination. As one 11-year-old girl argued: "There are boys that think that they are better than girls, so the *Spice Girls* try to prove that it is not so."[14]

The *Spice Girls* were structured as a group to represent the multifaceted ways of being a woman that have been emerging and so offers their fans new ways to define their female "me" and to construct and re-construct it constantly. Accordingly, the five "Spices," as members of the group referred to themselves, were perceived by the girls not solely as five different personalities that were objects of idolization or sources of identification, but also as five different definitions of femininity: A girl can be sweet and cute like Emma; wild and crazy like Melanie B; provocative and sexy like Jerry; snobbish and elegant like Victoria; even (!), athletic and "boyish" like Melanie C. Thus, each of the Spices presented these pre-adolescent girls with a legitimate form of femininity, each with its own identifying behavioral characteristics, facial expressions, clothing, hairstyle, and accessories. Here the *Spice Girls* were re-presenting to their fans, materially, the new ways and meanings of "being a woman" that were evolving in society and presented in the media and television programs in many cultures.

Interestingly, however, was the fact that the interviewees perceived all of these five options to be legitimate, but only as long as the model is also beautiful in conventional terms. The interviewees seem to think that a girl's beauty enables her to be anything she wants to be in television culture. While this is no surprise given what we know of the centrality of female appearance in our various cultures, it was unexpected to find that such a belief was taken for granted by young girls raised in well-to-do homes, with dual-career educated parents, and in an environment that was characterized by cultural wealth. Similar findings in other studies suggest that this may be a cross-cultural phenomenon: Attractiveness remains the most central criteria for identification with female characters and it is associated with feeling good about oneself.

Another central theme that appeared in these pre-adolescent Israeli girls' discourse was their active struggle with the conflicting meanings associated with what is referred to in feminist research as the virgin/ whore polarity. It seems that for some of the girls, particularly the younger ones, there was an almost obsessive need to see the *Spice Girls* as idols-but-whores. Some expressed strong reservations, even disgust with the singers' "whorish" appearance. Some also admitted gossiping with information collected from many sources about the Spices' alleged appearance in pornographic movies and magazines. Yet, at the same time, they expressed their deep admiration for them. Such polarized discussion reflects the internal struggles of young girls between forces of compliance with and resistance to traditional norms of femininity. Thus, the *Spice Girls'* open demonstration of sexuality created a "site of struggle" between the girls' desire to dismiss female sexuality as "whorish" and their desire for independence, freedom, and control over their lives. As in the case of Madonna, these sexual provocations can be seen as a form of mockery of the patriarchal dichotomies of virgin/whore and a challenge to traditional definitions of femininity.[15]

The *Spice Girls,* as a cultural phenomenon, revealed the girls' dual desires to be both "good girls" and "bad girls," at the same time. According to the feminist interpretation, this view is a result of the contradictory sets of values conveyed to girls in contemporary society: A main criteria for social esteem is to look as "attractive" as possible while, at the same time, actualizing their sexuality and attractiveness will be very negatively sanctioned. The *Spice Girls*, so it seems, represented both expectations all in one group.

The emphasis on friendship, togetherness, and sense of "sisterhood" was another central theme of female identity that emerged from the focus group interviews. One of the unique and appealing characteristics of the *Spice Girls* for many of the girls was the fact that they were promoted as a group of friends, who cared for and supported one another. As one 12-year-old interviewee said: " Yes, they are good friends. They support each other for sure [as] they are together all the time and during rehearsals... and for sure they have fun together. I think that it would have been extremely difficult to work together if they had not been good friends."[16]

Thus, in many ways, this pop music group offered the girls an opportunity to develop different aspects of their identity as young women and to confront society's conflicting expectations from them. Listening to the ways young girls interpret and integrate television portrayals of role models, each with its own individual life-story, offers us a glimpse into the stormy world of adolescence and the process of identity formation.

Following the development of general theoretical interests in masculinities, a parallel interest in the role of television in the construction of male identity has evolved recently as a separate field of research. Research in the general field has found that young males in many industrialized societies have low school achievements, a growing involvement in violence, high levels of substance abuse, a rising rate of suicide, and the like. By way of explanation, it has been proposed that boys feel unsafe and vulnerable trying to live up to expectations of traditional, stereotypical masculine behavior as projected in the "Boy Code" of toughness, emotional disconnection, and aggression. Researchers also posit that boys are pushed prematurely into harsh separation from an intense relationship with their mothers into proving their manhood. Further, in their struggle to become "ideal boys," they have a limited number of role models as their relationships with their fathers are usually quite restricted due to the latter's limited presence in the private sphere. Also, interaction with other male role models is episodic and associated with specific functions (e.g., soccer trainer, guitar teacher, etc.). Finally, the traditional images of men and masculinity that still dominate the media offer a very limited range of alternative options.

Within this complicated situation, boys often receive ambivalent feedback and conflicting messages from their social environment. Along with the traditional expectations, the new images of manhood prescribe expectations that they be more expressive emotionally and take upon themselves roles traditionally associated with women. As a result, they often receive contradictory or ambivalent feedback from their surroundings – family members, teachers, peers, and media. Thus, according to this developing line of research, boys may well be growing up with constant fears of inadequacy and ask themselves "am I man enough?"[17]

These difficulties are reproduced in research situations, which are themselves a form of social interaction. Here, too, boys are often reluctant to talk about their inner worlds, in general, as well as to expose the role television has in their lives and the many meanings it has for them, in particular. They adopt different strategies to avoid discussing their emotional reactions to television content or to share their viewing pleasures. For example, many adopt a mocking and condescending stance towards the viewing of soap operas and serials that are perceived as "girly," although it is quite clear that many are loyal viewers who apparently enjoy them. They disassociate themselves from programs dealing with interpersonal relationships, intimacy, and romance by relegating them to the "female" world. They report being more interested in traditional male programs, such as action-adventure, sports, and situation comedies. There is also research evidence that boys on the whole prefer closed narrative structures (i.e., story lines that pose a problem and solve it and bring it to closure) over open narrative structures (i.e., story lines that remain open and unresolved, such as in soap operas).

Super heroes that are popular throughout the world – such as Superman, Batman, and Spiderman – have a particular role in boys' development of male identity. In many ways, they are the embodiment of the "perfect" traditional man: they are physically strong, brave, always on the lookout to defend the weak, undefeatable, active in the outdoors, full of adventure, and are adored by women. As in the earlier discussion of the *Spice Girls*, super heroes are not automatically reproduced in boys' quest for their male identities. The heroes offer them an opportunity to examine possibilities and expectations and to challenge traditional views. Studies that analyzed interviews, drawings, and fan letters of boys reveal that they relate to media characters they admire on many emotional levels and have a deep concern for idols private lives, emotional worlds, aspirations, and behavioral motivations. Through these super heroes, they transpose their own desires and so create opportunities to discuss their relevancy to their own lives.[18]

At the same time, the story lines involving dominance and aggression situated in the context of conflict and threats restrict the boys developing identity and limit their ability to experiment emotionally and experience other possible social scripts. So it seems that most stereotypical popular media-fare constrain the inner worlds of both girls and boys and so reproduces a limited range of cultural expectations.

Gay identities

The identity development of homosexuals and lesbians is of particular interest due to the difficulties they encounter, in general, as well as in regard to our particular interest in the interaction between television, the construction of gender, and human sexuality. Clearly, this is a phenomenon with many sensitive dimensions, some of which are being discussed in most societies, if not contested in others. In contrast to the other social phenomena discussed in this chapter, most gay adolescents do not stand out as a group but rather are involved in individual, private processes often hidden within family lives. There-fore, unlike other social and ethnic minorities, they lack the support and solidarity of belonging to a social group. They also lack adult role models for imitation and identification, both in their everyday social life as well as in popular culture. Thus, television has the potential of presenting a world that is not directly accessible to them, while bypass-ing traditional socializing agents that might prove themselves embar-rassed, confused, non-supportive, or even covertly if not overtly hostile.

In recent years, portrayals of gays on popular television have been trickling gradually into our lives via the silver screen. In the past, most gay images were presented as a form of social, psychological, and/or physical deviation. Homosexuals were easily detected by their stereo-typical "hyper-feminization" – their appearance, tone of speech, body movements and hand gestures, and general mannerism and life style. While this has been gradually changing, with Western television now offering more diverse portrayals of gay people, they are still presented quite differently from heterosexuals. For example, gay youth are mostly portrayed as confused about their sexual identity, while heterosexuality is always presented as a natural, unchallenged state of affairs. Gay identity is often reduced to sexual activities devoid of any emotional relationship. Subtle messages reinforce the notion that homosexuality is a deviation that can be "cured" by a strong willed person and/or with the help of the ideal partner of the opposite sex.

The absence of diverse and constantly present alternative models and perspectives on television is exemplary of the mass communication concept of the "spiral of silence" regarding portrayals of gays (i.e., the de-legitimization achieved when a message is presented to be in conflict with dominant social norms that are continually reinforced by their absence in the media). While gay youth can increasingly find television texts in Anglo-European societies that reinforce their identity or inter-pret them in oppositional ways, they are mostly not offered through television a means of connecting to the rich and productive gay culture that is emerging currently in many societies, and with which they have the potential to be integrated and to find fulfillment.

Also, it is important to note that the emerging presence of gays on television may be playing an important role regarding changes in the orientation of the majority, heterosexual youth, in regard to gays. Finally, while we may have many questions and hypotheses regarding these processes, it should be recalled that actually we have very limited empirical data or empirically grounded insights about how these processes may be operating or their impact.[19]

Sex and sexuality

One of the more central issues regarding the social construction of gender is the role television plays in children's developing understand-ing of the role of sexual relationships in human relationships, their nature, meanings, and the differentiated expectations from the two genders. As discussed in Chapter 3, this is an excellent example of a realm of life that is initially encountered by many children through the media. The scope and nature of television's engagement with sex is, as we know, debated, often heatedly, and is, without a doubt, of public concern in many societies. Similar to the discussion over violence, there are many opinions regarding the types of sexual relationships that are appropriate for children to watch and at what age. These views vary not only from one society to another, but also among sub-cultures within them. For example, in some European countries, particularly the Nor-dic ones, there is a much more relaxed and permissive approach regarding the inclusion of nudity, erotic behaviors, as well as free talk about sex in programs that are viewed regularly by young viewers. In contrast, US television is as a whole much less permissive. Yet, it too, is perceived as overly revealing, indeed indecent, in comparison to many developing countries in Africa, Asia, and South America. Needless to say, when attempting to study this topic, one confronts considerable difficulties given the many sensitivities involved regarding young people's own sexuality, questions of morals, values, and religion, as well as children's inhibitions.[20]

Earlier, when in Chapter 3 we discussed the influences of television on sexual behaviors, we indicated that content analyses of mainstream media demonstrate that it is saturated with a wide range of sexual behaviors; from kissing and embracing, through love making, and full intercourse. Television also presents a variety of verbal engagements with sex including courting behaviors, expression of fantasies and desires, exchange of experiences, and sexual provocations. The spread of HIV-AIDS since the 1980s brought into public discourse as well as into families' private living rooms the discussion of casual sex, unsafe sex and use of contraceptives, homosexual sex, and the like. We have already discussed the influence television might have on sexual behaviors of young people, but here we inquire into the ways that the world of television sexuality is incorporated into the worldviews and ideologies of children and young people.

Studies that involved listening to children and adolescents talk about their views of the world indeed find that they use television's portrayals of sex and sexuality as a basis for conversations about its relevancy to their own lives. One such study conducted in the UK found that pre-adolescents and adolescents reported frequent encounters with sexual material in the media, valued the information received from it, and used it as a learning resource. The researchers noted, in particular, that interviewees demonstrated a range of critical skills in interpreting sexual content and evaluated such content through what they perceived to be sexual morality, views that were heavily influenced by their cultural backgrounds and gender.[21]

In general, there are many fascinating questions to which researchers have yet to find answers: How do young people relate sexual content to their own experiences? To what degree do they perceive television drama that dwells on intimacy as real, particularly in comparison to their own lives that are considered to be boring and void of romance? Do they compare themselves to the sexy television characters and feel that they have been unlucky in romance, lack beauty, or experience? What are the criteria they use to compare themselves and their partners to television characters? Given that personal experiences of all kinds often leave much to be desired in comparison with television's glorified, romantic, and problem-free portrayals, does the degree to which youth perceive such portrayals to be realistic influence their assessment and satisfaction with their own initial sexual experiences?[22]

By way of illustration, let us examine one particular study that investigated the role of television in cultivating sexual attitudes and beliefs among young people. The study included 343 18-year-olds in central USA. This age was selected since most 18-year-olds are either active sexually, to a degree, or close to being so. Participants in the study completed a questionnaire that inquired about the amount of television viewed; the degree of exposure to particular programs of various genres that include a variety of sexual behaviors; their consumption of erotic and pornographic materials; their attitudes regarding the relationship between love and sex; and their assessment of the frequency of the existence of various sexual behaviors shown on television in real life; such as, frequency of extra-martial sexual relationships and pregnancies; the consumption of drugs and alcohol before sexual intercourse; picking up partners in bars; as well as those elements commonly found in the more explicit sexual programs, such as orgasms, oral sex, erotic dreams, and the like.[23]

According to the study, accumulative exposure to sexual content, indeed cultivates young people's perceptions of existing sexual behaviors in reality. Heavy consumption of sexual content was associated with interviewees' predictions of the higher frequency of the behaviors depicted in them in reality. Exposure to explicit sexual material, such as erotic and pornographic movies, was the best predictor of perceptions of the prevalence of such behaviors in reality, while exposure to mainstream programs predicted perceptions of the prevalence of the kind of behaviors depicted in them. For example, exposure to soap operas that present mother-daughter competition over the same lover was related to a perception of this problem as prevalent in real life, too. And, similarly, viewing of MTV was associated with perceptions of male boasting about their sexual activities. This can be explained by the fact that many performers of pop and rock music demonstrate provocative sexual appearance, including self-caressing of intimate body parts, sexual talk, camera shots that cut back from the performers to sexy women in seductive positions, and the like.

This research, too, found that there were significant differences between young men and women in construction of sex-related perceptions. As expected, given the prevalence in most societies of double standards towards sexuality, girls expressed more conservative and traditional attitudes towards sex and assessed the problems associated with sex much more frequently than did the boys. It was postulated that gender differences are most probably influenced by other variables, such as the scope and kind of pervious sexual experience, religious and moral perceptions, and views regarding the degree of realism of the television representations. In addition, there is the rival interpretation that young people who are more active sexually are also more attracted to sexual television content and that their actual experiences, not their exposure to television, explain their perceptions.

Several other studies conducted in different countries applied various research methods and arrived at a similar conclusion: Exposure to television content that presents a variety of sexual behaviors may influence perceptions and value judgments related to intimacy and sexual relationships. Furthermore, children and youth who are active viewers raised in families with clearly defined values and who maintain open communication patterns seem to be least influenced by television values.[24] Such findings should not be too surprising given discussions in previous chapters.

Finally, this review would not be complete without paying specific attention to the question of pornography and its effect on perceptions and attitudes toward sex and sexuality, beyond the behavioral ones discussed in Chapter 3. Stated succinctly, analyses of the content of pornography suggest the following characteristics:

1 Pornography presents sexual relationships between people who have no intention to maintain a relationship following the sexual encounter.
2 Pornography presents a high frequency of sexual acts with a variety of partners that emphasize the physical and technical aspects of sex, rather than the human and emotional.
3 Pornography presents all types of sexual activities as providing ecstatic pleasures to the participants, including behaviors considered in many societies to be deviant, strange, and indeed violent.[25]

The prevailing feminist analysis of heterosexual pornography suggests that it presents a systematic portrayal of power-relationships between men and women, in which women are presented to be whores by nature, who enjoy pain and humiliation, and who are always available for sex under any conditions.

Do young viewers who are heavy consumers of pornography internalize such a worldview? A growing body of research (once again, on young people over 18, and mostly in the USA) suggests that, indeed, pornography does shape and reinforce undesired attitudes towards women in sexual as well as non-sexual contexts. Viewers of pornography, particularly of the more hardcore genres, were found in both correlation and experimental studies to have more negative attitudes towards women, to hold harsh and inconsiderate attitudes regarding the sexual needs of their partners, as well as, to play down the severity of sexual crimes and their consequences for women and children. While many of these studies were criticized on methodological and ideological grounds, there is enough evidence gathered to raise concern over the potential influence that pornography may have on sexual relationships.[26]

Body image and eating disorders

A medical problem particularly prevalent among female adolescents and young women, eating disorders (i.e., anorexia nervosa – starving oneself to death; bulimia – constant purging and induced vomiting; and compulsive eating) are complicated diseases that have psychological, physiological, and social aspects whose treatment involves many medical professions. These diseases are common in the more wealthy societies and among the more well-to-do classes, often times among talented, ambitious, good looking, and popular girls.

The cultural aspects involved with eating disorders emerged as a matter of social concern in the 1990s. Here, the possible contribution of popular culture, and particularly television, to this problem was the focus of much criticism due to familiar representations of women via unattainable portrayals of female beauty. Glorifying especially thin models and actresses as "sexy" and "glamorous;" presenting thinness as an expression of self-control and success; and constructing it as feminine and beautiful have been claimed by feminist researchers to be a contemporary form of gender inequality. According to this line of argument, the "beauty myth" enslaves girls and women of all ages to invest the best of their emotional, physical, and economic resources in a futile attempt to "fix" their appearance in a compulsory manner – via cosmetics, fashion, food, plastic surgery, beauty salon, fitness clubs, etc – in order to attain a resemblance of the beauty ideal that serves consumer culture.[27] The cultural norms projected through media images are presumed to create inner contradictions: between a woman's internal definition of "herself" and the definition of the "ideal me." In reality, the average female body in industrialized countries has been expanding gradually over the past half century, while its' representation was becoming thinner.

Researchers of the general phenomenon of the "beauty myth" have been asking questions, such as; how do images of thin, boyish-looking female celebrities, actresses, and super models whose bodily signs of femininity (e.g., full breasts, round thighs) have been erased affect self-body image and the self-worth of girls as they are growing up? What value do they attach to the nearly impossible ideal of a very thin, tall figure with slim legs and disproportionately large breasts?

A focus on eating disorders has developed particularly in the USA where eating disorders have become a serious concern. The intent of a growing number of studies is to deal empirically with the tangled relationships between the "beauty myth" and girls' self-body image. These studies employed both experimental designs for the study of short-term effects as well as correlation studies for the study of the longer-term accumulative effects. Overall they suggest that exposure to media images is one of a number of important variables that interact and that are involved in the development of eating disorders.[28] For example, the more dissatisfied with their bodies the teenage girls were the more they seemed to internalize the messages from the media. Accumulative exposure to stereotypical beauty models seems to contribute to a lower sense of body image, dissatisfaction with one's body, desire to lose weight, attitudes that are indicative of eating disorders (e.g., obsessive concern with one's weight, strong guilt over eating, and depression over one's appearance). Such characteristics have been measured using attitudinal scales attained by asking respondents to rank their degree of agreement with statements such as: "I think the ideal woman should be thin;" "I think of my body in comparison to the bodies of television characters;" or "I constantly think about wanting to be thin."[29]

Television seems to have both direct and indirect effects on body image. It shapes directly the way girls and young women process their own body image, but also indirectly by encouraging girls to internalize and believe in the thin body ideal. We may describe the relationships between viewing television and the symptoms of eating disorders in the graphic way shown in Figure 4.1.

At the same time, there is evidence of many other intervening variables in these processes. For example, girls who perceive television content to be less realistic, who are more critical viewers, who dismiss television's influence on their worldviews, and those who are more critical of the "beauty myth" – demonstrate resistance to such an influence.

So far we have discussed this phenomenon only in reference to girls and women, as thinness is mostly associated with the female body and eating disorders have been almost exclusively a female issue. However, there are signs that this is gradually becoming a male issue, as well, due to the developing changes in gender roles along with the economic and cultural pressures exerted on male audiences to become more aware of

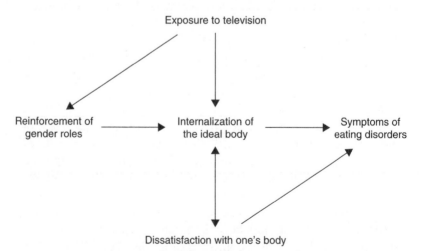

Figure 4.1 Relationships between viewing television and eating disorders[30]

their bodies and to join in the consumption of related products and services. Indeed, exploratory studies suggest that the same emotional mechanisms that operate on girls may well be activated in boys, too.

The discussion of television's contribution to eating disorders is an excellent example of a culturally embedded concern that has been studied mainly from an ethnocentric, Western perspective. The phenomenon itself may be completely irrelevant for societies where food is scarce or where women's bodies are mostly covered. The ideal of the "beauty myth" is clearly Anglo-European in origin. Even the few non-Anglo-European celebrities that have been framed as "exotic," are mainly a skin-colored version of the same ideal model (as are, for example, the colored Barbie dolls). Global television does not offer girls around the world alternative models of beauty – a fully rounded body of an African or Latin beauty or a small-boned Asian one. Light skin and hair and small facial features are still the norm, excluding alternative forms of beauty of the fuller facial features and curly dark hair of the African woman or the slatted eyes and characteristic nose of the Asian woman. While there is no systematic research to provide us with a satisfying answer to a question such as how this Anglo-European model is affecting girls and young women throughout the world, there is cultural evidence to point at the processes in action: the growing industry of facial plastic surgery (e.g., "correcting" eyes and lips) of Asian women, dying hair and whitening skin by dark-skin women, and the sucking of fat tissues from the hips and buttocks for a narrower look of Latin women.

The Social Construction of Reality

Our detailed discussion of television's contribution to the construction of gender can facilitate our understanding of other social issues in terms of the kind of questions asked, the kind of methodologies applied, the kinds of findings revealed, and so forth. Here, our general question is – how does the social reality presented on television shape the way young viewers come to view the social world in which they live, power relationships in it, dominant values that underlie it, as well as their own place in it in comparison to members of other social groups?

The "Mean World" hypothesis

The discussion of violence on television is one of the central issues regarding the role television has in cultivating a particular worldview.

Viewed broadly, we can say that violence is a way to present the social order and the division of power within it. Most popular television programs that are successful in the global market legitimate and reinforce white-male domination. Television violence and its consequences (and/or the lack of attention to them) provide viewers with "lessons" regarding those who can escape a crime without punishment, what are the dangerous and safe places, who are dangerous and who are safe people, what are the chances of encountering violence or becoming its victim, and the like. Proponents of the "Mean World" hypothesis argue that what viewers learn from television violence is fear, threat, distrustfulness, and a strong sense of vulnerability.[31]

Studies conducted according to this hypothesis measure attitudes by ranking responses to a host of questions on the "Mean World Index," such as:

- Do you think people are usually helpful or only concerned for themselves?
- Do you think people will try to take advantage of you if they get a chance or do they try to be fair?
- As a general rule, would you say that you can trust people or that you can never be careful enough?

In addition, interviewees are asked to state their degree of agreement with general questions regarding their social mood and sense of alienation, such as:

- Despite what some people argue, the condition of the average person is getting worse rather than improving.
- It is not fair to bring a child into the world given the current state of affairs.
- Most people in public office are indifferent to the problems of the average person.

Over the years, this tradition of research has arrived at the overall conclusion that heavier consumers of television see the world as much more cruel and dangerous and hold stronger attitudes expressing distrust, alienation, and depression than those who view less television. These researchers argue that we should be concerned about this conclusion because historical analyses of societies in distress suggest that people who feel insecure are much more dependent, easier to manipulate and to control, are more easily swayed by hard-line political and religious attitudes, are more open to accepting forceful solutions to social problems, and the like.

A related consequence of the Mean World hypothesis is the potential that constant viewing of television violence may desensitize viewers to the pain and suffering of fellow humans.[32] Here it is argued that over time viewers get used to violence, become less anxious while watching it, and so they gradually see violent actions as less extreme and voluntary. This in turn can lead to treating violent acts more lightly (e.g., as was discussed in relation to sexual crimes and pornography) and diminish a willingness to help victims of violence. This line of argument assumes that desensitization is a longitudinal process that affects all viewers over time.[33]

In general, there is limited evidence that offers us insights into the complicated nature of the relationships between viewing violence and cultivation of worldviews. For example, a study based on questionnaire surveys completed by high school students in Japan and participant-observation undertaken during viewing found indications of desensitization (e.g., laughter during violent sequences) and correlated such behavior with heavy viewing of violent programs.[34] In Australia, pre-school and elementary school children discussed television violence differently as a function of its realistic nature. For example, they were more critical about violence in sports programs that they perceived to be real, than they were about its appearance in a fictional family series. They also demonstrated disinterest in news, not only because news is "boring" according to them, but also because it presents realistic and scary violence.[35]

Of particular interest is a cross-national report prepared during the years 1996–97 for UNESCO on media violence.[36] The study investigated the role of media violence, television included, in the lives of 5,000 12-year-olds in 23 countries in a variety of regions and cultures in the world. The students filled out a questionnaire about their media consumption habits and preferences, and the social environment in which they live. The survey results suggest, among other things, that despite the many cultural differences, the media perpetuate the perception that violent behavior is normal and that it is associated with positive reinforcement. At the same time, media content viewed by the children offer very few non-violent alternatives (notice the similarity to the results of the analysis of violence in TV programs presented in Chapter 3). A major contribution of the UNESCO study is evidence that the consequences of media violence are related to the social reality in which children are growing up. For example, violent media messages reinforce the life experiences of children in the study who were living at the time in more violent environments (war zones or urban areas with high crime rates). These children were also more attracted to famous violent characters (e.g., Sylvester Stallone in the role of Rambo; the many roles of Arnold Schwarzenegger). While children who were living in non-violent environments demonstrated similar perception, they did so to a lesser degree.

Based on the initial, albeit limited research efforts undertaken to date, we can conclude that there seem to be many intervening variables in the relationship between viewing television violence and internalizing a particular worldview. Among these variables are the degree of realism of the violence portrayed, the real-life circumstances of the children, and the type of gratifications that children derive from the viewing.

Perceptions of the social "us" in comparison to "others"

Content analyses of popular commercial television programs traded around the world suggest dominance of the life styles and culture of the white middle class. Other ethnic groups are generally absent. When they do appear it is as minorities in Western television where they are assigned stereotypes that represent the western-European point of view. For example, while American television has become gradually more inclusive of multiculturalism, it still mainly divides the social world, racially, into white and non-white. Large minority groups of color in the USA, particularly African-Americans, receive their own "ghettoes" on television (e.g., an all black situation comedy or rap-music program) with interaction with the white world being restricted.[37] Other large minority groups, such as the Latino and Asian populations, appear rarely. Neither is the diversity within these groups recognized (for example, Mexicans, Argentineans, Peruvians, and the like within Latino ethnicity; and Chinese, Japanese, Korean, and the like within Asian ethnicity). Pressures to be more inclusive have resulted in the last decade in some significant changes. However, the appearance of non-white persons on the screen has been criticized often as a form of "tokenism."

Local productions of television are a different matter, as they represent local populations and cultures. Indeed, it is important to note that audiences all over the world express great affinity for locally produced programs and, consequentially, their ratings are usually high. However, the expense required in the local production of one episode, including the human and technological resources, is usually much greater than the cost of the station's purchasing a year's worth of old re-runs of an American series. As a result, television all over the world is heavily dominated by American television. In addition, there are indications that even young viewers notice the often lower production quality and aesthetics of their own country's productions in comparison with those made in USA (for example, less sophisticated use of photographic techniques, sparser settings, less professional quality of actors and actresses), thus reinforcing the supremacy of American television and the social world it represents.[38]

Again, what is the contribution of such portrayals of the social world in the social construction of reality by children all over the world? Do white, middle class European-American children perceive their own dominance on television over other social classes and ethnic groups? What influence does television have in the emerging self-identity of the non-white minority child in the USA, France, or in Africa, or for an Asian child growing up among a majority within his/her society, yet a minority within the global television fare? What are the consequences of the absence of images that are similar to a child's self-definition or the stereotypical presentation of it in the child's emerging self-image?

Here, some research evidence suggests that minority groups in the USA consume television in a different manner than the white population: they had their own orientation, tastes, and preferences for specific programs, mainly those portraying their own ethnic group. They reacted differently to the images appearing on television, perceived the degree of realism that portrays the unfamiliar aspects of the white world to be higher, and used it to learn about this inaccessible reality. The same held true for white children's reactions to black situation comedies: They perceived them to be more realistic, accepted the stereotypes of African-American people as funny, and trusted that the occupations presented on television reflected the kinds of occupations with which African-American people are actually involved. That is to say, that television viewing both shaped and reinforced believes children had about other ethnic groups. Children who believed that African-American inferiority on television reflects real life tended to be reinforced by such attitudes as a result of induced viewing in the research situation. However, television seemed to have a stronger effect on the visibility of the African-American minority on children: The more children viewed programs that had African-American people in them, the higher they estimated their proportion in society, and the more they assigned television a role as a source of information about them.[39]

The type of television programs viewed, too, is of importance. Heavy viewing of television fiction that portrays African-American people is associated with over-estimating the social, economical, and educational status of African-American people in reality; while heavy viewing of television news was found to be related to perceiving the status of black people to be much inferior to that of the white population. In addition, viewing educational television that was aimed at boosting African-American children's self-esteem had a particularly strong appeal and attracted identification. As in other areas, this research reveals that television has both reinforced existing attitudes as well as added new information when no prior knowledge existed. Additional support for these conclusions came from studies concerned with other kinds of social minorities, such as disabled people. For example, a study of children's reactions to portrayals of blind people in a documentary film demonstrated a positive change in viewers' attitudes; that is, television contributed in this case in a positive manner in an area in which children did not have prior first hand knowledge.

Clearly, when the reality portrayed on television is similar to the real experiences of the young viewers, they are much more critical and realistic in their evaluation of the program. And, conversely, when it presents a reality that is removed from them (e.g., a white world to black children and vice versa), they lack the skills and experience to evaluate it critically. For example, African-American youth were found to believe that television's social world is realistic, except when it referred to their own ethnic group. Similarly, African-American children expressed a desire to identify with white characters, to whom they assigned positive personality traits and a much higher social status than to their own group. Japanese students who had just arrived in the USA and who had not had any first-hand contact with African-Americans were much more "vulnerable" to their portrayals on television in comparison to local white Americans who had first hand experience with African-American peers.[40]

Unfortunately, we do not have enough research-based knowledge to assess the contributions of new images of a variety of ethnicities that have begun to appear in more recent American television programs. Research studies that could be advanced include the following questions: How do portrayals of actors and actresses of African, Asian, Latin, or indigenous people on television in typical high status television roles such as medical doctors, lawyers, journalists, detectives, contribute to the development of a positive self-image and future aspirations among children? Does the presentation of a multicultural world (i.e., where in the same emergency-room, law-firm, or police station there are professionals of all ethnicities, ages, and disabilities working side by side, making friends, having fun together, falling in love, and having sexual relationships) contribute to the social integration and reduction of prejudices among viewers? Do African-American girls take pride in an African-American woman-judge who appears on television and does such a role encourage them to believe in such professional possibilities for their own career aspirations? How does a boy in Japan perceive a Japanese surgeon in an American television program?

The little that we do know from research relates mostly to ethnic minorities in the USA, and in particular to African-Americans. However, the same questions need to be pursued regarding different social minorities that, too, are discriminated against on the basis of age as well as physical or mental disabilities. What does the portrayal of a lame female chief of emergency room, a deaf political advisor, or a grandmother holding a political office do to perceptions of disabilities and ageism?

Although all of these images may be inspiring and appealing, due to lack of empirical research we can only surmise about the influences of these changes in television portrayals. However, existing theories can help us make intelligent predictions: The "cultivation hypothesis" suggests that viewing such images on a regular basis is likely to contribute to the cultivation of a multicultural worldview tolerant of difference. According to the "uses and gratifications theory," we can assume that the reasons for watching the specific programs and the gratifications provided by viewing will mediate between the child and the perception of the realism of the program viewed. Cultural studies will help us understand the active role the child has in making meanings of these images. However, as noted, these and other theories await exploration in future studies.[41]

Perceptions of a rich, violent, United States

Children all over the world who live in very different cultures, each with their unique social perceptions, values, and traditions are processing similar images of American society in their very own way. The dominance of American programs all over the world raises another interesting question: How does television contribute to the construction of the concept of "America" in the minds of children who have never been there? This question provides a unique opportunity to inquire about the role of television in the construction of social reality when there is a void in real-life experience.

A series of studies devoted to this very question conducted during the 1990s present revealing conclusions.[42] For example, a small study based on focus groups with adolescents in Germany found that viewers apply four categories when engaged in critical viewing of American programs[43]:

- *Naive acceptance*: The viewer does not distinguish between the text and the reality and accepts the program messages as factual.
- *Sophisticated acceptance*: The viewer accepts the attitudes presented in the program, but is aware of alternative arguments based on his or her own life-experiences and/or the program itself.

- *Sophisticated rejection*: The viewer does not accept the program as is, argues with it on the basis of his or her own experience and additional thoughts derived independent of the program itself.
- *Deconstruction* (i.e., breaking down messages into their components and roots): The viewer expresses awareness that the program is a text constructed by professionals who have their own attitudes and perceptions.

The adolescents in the German study were aware that the programs were produced in the USA, but were not terribly preoccupied with this fact. When discussing the inter-personal relationships presented in the programs, they did not refer at all to the culture in which these relationships took place. The fact that the characters were American did not prevent the interviewees from identifying with them and feeling emotionally close to them. Many of these youth related the social issues addressed in the programs to similar ones in their own familiar social environment: The desire for equality within a couple in a situation comedy, inter-relationships among family members, or friendship in a soap-opera. These were interpreted and related to through the background of their own contextualized experiences and values. One focus group, for example, related a story line presented in a soap-opera involving the relationship between a white teenager in the rich California neighborhood of Beverly Hills with an African-American to their own relationships with immigrants to Germany. While many of the interviewees demonstrated considerable ability in deconstruction of television texts, most of them did not apply this capability when asked to talk about and to respond to these programs. Rather, what they preferred to do was to claim that they like to view some American programs and that these programs have much relevancy in their own social and ideological world, regardless of their production origins. The American identity of the programs, so it seems, was not a significant element for their analysis of the social world presented to them.

The findings of the German study are not unexpected, given the European-Christian nature of the culture and similarity to the USA, as well as, the selection of programs that center on universal themes of relationships in the family, between friends, and couples. Thus, it is interesting to examine these issues in a culture that differs significantly from the USA. A study conducted in India, for example, included a survey of 450 youth in three large Indian cities that focused on their acquaintance with American characters and their perceptions of American society and culture.[44] The study found that the most residual aspect of American culture was that the youth had specific recall of the brand names of American products (e.g., brand name products such as Coca

Cola and Levi jeans), as well as, names of celebrities in the film and pop music industries. The specific choices made by the interviewees reflect the particular timing of the study (in late 1990s) when the most popular American programs were soap operas and Disney movies. Above everything, it appears that what viewing these programs achieved was to reinforce the popularity of American cultural products in the non-western world.

In addition, 80 percent of the interviewees in the Indian study claimed that television was their central source of information on the USA. They recognized mainly the names of famous American white males; believed that Americans enjoy a very high standard of living, had powerful media, and advanced technology. They perceived the USA's scientific progress as the most important contribution to the world, with building nuclear weapons as among its chief achievements. Seventy-two percent agreed with the claim that "America is a racist country;" 53 percent agreed that "America symbolizes equality of opportunity" (which also means that about half of them did not believe this was the case); 41 percent agreed that "American involvement in international politics is justified" (which means that most (59 percent) did not agree – and this was before the many international crises involving the USA at the beginning of the third millennium, in particular the war in Iraq); and only 20 percent agreed with the statement that "America is a male dominated society."

In Greece, two-thirds of 508 youth who completed questionnaires reported that American programs constitute most of their viewing diet, second only to Greek programs.[45] They perceived people in the USA to be living a comfortable life, but over-estimated the ability of an average American family to allow itself to take an annual vacation in Europe or to purchase a luxurious car. At the same time, about half thought that Americans lead boring lives. They also believed that Americans are happy with their lot, friendly, and trustworthy, and that youth their age in the USA enjoy more personal freedom. The more those surveyed viewed American programs, the more they believed these programs to be realistic; the more they liked them; the more they described American society and American characters in positive terms and rated its wealth to be at a high level. Age was an important variable in these correlations: younger viewers (who obviously had less experience and alternate sources of information) had less accurate evaluations of both the crime rate and levels of wealth in the USA.

Given these and other findings, the study concluded in a manner similar to other studies of social perceptions that the quantity of television viewing in and of itself does not predict the attitudes. Viewing American programs does not directly produce an effect of a particular perception of American society, but rather there are additional variables that intervene in this process such as the attractiveness of the program, the perception of its realism, the particular programs watched, the age and gender of the viewers, and their social status. According to this study, the most salient variable was the strength of their Greek identity – adolescents who watched a lot of Greek television, felt a strong sense of personal safety in Greece, and expressed positive attitudes towards the culture and values of Greece, viewed American society as less rich and more violent, the standard of living as less comfortable, thought Americans to be more bored, and American youth enjoyed less personal freedom.

A study conducted in Israel of 901 elementary children's viewing of wrestling programs produced by the World Wrestling Federation (WWF) revealed, as well, that some of the stereotypes of the USA prevalent throughout the world seemed to be reinforced by viewing these television programs.[46] For example, in the personal interviews, children used a variety of reasons to explain that the program was American by including statements about it being the richest and most developed country in the world: "It's the kind of country...they do everything big – not a small amusement park, but Disneyland," argued a sixth-grade boy. Similarly, a fifth-grader said: "Many stars come from there. America is 'The' – it's the most developed.... it is very big and all the big things are in Hollywood." At the same time, they perceived the USA to be the most violent and dangerous country: "When you walk in the streets in the United States you don't know what will happen, anyone can attack you," explained a fifth-grade girl. The Americans, according to these interviewees, were perceived as the most violent of all people. They lack self-control and live according to behavioral norms that are not acceptable anywhere else in the world. At the same time, the USA was admired for its innovativeness and the potential to fulfill the "American Dream," as one fifth-grade boy explained: "America is the country where everything new enters.... Let's say I wake up in the morning with a new product or a new television program and I have the power to make it, it will become popular very quickly if I have commercials."

Interviewees specifically named movies and programs as their sources of information and "proof" of their claims. "There are many movies about America fighting. Everyone there is strong," explained a third-grade girl. A friend of hers added: "America. They are strong. I see in the program. Especially in action movies." Names of famous actors at the time the study was conducted (such as Sylvester Stallone, Arnold Schwarzenegger, Jean-Claude Van Damme, Chuck Norris) were given as evidence of American violence. The news, too, was an important source of information for children who cultivated such a worldview: "There is more violence in America than in Israel or in other countries. You can see it on television in the news and everywhere," argued a sixth-grade boy. Interestingly, interpersonal sources (e.g., relatives who have visited the USA and related their experiences) only served to reinforce these views.

Here, too, the interpretation of WWF was deeply contextualized in the life circumstances of Israeli children who recruited the Israeli–Arab conflict to explain why the program could have never been a local one: "We already have enough fighting between Arabs and the Israelis, so we don't need WWF. In the United States they need it, because they don't have enough," explained a third-grade boy.

We can conclude that popular television programs viewed all over the world, such as the WWF, contribute to cultivation of a worldview which in turn shapes expectations and perceptions regarding American society within which new information – from additional media sources as well as from first hand experiences – is absorbed. We may choose to describe this as a type of "self-fulfilling prophecy."

A unique opportunity to examine these conclusions was undertaken in an extensive cross-cultural study called the *Global Disney Audiences Project*. In order to assess the place of *Disney* culture in societies around the world, this study employed standardized questionnaires, interviews, and participant-observations in 17 countries outside the USA and at 5 locations within it.[47] Responses, mainly by young adults, to the question – "Is Disney uniquely American" – varied greatly from country to country. Overall, approximately 50 percent thought Disney to be uniquely American, suggesting that it was an American prototype (e.g., the American dream) and/or perceiving it to be culturally imperialist. Interestingly, those who expressed the opinion that *Disney* is not uniquely American argued that it is "Western," "universal," or even "mine." This interpretation suggests that their perception of American is interchangeable with terms such as "Western" or even "universal" and as such represents the interviewees' own existential experience. If indeed non-American children understand new experiences, among other things, through an American worldview presented in American programs, then it may be an argument in favor of the "Americanization" of popular culture thesis.

A related illustration comes from China, where VCDs with Disney characters, songs, and stories are used in order to teach children the highly valued English language. While it is unclear how much English is being retained, it is clear that Disney products are growing in popularity in China as are many other popular texts originating in the West. The rival interpretation to the Americanization thesis challenges notions of the development of a cosmopolitan perspective, as it suggests that Chinese children, while deriving great pleasure from these texts, are consuming them within a particular domestic political allegiance.[48] This argument clearly echoes the concept of "glocalization" discussed in the introduction.

Cultural integration of immigrant children

A particular case of interest in regard to the social construction of reality is the emerging research interest in the roles television serves for immigrant children, as part of contemporary migration movements. Initial conclusions suggest that these roles are not unequivocal and often have conflicting influences. On the one hand, viewing TV assists children to adjust and integrate into a new society, while on the other hand in doing so it works counter to the desire, particularly of adults, to preserve the homeland cultural identity and social segregation. Similar research on adults suggests that exposure to the host media plays an important role in the immigrants' learning about the new society and taking part in it. Yet, the host media are a powerful tool in shaping and nurturing negative stereotypes of new immigrants, thus causing the latter's sense of alienation and social isolation.

Similarly, television in the immigrants' language (via either special broadcast channels or broadcast delivered through satellites from the original country) play a double role. First, channels based in the new residence country serve as a tool for learning about the new society and how to accommodate to it. Second, both types of broadcasts preserve the immigrants' cultural heritage and strengthen their inter-group solidarity. In the era of globalization, the mass media and advanced communication technologies enable immigrant communities of the same origin, dispersed over different countries, to retain ties with the "motherland" as well as with their fellow-ethnic in other countries. That is to say, the global media are one of the main factors that shape and nurture transnational diaspora communities.

This having been said, very little is known empirically about the various roles that media actually play in the lives of immigrant children who undoubtedly face unique personal and social challenges, as well as, inter-generational tensions. More than their parents, these children are expected to handle two cultural identities, to speak two languages, and to be able to negotiate between two cultural worlds. The little empirical evidence that exists suggests that, in comparison to children born in the USA, immigrant children spent more time watching television and expressed a more positive attitude toward educational/informational programs. Moreover, foreign-born children appeared to use television

more for learning about others and themselves and exhibited significantly greater identification with television characters and expressed
stronger beliefs in the televised reality of people and events.[49] It seems,
then, that for immigrant children, television is an important source of
education and information about their new society, particularly during
the first few years following immigration when they suffer from isolation and lack of close relationships with local children. Hence, television characters probably were among the first Americans to whom they
were introduced and with whom they could easily "interact." In short,
the immigrant children experienced indirect interaction with surrogate
Americans.

Initial evidence from a European study suggests that young children
involved in immigration to various communities (e.g., from North
Africa into the south of France; from Turkey and Somalia into Denmark; from former Soviet Union to Israel) often resist parents' efforts
to interest them in media content from their countries of origin.
Researchers argue that what serves as a tool for immigrant parents'
retention of their original cultural identity, may be perceived by their
children as an obstacle to their own full integration into the new
homeland. Nevertheless, the children do become part of "Sunday
culture" when they join their parents to watch television programs
from their former homeland for the sake of family togetherness.[50]

A more focused ethnographic study conducted among young
Indians in London focused on the interplay of different media content
and its crucial role in the construction of their cultural identity. Here
researchers found that exposure to Indian movies and dramas ensured
a degree of preservation of traditional norms and values, while the
exposure to British and transnational television content enabled these
teenagers to challenge the traditional values and norms of their parents
and to develop a new cultural identity that supported their efforts to
integrate into British society. Another small study of 5 first-generation
Indian female adolescents in the USA also provided evidence of the
multi-roles that both American as well as Indian TV play in the
construction of ethnic identities, and how those are intertwined with
gender and sexual ones.[51]

Similar processes have been identified in a comparative study of
immigrant children from the former Soviet Union to Germany and
Israel. The study revealed that television plays a significant role in
immigrant families in both countries. In this context, cable and satellite
channels originating in the former Soviet Union are of special interest.
Parents wishing to preserve their children's affinity for the Russian
language and culture encourage joint viewing of programs broadcast
from Russia. Although the children themselves were not too eager to

watch television in Russian, they usually acceded to their parents' request in order to maintain smooth communication with them. A similar pattern was found in some of the families regarding the local channels, as watching the programs in the host language seemed to assist in bridging the cultural gap between immigrant children and their parents, since parents' integration into the host culture was much slower. At the same time, television was found to have a central role in immigrant-children's sense of fitting in the local and global culture and in constructing their new identities.[52] Also related is the evidence that suggests that television serves an important role in second-language acquisition of immigrant children. This will be elaborated in Chapter 5.

As you may well have recognized by now, a major thread interwoven in our discussion of the roles served by television in the lives of immigrant children highlights, again, the interplay between television, identity issues, and cultural context. Television, we have seen, is much, much more than the populist acclaimed wasteful entertainment. Indeed, among its many roles, it is an alternative form of "schooling." This conclusion reinforces the need for producers to realize and to manifest the responsibility involved in producing quality television for children. Furthermore, such an understanding reinforces the need for such programming as one of the goals of a responsible television industry concerned about the cultural ecology of their children.

The Construction of Political Reality

The political world is an instructive example of that part of reality that most children are detached from, yet are directly influenced by as well as expected to influence in due course, when they become active, involved citizens. With the aid of television, very young viewers learn to identify their own as well as other countries' political leaders; listen as they give political speeches or argue before their governing bodies; follow demonstrations; and recognize major issues on their national political agenda. Aside from these general claims, what roles do television together with other socializing agents play in the process of children's emerging understanding of political reality?

A series of studies conducted on this topic in the 1970s in the USA suggested the following conclusions[53] :

1   Media serve as the primary source of political information for young audiences.

2   Most political learning by children was assisted by newspapers and television. Younger children were more dependent on television and, as they matured, newspapers were added as a source of information about news and current events on television. Television remained as the central source of political information for young viewers from lower social economic classes.

3   The adolescents themselves identified the media as a significant influence in shaping their political perceptions, in addition to its serving as a central source of information. According to their self-reporting, the media influence their attitudes in specific areas and in some cases even more than their parents, peers, and teachers.

4   Adolescents with more interest in news and current affairs obtained in part via the media tended also to discuss it more within their family. As a result, in their case, the socializing agents reinforce one another.

5   The main contribution of news reporting in both newspapers and television was to attitudes and knowledge, and not to actual political activism. Several studies suggested that there was no clear relationship between the shaping of knowledge and attitudes following exposure to the media and their practical application in various forms of political activities.

6   Adolescents did not necessarily adopt their parents' habits of consuming political content via the media, nor their parents' political attitudes.

Not surprisingly, one of the foci in this research area is the direction of the influence. In this regard, studies have found that youth who have a greater interest in political issues approach the media more selectively in their search for relevant information. Furthermore, youth who report heavy consumption of news are also those who have more political knowledge. This leads to the question – is heavier consumption of political content on television dependent on other variables (such as political interest, family background, education, gender) or is it an independent variable on which other variables depend (e.g., knowledge, attitudes, political involvement)? Apparently, there are longitudinal interrelationships between all of these variables: parents and peers interact with the consumption of television. This in its turn interacts with political values and attitudes (see Figure 4.2). Youth who are more involved socially, and, therefore, more exposed to the attitudes and interpretations of their peers, also use media more as sources for information and attitude formation.

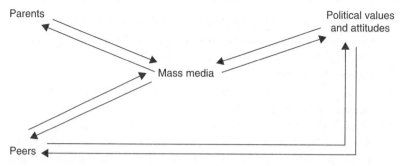

Figure 4.2   The inter-relationships between different political socialization agents[54]

There are many questions that require further inquiry in this domain, as well: Can television encourage the development of a particular kind of political society? How can parents and educators take advantage of the potential contribution of television for political socialization? What is the nature of the relationship between the political information transferred in the media and the emotional aspects of affiliation with a particular political movement or identification with a particular ideology? These and other questions are often considered to be controversial and value laden in some societies. On the one hand, if youth will not be exposed to political issues in the media, their knowledge and involvement in these areas will be deficient. This is undoubtedly an undesirable situation for a society seeking, even committed, to developing an active citizenship in the public sphere. At the same time, if indeed children are informed by media content, they may be exposed only to particular frames of references to reality, to particular political ideologies, to a limited social agenda, and to the exclusion of specific social and ideological peripheries. When other socializing agents do not fulfill their duties in an active way, media reports become the primary political reality for them (i.e., there is an absence of alternative sources of information).

A more specific study on the role of news in the making of citizens in the USA and UK employed a qualitative methodology in interviewing adolescents and in analyzing news programs designed for them.[55] The interviewees wanted to be more informed about the world and to be treated respectfully, but at the same time they expected to be entertained and stimulated. The researcher concluded, among other things, that there is a need for innovation in traditional forms of news presentations in order to stimulate young people's engagement and to penetrate the wall of apathy and cynicism that they often exhibit.

This research was related to discussion of the formal exclusion of youth from the public sphere and the absence of their ability to realize their political rights. Here, too, we find strong traces of the debate over children as "being" versus "becoming;" that is, the assertion that youth should be treated as actual citizens ("being"), rather than as "citizens-in-the-making" ("becoming"). If so, they need access to the mediated public domain of television news – both as an audience whose needs and interests are taken into consideration as well as participants whose opinions and concerns are being voiced.

The construction of conflicts

Of special interest is research regarding political socialization conducted in societies during times of war and armed conflict. If in the past attempts were made in some societies to shield the young from war and other forms of political violence, today, as we have already argued, children worldwide are exposed through television to traumatizing events and the many violent conflicts that have and are taking place at the time of this writing in Afghanistan, Chechnya, Iraq, Palestine, Sudan, the former Yugoslavia, to name but a few. Researchers have found that children learn about such events, react to them emotionally, and construct their worldview of politics through them. Clearly, here, too, their media experiences are mediated through the political environment in which they live. Not surprisingly then, a comparative study of children's reactions to the war in Iraq conducted on its outset in the spring of 2003 revealed that most American children supported whole heartedly the attack, while German children who were exposed to the strong European opposition to the war expressed views similar to those of the adults. Israeli children, who were being prepared at the time for the possibility of their country being a target for Iraqi missiles (as was the case in the 1991 Gulf War), interpreted the war as entangled within the complexities of the enduring Israeli–Arab conflict. These and other studies of children's reactions to the war in Iraq underline how interested and involved they wish to be, as well as how hard children endeavor to assimilate the fragments of information they receive, but yet how limited is the availability of appropriate resources with which they can undertake this complex process.[56]

More specific is the role of television for children growing up in societies divided by deep, enduring conflict. A series of studies on the political socialization of Israeli youth, who are growing up in a society divided by the Arab–Israeli conflict, provide us with interesting insights. One study correlated the attitudes of Jewish-Israeli youth with the news coverage of the conflict and found that television had a central role in shaping the subjective perceptions of adolescents regarding the political agenda in Israel, the dimensions of the conflict, and the stereotypes associated with the Arabs as an enemy. Such processes were related to the amount of time the adolescents devoted to viewing television news and their attitudes towards the medium, such as the willingness to learn from television, dependency on television as a source of political information, and the perception youth had about the degree of influence television had upon them.[57]

Another study emphasized the role of family communication patterns in political socialization (see the discussion in Chapter 1). The study suggested that, as a general rule, teenagers held more extreme political views than their parents. Peer-pressure as well as adolescence, as a period in which ideas, values, and options are being tested, may partially account for these findings. However, a complementary explanation offered was that the extreme nature of the coverage of the conflict (e.g., dwelling on violence and on negative aspects rather than on possible solutions and cooperation) reinforced negative attitudes towards Arabs, in general, and their role in the conflict, more specifically. The results also indicated that teenagers raised in families that do not conduct critical discussions about television coverage of the conflict may be more influenced by its content in the shaping of their worldview.[58]

Whether research has emphasized the role of television or the role of the family, all agree that television does not operate in a social vacuum, but as part of complicated social contexts that work sometimes cooperatively, sometimes in conflict, but always within a process of negotiation of meaning. This conclusion, too, sheds light on methodological and conceptual concerns involved in the study of children and youth. Analyzing transcripts of conversations conducted with families involved in watching the news suggests that opinions and attitudes are formed and contested during the viewing itself. Political opinions, shaped and reshaped during conversations and debates, which are often full of contradictions, constantly undergo a dynamic process of reconsideration and consolidation.[59]

In contrast to the dynamics revealed to be part of the process of constructing meaning as well as consolidating values and worldviews, research involving completion of questionnaires requires that participants take a stance in regard to each question (e.g., fully agree with the position, somewhat agree with the position, disagree with the position) and thus portray themselves as having clear-cut opinions. In contrast, recorded actual conversations reveal that participants in the research have much more ambivalent and fluid positions. Accordingly, the role of television in the political socialization process uncovered in such conversations is not linear – from television to young viewers, but involves dynamic, dialectical, and reciprocal processes as well as conservative and subversive undercurrents. The implications of such understanding have import not only for understanding the roles of the media in political socialization but also for questioning what are the most fruitful and appropriate ways to study such processes.

Peace-building interventions

The complementary side of the same issue is the employment of television for peace-building interventions. The most notable of these efforts has probably been the experimental work initiated by *Sesame Workshop* with co-productions in the Middle East. An early initiative in the 1990s, which coincided with what seemed at the time the beginning of a peace process in the region, was aimed at pre-school children in Israel and the occupied territories of Palestine in Gaza and the West Bank. While the basic production model followed the classic *Sesame Street* format (see Chapter 5), it deviated in developing story lines in two separate "Sesame Streets" (*Rechov Sumsum* and *Shara'a Simsim –* *Sesame Street* in Hebrew and Arabic, respectively) representing the two-states solution of nations destined to live as neighbors and with two sets of characters speaking in two languages (Hebrew and Arabic). The curriculum that accompanied the program included focusing on mutual respect between and within Israeli and Palestinian societies, modeling pro-social interactions, visits to each other's street, presentation of conflict resolution by positive and non-stereotypical characters, and highlighting similarities and differences between the two nations.

A joint team of Israeli and Palestinian researchers examined the reactions of 600 pre-school children (Jewish and Arab Israelis, and Palestinians) to selected segments of the co-productions. They were interested, in particular, in the level of knowledge and attitudes children of each group held towards the other as well as, with their familiarity with their own culture. For example, a segment titled "Embroidery" documented a Palestinian girl following her grandmother as she embroidered a traditional dress. This segment was presented to Palestinian children in Ramallah in the Palestinian Authority as well as in Jerusalem in Israel. The researchers evaluated children's attention to the segment as well as its attractiveness to them. Following the viewing, each child was asked to spontaneously describe the segment, to answer specific comprehension questions, and to pick favorite and less favorite elements. The study found that children's attention was generally high, that they were able to follow and describe the plot line, and that they had a high level of recall. These findings were perceived as evidence for the potential of educational television to present authentic and positive portrayals of both the Palestinian and Israeli cultures to children of both groups. The fact that many children related the different segments to their personal experiences and were very involved in the viewing was an encouraging indication that the producers were reaching their educational goals. Thus, the study provided support for the claim that television does have the potential to challenge negative stereotypes by exposing children through television to the everyday life of peers on the other side of a conflict. The mere presentation of peaceful, normalized relationships between groups constantly portrayed on television news as violent enemies offered momentary relief from reality and a vision of an alternative future.[60]

This project was terminated following the deterioration of the situation in the Middle East from the beginning of the twenty-first century. Instead, a new co-production coordinated between Israeli, Palestinian and Jordanian television stations has been introduced. The preliminary findings available at the time of this writing suggest that these programs, which are developmentally appropriate, can be effective in promoting pro-social reasoning in the young viewers following the use of repetition within the programs as well as multiple showing. They provide support to the potential of such media interventions to help foster values such as mutual respect and cultural understanding, while reducing prejudice, stereotypes, and negative attitudes.[61]

Inspired by the Middle-East co-productions of *Sesame Street*, another initiative designed to encourage mutual respect and understanding among ethnic Albanians, Macedonians, Romas, and Turkish children aged 7 to 12 was developed in Macedonia. *Nash Maalo* ("our neighborhood) featured a multiethnic case of four children-friends and employed about a fifth of the dialogue in the languages other than Macedonian (accompanied with subtitles). A pre-test/post-test comparison of knowledge and attitudes of 240 children (60 10-year-olds from each of the four ethnic groups) who viewed the series over the course of several months in 1999 revealed many gains: Children's negative stereotyped perceptions and attitudes toward the various ethnic groups were reduced; they were better able to identify the three minority languages; and were more willing to invite children from other ethnic groups to their homes.[62]

These encouraging results led to a similar effort by *Sesame Workshop* in Cyprus, *Gimme6,* designed to provide positive images of the Greek Cypriot and Turkish Cypriot communities, to highlight their similarities and differences, and to disperse negative stereotypes. Following in the footsteps of *Rechov Sumsum/Shara'a Simsim* in Israel and *Nash Maalo* in Macedonia, here too, the goals focused on developing mutual understanding and conflict prevention and resolution. At the time these lines are written, negotiations are also being held in regard to the development of a similar initiative in Northern Ireland in order to contribute to the reconciliation between the Catholic and Protestant communities there. An earlier local attempt to address the Northern Ireland "troubles" (i.e., the common term used to describe the conflict), *Off the Walls,* was a series of five 20-minute programs for use in schools and youth clubs designed to promote mutual respect and tolerance among Northern Ireland youth. Similarly, *Respecting Differ-ence,* a more recent media initiative for pre-schoolers aims "to promote an understanding of and positive attitudes toward those who have similarities and differences, through respect for self and others within the diverse community of Northern Ireland."[63]

While there are few research efforts associated with these and other pioneering efforts around the world, the results in hand do indicate that there is a need and desire to involve television in a much more proactive way in facilitating peace building, mutual understanding, prejudice reduction, and conflict-resolution efforts.[64]

"Edutainment" Genres and Construction of Social Reality

The potential of television in children's construction of social reality has been attended to quite differently in different parts of the world. In sharp contrast to many of the dramatic and reality programs produced in Western countries, a trend has developed in other parts of the world – including Africa, Asia, and Latin America – to deliberately incorpor-ate social issues in the entertainment programming (such as soaps and telenovelas as well as cartoons and reality TV genres) viewed regularly by children and youth. A variety of issues are addressed including health, literacy, and social dangers.

This latter approach to using popular television texts in order to advance awareness of social issues, even social change, seeks to contrib-ute to the empowerment of young viewers by providing them not only with information and knowledge, but also with role models, reasons, values, and the motivation to be involved in shaping attitudes and actions that can be incorporated in their own everyday lives. In South Africa, for example, entertainment-television was recruited as part of the *Soul City* project for health training regarding contraception during the pressing social and health problem of HIV-AIDS. Also, the *Yitzo Yitzo* ("this is how things are") series tackled complex problems that are the reality of life in South African schools in the black townships including violence, sexual harassment and rape, drug-abuse, and HIV-AIDS. The latter example led to a heated public debate about the program's blunt treatment of these problems. A research project that evaluated how young viewers engaged with the program found that it was a source of both redemption from the hardships of their everyday lives, as well as, a source of inspiration for ways to seek a better future for themselves. This series demonstrates the complex issues involved in television's efforts to present reality to children and youth via dramatic formats. For example, could it be claimed that the presentation of violence, drug abuse, and sexual crimes serves to normalize these behaviors and continue to perpetuate them as legitimate, particularly in the current South African context in which they are raised?[65]

Degrassi Junior High, a much acclaimed early adolescence series from Canada, is an interesting example of a program that became popular in other countries, as well. Located in a school, the series dealt with many of the issues that presumably were of concern to North American adolescents, such as drugs, alcohol, sex, interpersonal relationships, peer relations, etc. An experiment that compared viewers to non-viewers found that the series was successful in raising viewers' awareness of many of the issues addressed and encouraged the viewers to reflect over them. Class discussions of these issues proved to be particularly beneficial in encouraging such processes.[66]

Of special interest are two gender-related initiatives. The first is the popularity of *Meena,* a popular cartoon figure of a South Asian girl. Originating in Bangladesh in 1991, it has since spread to India, Pakistan, Nepal, Sri Lanka, the Maldives, Bhutan, and Southeast Asia. This is an example of a television intervention as the series that features Meena was created with the intention of fostering social change by specifically addressing issues of gender discrimination (e.g., in food, education, and domestic workloads). One of the unique features of *Meena* is the fact that it was formulated following extensive formative research involving creators, programmers, researchers, and communities of potential audiences. Based on a lovable cartoon girl-figure that stimulates identification, *Meena* stories have succeeded in presenting a role model that challenges traditional value systems without threatening the audience.[67]

A more recent example comes from Egypt where *Gelila* – an Arab female cartoon superhero – who appears in printed comics has been gaining fans around the Arab world. *Gelila* represents the new liberated Arab woman. She combines traditional roles (e.g., she raises her two siblings following the death of their parents in a nuclear disaster) with a career as a brilliant scientist during her day job, who turns superhero at night when she is called upon to save the innocent from evil forces. The content of the cartoon series departs from the topics related to the Middle-East conflict as well as fundamentalist religious aspects of the Moslem world. They are designed to give Arab children culturally relevant superheroes to which they can aspire in the context of a positive future for the Middle East. At the time of this writing, the producers of *Gelila* were experimenting with pilot episodes for a television series.[68]

Many other creative, well-intended and produced quality edutainment programs for children are being developed world-wide. A selection of exemplary programs are presented in special international events such as the Prix Jeunesse in Germany and the Japan Prize. The entries to such events are illustrative of the breath and depth of quality television for children as well as its grounded cultural nature. For example, in 2004 several programs presented at the Prix Jeunesse from African countries dealt with helping young children who had lost their parents to AIDS to deal with their loss, while other programs impressed upon viewers the importance of being more tolerant of peers who have HIV. Programs from Scandinavian countries were concerned with allowing boys to express their inner worlds during puberty, discuss their sexual development, and their yearning for intimacy. Several Asian programs brought up the issue of equal schooling and literacy for both boys and girls. A Palestinian-Jordanian co-production dealt with the life of one family under the Israeli military occupation, while one from Israel presented the life of an immigrant family whose daughter was killed in a suicide-terrorist attack. Some Latin America producers struggled with infusing anti-"macho" values in their programs as part of a campaign against domestic violence.[69]

Overall, we can say that there is a very long list of social goals that television producers all over the world are setting for themselves. The effectiveness of most of these programs has yet to be studied in a systematic, comprehensive manner, although the knowledge we already have at our disposal from the previous chapters should suggest to us that such an approach does have great potential to contribute to the well being of children-viewers.

Concluding Remarks

In summarizing the role of television in the construction of social reality, we return once again to the conclusion that viewers, even the young ones, located as they are within social and ideological contexts, are selective in their viewing of content and active and creative in their interpretations of it. They gain pleasure from their use of television texts, be they soap operas, reality TV, quiz shows, or cartoons. They learn and accept advice from them in a variety of ways; recognize themselves and feel self-affirmed, and complete (or conceal) what is missing in their own life-worlds. Viewing television, too, serves as an outlet for their expression of feelings and fantasies and as an important activity that enables them to reconstruct the meaning of everyday life.[70]

However, we need not be too hasty in our celebration of the symbolic creativity of young viewers and to under-estimate the potential political and social implications of television for these audiences in contemporary societies. The interaction of viewers with television texts is complicated and incorporated with many other socializing forces. We find that the academic discussion of this area shifts between the overemphasis on the power of television to construct the social world of "captive" young audiences, on the one hand, and the dismissal of the power of television, on the other hand. This may be due to the glorification of young viewers as critical consumers who debate the content and struggle with the many interpretations embedded in the text. Such views emphasize the role of cognitive processes in their estimation of the attention devoted to television, to the analysis of the texts themselves, its content and power to construct reality, or focus on the audience as an ideological product of the text.

We should remember that it is impossible to separate the discussion of the role television has in the construction of reality from those of other media, as they all deal with the same realms of life and reinforce each other by creating an incorporated worldview. All such media-related research reveals that the relationship between exposure to television and the construction of reality is complicated and multifaceted.

Study of most of the issues raised throughout this chapter are far too underdeveloped and understudied to arrive at the overarching conclusions sought by many parents, educators, and politicians, as well as media producers. However, even so, society cannot be relieved from being responsible for the content of television programs offered to children or to leave it unchallenged. The reinforcement of similar messages in many television programs makes it very hard for young viewers to resist or to undertake an oppositional process of negotiation with them. The implications of these issues for education and broadcast policy will be discussed in Chapter 6.

Notes

1   Van Evra (2004).
2   From the vast literature in this area, see, for example, Carter and Steiner (2004), Gunter (1995), Meyers (1999), Ross and Byerly (2004), and Van Zoonen (1994).

3   De Beauvoir (1989[1952]).

4   See, for example, Barner (1999), Browne (1998), Ditsworth (2001), Dobrow and Gidney (1998), and Mazzarella and Pecora (1999).

5   See, for example, Atkin, Greenberg, and McDermott (1979), Frueh and McGhee (1975), Signorielli (1990b), and Wroblewski and Huston (1987).

6   See Gunter (1995) for an integrative summary.

7   Morgan (1987), Signorielli and Lears (1992).

8   See Durkin (1985).

9   See, for example, Drabman, Robertson, Patterson, Jarvie, Hammer, and Cordua (1981) and Pingree (1978).

10 Bachen and Illouz (1996).

11 Ang (1985), Modleski (1984), Radway (1984).

12 See such discussions in Currie (1997), Douglas (1994), Frazer (1987), Mazzarella and Pecora (1999), and Peterson (1987).

13 Lemish (1998b).

14 Ibid., p. 154.

15 Fiske (1989), Schwichenberg (1993).

16 Lemish (1998b, p. 160).

17 Pollack (1998), Seidler (1997).

18 Dyson (1997), Götz, Lemish, Aidman, and Moon (2005), Lemish, Liebes, and Seidmann (2001).

19 Kielwasser and Wolf (1992).

20 Based on interviews with producers of quality television programs for children who participated in the *Prix Jeunesse*, June 2004, Munich (Lemish, work in progress).

21 Buckingham and Bragg (2004).

22 Baran (1976), Greenberg, Linsangan, and Soderman (1993).

23 Buerkel-Rothfuss and Strouse (1993).

24 Gunter (2002), Lee (2004).

25 Zillman (1994).

26 Lyons, Anderson, and Larson (1994), Weaver (1994).

27 Barky (1988), Wolf (1992).

28 See, for example, Harrison (2000a, 2000b), Harrison and Cantor (1997), Myers and Biocca (1992), Posavac, Posavac, and Posavac (1998), and Tiggermann and Pickering (1996).

29 Botta (1999).

30 Based on the model proposed by Stice, Schupak-Neuberg, Shaw, and Stein (1994).

31 Based on Gerbner and Gross (1976) later summarized by Signorielli (1990a) and Weimann (2000).

32 See also Sontag (2003).

33 Donnerstein, Slaby, and Eron (1994), Wilson, Kunkel, Kintz et al. (1996).

34 Kodaira (1998).

35 Durkin and Low (1998).

36 Groebel (1998).

37 Greenberg and Brand (1994).

38 Lemish, Drotner, Liebes, Maigret, and Stald (1998).
39 See, for example, studies such as Graves (1993), Lichter and Lichter (1988), and Stroman (1986).
40 Fujioka (1999).
41 For a list of possible studies see Berry and Asamen (1993) and Cortés (2000).
42 See, for example, Kamalipour (1999).
43 Palmer and Hafen (1999).
44 Das (1999).
45 Zaharoponlous (1999).
46 Lemish (1999).
47 Wasko, Phillips, and Meehan (2001).
48 Hemelryk (2005).
49 Zohoori (1988).
50 Lemish, Drotner, Liebes, Maigret, and Stald (1998).
51 For the UK study see Gillespie (1995); for the US study see Durham (2004).
52 Elias and Lemish (under review).
53 Chaffee and Yang (1990).
54 Based on Adoni (1979).
55 Buckingham (2000).
56 Lemish and Götz (forthcoming).
57 First (1997).
58 Liebes and Ribak (1992).
59 Ribak (1997).
60 Cole, Arafat, Tidhar et al. (2003), Cole, Richman, and McCann Brown (2001), Killen and Fox (2003), Killen, Fox, and Leavitt (2004).
61 Brenick, Lee-Kim, Killen, Fox, Raviv, and Leavitt (forthcoming).
62 Shochat (2003).
63 See Kelly, Logue, and McCully (1996) and NIPPA (2004).
64 Fisch (forthcoming), Graves (1999).
65 Gultig (2004), Sherry (1997), Smith (2004), Tufte (2003).
66 Singer and Singer (1994).
67 McKee, Aghi, and Shahzadi (2004).
68 Based on a news report by Ben Wederman broadcast on CNN August 13, 2005.
69 Based on interviews with producers who participated in the *Prix Jeunesse*, June 2004, Munich (Lemish, work in progress).
70 Götz (2004), Götz, Lemish, Aidman, and Moon (2005).

5

Television and Learning

In the previous chapters we learned that television is among the most significant of the socializing agents of our times. It teaches children and youth facts, behaviors, values, norms, how the "world works," and it contributes to the formation of worldviews. All these take place even when broadcasters have no educational or instructional intentions, a clear curriculum, or a formalized set of educational goals. In many studies, children report that they use the entire range of television programs as a learning environment. If this is the case, it is particularly interesting to examine the potential television has when it is intentionally used for such purposes. This will naturally lead us to discuss the relationships between television and the school system – the formal socializing agent designed by societies all over the world to teach and instruct children and youth. What are the advantages and disadvantages of television as an educational and instructional tool in comparison with schooling? In what ways do they compete and complement each other? What are the possibilities of integrating television within school systems and for integrating formal schooling within television? How effective is learning from television?

Television and School – Two Educational Systems

Though many writers see television as an alternative form of schooling, as educational systems, the two are fundamentally distinct: aside from the differences in their content preferences, they represent two dissimilar technologies and, indeed, two different cultures. This line of argument follows the theoretical claims of technological determinism according to which human civilizations are shaped to a large degree by their technologies.

An integrated list of the major differences between the two schooling systems that apply to most societies includes: institutional goals; language; hierarchy; unity of time and place; compulsion; peers; activity; and delay of gratifications.[1]

Institutional goals: School systems have been established with the primary purpose of functioning as an educational and instructional setting. This goal drives everything that happens within the system. As an over-generalization, one can argue that most schools seek to teach specific skills, knowledge, and values that are delineated in formal curricula. Most learning, even the most democratic and open forms, takes place through a process of interaction primarily with teachers who are required by society to undergo training in order to qualify for teaching credentials that attest to their having achieved the requisite education, skills, and knowledge. In all societies, the office in charge of education (be it a national ministry of education, a community educational board, or a private organization) applies different forms of centralized supervision and testing to insure that schools operate according to goals determined for them by society.

In contrast, commercial television stations disavow having any educational responsibilities. Above all else, their *raison d'être* is to make a profit by attracting as wide an audience as possible in order to sell advertisers' products. Accordingly, the sole measure of a program's influence is its' "rating," that is the size of the viewing audience.

Language: Learning in schools is directed primarily to verbal languages – in spoken, written, print modes. At its core, all verbal languages are abstract, their signs are social conventions, and their interpretation involves assigning meanings to the signs (be they written letters or audio sounds). Verbal languages are linear, as they require expression in a particular word order (according to each language's grammar and syntax) and their comprehension as well as interpretation requires systematic scanning of either written or spoken texts (e.g., one needs to listen to the sentences or read the lines in order to make sense of the content).

Television, on the other hand, is based on the audio-visual language. Its visual dimension is material with comprehension moving from perceiving the concrete to abstract interpretation (e.g., from perceiving interlocking glances to the abstract concept of love). It is simultaneous, holistic, and non-linear. One interprets the moving pictures (changing in front of our eyes over 20 times per second) as a whole entity, since the detailed linear analysis undertaken with verbal texts is impossible.

The fact that the two systems emphasize different forms of expression requires that children apply different cognitive skills in their engagement with the text: dominance of the verbal in the school culture and dominance of the visual in the television culture.

Hierarchy: Schools are hierarchical institutions that are based on pupils' accumulative knowledge and skills. Since schooling is mandatory in most societies, children must progress through a unified course of study from kindergarten, or even earlier in some societies, and continue on in a fixed order (e.g., first grade, second grade, and so forth, with few exceptions of those who either skip a grade or are held back) to the grade or achievement level mandated, or until the mandated school leaving age. For example, it is impossible for most children to learn to multiply numbers without having mastered the basic motor skill required to hold a pencil, visual recognition of numbers, and the complex concept of the function and value of numbers. Similarly, it would have been extremely difficult to learn details of the history of African nations in the tenth grade without having mastered reading and writing skills in the first and second grades, and so forth.

Television, on the other hand, is not a hierarchical institution. One can participate in any one of its "classes" (i.e., programs) without skills and knowledge prerequisites, at any age, or having earned specific graduation certificates.

Unity of time and place: Most schools and most of the activities that take place within them are characterized by unity of time and place; i.e., most of the pupils in a particular class engage in the same topic during a predetermined time period. For example, the school day starts at a specific hour and pupils are expected to be on time. A math class starts exactly when the bell rings at 9:00 a.m. in the home classroom of the fifth-grade class. All students are to be engaged in math-related activities. Any attempt to be involved in another activity is negatively sanctioned (e.g., doodling, drawing, chatting, sending a note to a friend, talking on the mobile phone, eating, reading a book, doing homework for another class, or even day dreaming).

In contrast, though television channels offer the audience a predetermined schedule, viewing lacks any uniformity of time and place. No one has to view the same program at the same time and at the same place. On the contrary, most viewing is done independently. Each child can view according to his or her own schedule and preference, can stop viewing in the middle, switch to another "class," delay viewing, and be involved in many secondary activities at the same time.

Compulsion: Formal schooling is a direct intervention into children's lives. They hardly have any say in the matter, certainly not in societies that impose mandatory schooling, leaving parents with at most the choice of schools. Furthermore, upon becoming a participant in this system, children are required to assume a host of responsibilities and tasks that are undertaken through a normalized system of positive reinforcement and negative sanctions (e.g., complements, grades, punishments). And, throughout their schooling, children are almost completely under the control and supervision of adults – especially during their early years.

Television viewing, on the other hand, is mostly undertaken voluntarily, with limited adult supervision. It does not make any demands nor involve obligations. It neither tests achievements nor motivation, does not impose itself, and is more often than not very enjoyable for the viewer.

Peers: In mass schooling contexts, children learn from and are influenced directly and indirectly by their peers, in terms of ideas and experiences shared, the pace of learning, disturbances, and so forth. Most children in each class are of a similar age and often quite similar in regard to other demographic variables, such as socio-economic status, ethnicity, and religion. Most contemporary schools direct pupils' learning according to non-pupil-specific learning goals, general curricula, standard achievement levels, and so forth, developing the individual needs, learning style, and abilities of each student. Alternatively, individual tutoring is often undertaken in progressive educational systems accompanied by reduced class size, small group work, and division of pupils according to their interests, needs, and/or achievement levels.

In contrast, learning from television is usually undertaken in isolation from one's peer group, occasionally in the intimacy of one or two close friends, or within a multi-age family unit. Television's "curricula" is far from being tailored individually. On the contrary, often it aspires to be as global as possible, to attract as wide and diverse an audience as possible. For example, *Pokémon*, a popular Japanese animation series, is a program that is directed to children all over the world, indiscriminately, albeit with language and some minor cultural adjustments. That is, there is no special version of this popular animation series for exceptionally bright children in Nepal, for Chicano children who have immigrated to the USA, or for children of the Islamic faith in Algeria. In summary, programs that are popular globally are broadcast to the entire population of children in the world, regardless of age, culture and socio-economic differences.

Activity: Active forms of learning accompany or are required for many schooling activities; for example, homework, practice, participation in group discussion, field trips, work on projects, and the like. Here the contemporary assumption of educators is that active learning is more efficient and has the potential to be more meaningful for pupils.

In contrast, learning from television is mainly a product of cognitive and affective processes initiated by the viewing, with occasional reinforcement through conversation. Beyond early childhood, most children are not physically active during the viewing itself, do not "practice" what is being learned while viewing, do not process the concepts and skills through writing homework assignments or preparing for tests, and do not go on field trips to the places portrayed in their favorite programs.

Delay of gratifications. Studying in school requires an ability to delay gratifications. The efforts invested in a language, physics, or geography class are part of a long process undertaken by the child to attain an education and skills necessary for what is, admittedly from the child's point of view, a vague and unclear future that is often described to be something that will be satisfying and economically sufficient. However, even receiving gratification from reading a book, completing an assignment, or earning an award require long-term investments by the child.

Viewing television, on the other hand, is characterized by immediate satisfaction, as well as, deriving pleasure and expressing a variety of emotional reactions – laughter, suspense, identification, excitement, sadness – that do not require self-restraint in favor of some kind of a future.

These and other substantial differences point to the many advantages of television over school as a medium preferred by children. From their point of view, this is an activity, indeed a culture that they enter voluntarily. It makes no demands upon them and provides pleasure and fun all of which they control. Furthermore, television's preoccupation with interpersonal relationships, struggles of good and evil or love and hate among other themes may seem to many children to be much more relevant, attractive, and exciting than many of the topics studied in school that often seem irrelevant and removed from children's reality. Television, thus, seems to offer an alternative way of learning about the world and oneself that threatens the central place that the school system has had in the education of children.

Viewing Television and Performance in School

In reality, most children spend considerable time in both educational systems – school and television. On most days they pass from one to the other having learned to manage the differing expectations and conventions of both worlds. Most of adults' concern is about how viewing television might affect performance in school. Four different hypotheses regarding this relationship exist in today's research literature[2] :

1 *Displacement*: Discussed in Chapter 3, we recall that this school of thought claims that television may displace other activities, including reading, doing homework, and completing other intellectual assignments. As a consequence, skills required for achieving satisfactory performance levels in school are thus left unpracticed and neglected.

2 *Information processing*: This school argues that accumulated viewing of television may affect children's cognitive abilities, as it requires different forms of information processing deemed irrelevant for school-based learning.

3 *Gratifications*: According to this line of argument, heavy viewing of television affects the expectations that children have from the process of learning at school. They learn from viewing television to demand innovation and surprise, expect a quick pace, constant stimulation, and immediate satisfaction. These expectations stand in stark contrast to typical learning processes in school, which are relatively slow paced and oriented to long-term goals. As a result of this gap, children – so the argument goes – are impatient, have difficulty delaying gratifications, are bored, and consequentially, demonstrate negative attitudes toward schooling.

4 *Stimulate interest*: An opposing school suggests that television may be encouraging learning, as it stimulates curiosity, widens the child's interests, and reinforces a desire for learning. It may enrich the child's world in specific subject areas, including those studied in school (e.g., vocabulary, civic studies, science, geography, culture).

To date none of these approaches has a solid empirical base and thus they are debated through philosophic, even ideological, arguments. Research attempts to tackle these questions have been limited in scope, short-termed, and non-systematic. Many researchers would argue, too, that it is not the medium itself (as the deterministic approach would have had us believe) that determines the nature of effects on learning, but the learning environment of the family.

This having been noted, there is some evidence to support the negative association between heavy viewing of television and basic literacy skills (i.e., reading, writing, and math) and school achievement more generally. For example, several large-scale research projects conducted in the 1980s in the USA provided evidence that heavy television viewing was associated with lower scores in reading, writing, and math tests in all age groups, regardless of gender and socio-economic

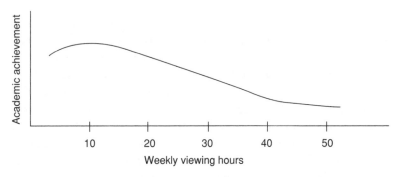

Figure 5.1 Relationship between viewing television and academic achievement

status.[3] However, very light television viewing, too, was associated with lower scores! The conclusion might be that we are facing a typical "bell-shaped" phenomenon: there is a positive correlation with achievements for up to an optimum number of viewing hours per week (some suggest around 10 hours), but over 10 hours this relationship reverses itself and becomes more negative as the number of viewing hours increases (see Figure 5.1).

These findings, of course, cannot provide us with an answer regarding the direction of causality. Is heavy viewing of television responsible for the low achievements? Or, perhaps, more viewing hours are a result of low achievement in school? And, perhaps, both heavy viewing, as well as, lower achievement is associated with an external variable (e.g., learning disability, emotional difficulty, social problems)? We can even complicate this question further by suggesting that perhaps good students are more aware and more in control of their own cognitive processes and their allocation of attention and, thus, manage their studies as well as their television viewing more efficiently.

An exceptional, multi-year study conducted in Sweden followed 194 children from the age of 6 to 12, as well as their parents, in an attempt to examine long-term relationships between viewing television and school achievement.[4] Rather than asking whether viewing television in general effects school performance, they examined the kind of uses and gratifications that children had from their specific viewing. For example, they argued that the findings reveal that higher achieving children used television more as a medium that complemented their school studies, while children with lower achievements used it more for entertainment and passing time. The relationship between viewing and achievement was understood to be reciprocal. Thus, pre-school children whose parents supervised their viewing, discussed programs with them, and encouraged them to view programs appropriate for them tended to perform better in their first-grade examination, and this in turn affected their television viewing choices and, vice versa, resulting in better performance in the sixth grade, as well. In contrast, pre-school children whose parents did not supervise their viewing nor encouraged viewing programs appropriate for them were involved in a negative vicious cycle: they viewed more fiction programs unsuitable for their age level and earned lower grades in school which led to more viewing of television and so forth. As a result, they achieved lower grades in the sixth-grade examinations. Social-economic status seemed to remain the most important predictor of a child's performance. Success in first grade, which in itself is dependent to a large degree on the child's family environment, was the best predictor of success in the sixth grade. These findings clearly point out to the responsibility of parents in creating a television environment that is best suited to the needs and abilities of children in different stages of their lives.

Support for this pattern comes from additional studies conducted in the USA and Europe that concentrated specifically on the relationships between viewing television, academic achievements, and reading skills.[5] As a general rule, over 2–3 hours of viewing per day (the numbers may fluctuate according to the method used) was associated in all age levels with the lowest reading grades, while viewing less then 2 hours per day was correlated with higher scores. The home environment plays a central role here as well: for example, children who are raised in a reading culture at home receive more encouragement and assistance from their family. Having a television in a child's bedroom was found to be negatively associated with test scores. Most importantly, several of the studies suggested long-term effects of early heavy exposure to entertainment television on educational aspirations and achievements.

The reciprocal nature of this relationship suggests that viewing television is particularly attractive to those children who find practicing reading demanding (perhaps those less intelligent or having learning disabilities). As a result, children experiencing difficulties in school continue to have less enjoyment from reading, engage in it less, and spend more time viewing television. Researchers believe that this argument explains the findings that by the time they reach high school, children with the lowest performance level score less on intelligence tests, are from a lower social-economical level, read less, and view more television. Accordingly, claiming that limiting viewing time alone will improve children's performance is inaccurate, as raising children who advance in accordance with their capabilities also need parents who are willing and able to encourage as well as to facilitate their children's reading behaviors. In addition, other studies highlight the fact that it is not necessarily the amount of viewing time alone that is associated with a host of literacy skills, but the kind of programs viewed, on one hand,

and the kind of books read, on the other hand. For example, heavy viewers of light entertainment and violent cartoons were often designated as scoring lower on a host of tests and the little reading they did was found to be television-related (e.g., easy-reading books developed around popular television series).

In summary, there is a body of research that points out the possibility that there is a negative relationship between amount of viewing television, combined with specific kind of television genres, and performance in school, including literacy skills. Furthermore, no evidence has accumulated so far regarding the possibility of there being a positive contribution of television to school performance (option 4 above). It is interesting to note that the research evidence coming from the more medically oriented literature is much more unequivocal about the adverse effects of television viewing. As we will find out later in this chapter, this conclusion is completely reversed when it comes to a discussion of educational programs designed to advance learning. Researchers agree that the relationships are reciprocal, certainly not unidirectional, and are complicated by a host of variables, such as the socio-economic status of the family, media access, family communication, parental mediation, and specific attitudes towards both viewing and reading. In short, viewing television is probably only one activity of many that take place in the home environment that have significance for the development of children's cognitive skills and educational achievements.

Television and Language Acquisition

A related concern of which we also know very little, is the possible relationship between viewing television and language acquisition. Critics of television argue that the quality of verbal engagement with television is low, since most of its popular programs are linguistically under-developed and use a limited vocabulary with dialogues consisting of short sentences. Furthermore, the visual aspects of television often dominate the viewing experience. Finally, the nature of the viewing experience does not allow for reciprocal interactions; that is, language on television is incapable of adjusting itself to meet the needs or interests of each particular viewer or to provide feedback and appropriate reinforcements. All these characteristics may lead us to the intuitive conclusion that television may not be a valuable source of language acquisition.

However, the current literature on the development of language skills presents an accumulation of research evidence that it is also possible to acquire language through observation of the verbal interactions of others. Such interactions are plentiful on television, take place in a wide variety of social situations, and in formats that become familiar, repeat themselves, and are thus easily learned by the child. In addition, observational studies of young viewers suggest that they are often active during viewing, including verbal actions, such as talking and singing.[6]

What then is the contribution of television viewing to the development of linguistic skills? Do children learn language from viewing television? Does viewing inhibit the development of language? The answers to these questions are complicated; as such learning is dependent, among other things, on the type of linguistic skill examined. For example, is the influence of television viewing on the development of grammar different from its influence on development of vocabulary? Development is also related to the type of programs examined: Do programs directed at a wide audience affect language development in a manner different from those aimed specifically at certain age groups and do these programs adapt their linguistic level accordingly? Finally, we need also to distinguish between the child's acquisition of native-tongue and an acquisition of a second language, usually later in life.

Acquisition of native language

Several studies conducted in the USA examined the relationships between viewing television and native-English-language acquisition in the early formative years.[7] Following our discussion of literacy skills, we should not be surprised to learn that the research demonstrated that heavy viewers had poorer language skills, and vice versa. The researchers also learned that the type of viewing is crucial: children with limited verbal skills tended to watch programs that were verbally limited, while children with rich linguistic skills, watched programs with rich language. As in previous cases, we understand that these findings are reciprocal: Young viewers with limited verbal skills are attracted to programs that are more comprehensible to them, thus reinforcing their limitations. We can also argue that those children who spend a lot of time viewing television have fewer opportunities to practice social interactions in real life.

However, studies that examined educational programs designed to enrich young children's lives and facilitate linguistic development demonstrate significant achievements. Such programs adopt linguistic styles that facilitate learning: repetitiveness, clear yes and no questions, specific "Wh" questions (who, what, where, when, and why), verbal descriptions that are synchronized with the visuals presented, pacing similar to the one often used by parents reading a story, and the like. These presentation styles were found to be effective in research situations: Young viewers learned unfamiliar vocabulary (both nouns and verbs) following exposure to television programs, both in short-term experiments (where children were presented with a video segment only once) as well as in longer-term ones (where children were exposed to a series of programs for several weeks).[8]

In a longitudinal study of *Sesame Street* illustrative of this line of research, American researchers examined the vocabulary of 3- and 5-year-olds in mid-America using the Peabody Picture Vocabulary Test (PPVT).[9] In this standardized test that requires children to name objects appearing in test pictures, a child who is able to distinguish between a cow and a horse, for example, is rated as more advanced linguistically than a child who names all four-legged animals "dog." Parents filled in weekly viewing diaries once every six months (i.e., a diary providing information of all programs viewed by the child, usually in 15 minute intervals) for the children for a period of two and a half years at which time the children's vocabulary was tested once again. The most interesting finding for the purpose of our discussion is that 3-year-olds who viewed *Sesame Street* frequently improved their vocabulary much more significantly in comparison to those who viewed it much less. These findings remained valid even when other related variables that could affect both the viewing of *Sesame Street* as well as language development were considered (such as parents' education, number of siblings, performance on the first PPVT). The researchers suggested that this may be an indication of the direction of causality: Viewing of *Sesame Street* contributed to vocabulary development and not the other way around; that is, it was the case that heavier viewing of the program lead to better scores on the PPVT, and not that better language skills lead to more viewing of the program. Interestingly, these findings were not found for the older group that started the study at the age of 5. Since the program's linguistic level was aimed at pre-school and kindergarten age children, it is possible that it did not contribute anymore for older children.

Another longitudinal study was aimed at even younger children.[10] It found that infants and toddlers benefited most from viewing programs that applied specific linguistic strategies that are appropriate for this target age group; such as, the actors speak directly to the child-viewer, encourage their participation, engage in object-naming, provide opportunities for the child to respond, and the like (e.g., *Blue's Clues*, *Dora the Explorer*). Watching programs that use attractive storytelling formats was also found to be associated with positive language development (e.g., *Arthur*, *Clifford*, and *Dragon Tales*). Interestingly, another popular program of this age group, *Barney & Friends*, was found to be negatively associated with the acquisition of vocabulary, but at the same time positively associated with the production of expressive language in play situations.

Indeed, anecdotal parental accounts and the few observational studies that followed the language development of babies and toddlers in their home environment suggest that parents use television as a "talking book" with their young ones. They practice linguistic skills during television viewing, particularly with programs aimed at the very young. For example, both children and parents designate objects and characters on the screen by name (e.g., balloon, butterfly, Ernie [*Sesame Street*], Po [*Teletubbies*]); they ask questions (e.g., Where did they go? What is she doing?); repeat messages, including commercials and slogans; and describe what they see (e.g., "He is sad;" "They are playing with the dog").[11] Accumulatively, these and other findings suggest that it is not viewing television in and of itself, but rather the type of television content, viewing circumstances, and form of parental mediation that determine the nature of television's relationship with language development.

Aquisition of second language

If indeed television does have the potential to contribute to linguistic development, even in ways limited to specific skills, it also makes sense to examine it in relationship to the acquisition of a second language. This is particularly relevant to children growing up in small-language communities when imported programs use subtitles (i.e., they are not dubbed into their own language). This is also a very important process for minority groups whose native tongue is different than that of the majority population as well as for immigrant children who move into a different linguistic culture. This has become a common experience for many children today due, on one hand, to economic and cultural globalization processes as well as Americanization of popular culture; and, on the other hand, by growing mobility of populations from one culture to another.

Viewing television at home provides many varied opportunities in a non-threatening, non-demanding social environment to explore new languages that are embedded in local cultural and socio-linguistic contexts. Anecdotal data from around the world suggest that such viewing does assist in the acquisition of a second language. Indeed, English teachers have argued that their pupils of English as second language are much more proficient when there is a dominance of television programs in English in their country's TV fare. Similarly, the popularity of Spanish among children has been given an unexpected reinforcement through the popularity of Latin telenovelas around the world. But what does systematic research suggest?

The few existing studies that have been conducted support the view presented above. Chicano children in the USA (immigrants from Mexico) who had some basic English skills benefited from viewing American television.[12] The series *Carrascolendas* was produced in Texas USA in the early 1970s for these Chicano children who where starting their schooling in the new culture. The series employed bi-lingual puppets, skits, singing, and animation to help preserve the Spanish language and affinity for the unique cultural heritage of Chicano viewers. Research of the series found that viewers improved their knowledge, pride in their cultural and historic heritage, and their Spanish language skills. Similarly, English-speaking children in the USA have learned Spanish vocabulary from the many pre-school programs that have included Spanish-speaking characters. For example, the highly popular series *Dora the Explorer* (on the Nick Jr. channel of Nickelodeon) features a 7-year-old bilingual Latina girl, Dora, who uses both English and Spanish as valuable tools in her adventures.[13] Similarly, children in The Netherlands who had been viewing American programs with Dutch sub-titles improved their English vocabulary.[14]

Such incidental learning of a vocabulary of a second language seems to fit well with current theories of second language acquisition. First, research evidence suggests that learning a language does not necessarily require practice. "A quiet" period seems to exist during the learning process within which a child absorbs linguistic inputs without neces-sarily using it or demonstrating this knowledge. The prior existence of a native tongue serves as a general infrastructure supporting the learning of any additional languages. At the same time, many variables interact during the process when a child learns a second language. Some of them are cognitive – such as developmental level, intelligence, linguistic awareness, and general knowledge of the world. Other variables may be personality related – attitudes toward learning, self-confidence, verbal ability, openness, and motivation to learn. There are also social vari-ables – opportunities to interact with the speakers of the second language, receiving corrective feedback, difficulty level of the inter-actions; and more general cultural variables – ethnic identity, status of the linguistic community, and so forth. All of these variables interact with one another in the complicated processes of second language acquisition, with television exposure being just one among them. Perhaps, under circumstances where the second language and its speakers are perceived to have a high status, personal benefits of learning that language are perceived as high, and so is motivation for learning. In such cases, television may have a more central role as an effective teacher. Such may be the case around the world in regards to children's incidental English learning through television viewing (as well as use of other English-dominated media, as is currently the case with the Internet). Systematic exploration of this intriguing possibility has yet to take place.

The Audio-Visual Language and Cognitive Skills

As mentioned previously, one intriguing hypothesis suggests that different media cultivate different cognitive skills and, therefore, also affect different learning processes. What are the skills included in the concept of "visual intelligence?" How can they be measured? How do such skills compare with those attained via verbal intelligence? Research of such questions has sought to point out the differences in comprehension and learning that can be attributed to the structural components of the dominant languages of each medium. These studies are supported by evidence from neuro-psychological research that suggest that different symbol systems are processed in different parts of the human brain. For example, the left hemisphere processes sign systems, including verbally transmitted information, while the right hemisphere is more active in processing numerical and figurative information.

A few central assumptions lie at the heart of this field of research regarding the nature of the audio-visual language: As a medium, television is distinguished from print forms by combining various forms of expression: pictures, speech, voices, music, print. Its audio-visual language employs systems of signs that represent meaning quite similar to verbal language. This language has its own codes and conventions that are used for the expression of various domains of content. For example, the codes and conventions employed in many popular music videos are quite different than those applied in news broadcasts.

When we interpret visual images, including those on television, we do so in a manner similar to the way we perceive the reality of the physical and social worlds. More than our acquaintance with the codes and conventions of television, it is our ability to elicit references from representation that forms the basis of our ability to make sense of it. This is in contrast with the way we make sense of other languages – such as verbal or mathematical, where we are dependent on familiarity with the signification system (e.g., letters, numbers). Put differently, making sense of television content (at least on a basic level) does not require learning pre-requisite skills, as do other languages, as we practice interpreting visual messages in real life constantly. This characteristic helps to explain why, for example, very young babies already show an interest in television without any training (e.g., in contrast to being able to read), as do children who have difficulties interpreting other forms of significations, such as those associated with language.

Furthermore, the special characteristics of visual language, which are fundamentally concrete, are assumed to restrict the development of abstract thought. Visual language is limited in its ability to refer to the non-visual (e.g., a strong smell), abstract terms (e.g., conclusion), terms of negation (e.g., the absence of something; "never"), and the like, although it can arrive at an understanding of the meaning indirectly or through a concrete example. Thus, while the picture on the screen can present specific instances (e.g., a specific house), words can express the systematic regularity of an entire group of incidences (e.g., the concept of "home"). Visual language, according to this line of argument, deals with representing reality, but does not have the ability to make propositions regarding it. The individual viewer is left with the task of bridging between the concrete picture and the abstract idea behind it.

Finally, we can add that while most humans learn not only to understand verbal language as well as to produce it (i.e., not only understanding but also speaking), such is not the case for the visual language of television: Most children are capable of interpreting television messages, but only few ever have the opportunity to actually produce them in a television program.

Granted we have barely touched upon the complicated and tangled nature of different languages, but suffice to say that as a result of these assumptions, many argue, that television's visual language does not necessarily expand our cognitive skills to the same degree that verbal languages do. This having been noted, the central question of concern to us here remains unanswered: What, if any, cognitive skills are acquired through our experiences with the visual language? Such a determination can be made in at least two different ways: First, by studying cognitive processes activated during television viewing with a view of seeking to understand how their repetitive use cultivates the skills necessary for making sense of television content. Second, by tracing the use of skills required and acquired that are applied for other purposes aside from watching television, such as remembering information or using television content in mental processes independent of television.

The development of special viewing skills

Due to the theoretical and methodological complexity of the topic, the study of the cognitive implications of visual language has focused on specific skills and not general thought processes. These skills are understood to be part of "spatial intelligence," a domain of intelligence that involves the ability to mentally represent spatial relationships accurately and to imagine the implications of changes within them (e.g., the ability to visually represent walking from one place to another).

In seeking to determine if viewing television cultivates skills that constitute spatial intelligence, several studies focused on television and film's capabilities of presenting various points of view (e.g., to observe the same character from different angles). For example, one such experiment presented children with video segments in which the camera moved from one point of view to another. This tested the children's abilities to mentally represent such movements by applying it to new situations outside of viewing (e.g., in picture-cards). The rationale for this approach was that the camera movements on the screen in fact imitate the mental process required from the child engaged in the spatial intelligence task, thus facilitating it. Indeed, the results supported the hypothesis that viewing such movement improved children's task performance.[15]

However, correlation studies produced contradictory evidence that did not support this finding.[16] The rival explanation suggested that due to editing television does not provide the whole range of visual experience of changing points of view that occurs in reality. It also limits the range of points of view and does not offer the child an open space for active experimentation with all options. This argument is particularly relevant for young children, as visual skills developed at this age are dependent on physical experiences in real spaces. It is possible that following the acquisition of these skills, they can be further developed by mediated experiences, but there is no evidence to date that these can replace actual real-life experience.[17] An interesting question that arises from this line of argument is whether virtual experiences in the new technological environment (e.g., driving a virtual car in a video or computer game) contribute to the development of these skills?

A somewhat different, but related concern focuses on the investment children make in interpreting television content. The mere exposure to television is a necessary but not sufficient condition to giving control of visual language. It can only affect cognitive skills when children attempt to interpret and make meaning out of it. That is, the more children invest mental effort in processing information, the more they get out of it. In this as in other cognitive matters, age is a significant consideration: younger children have a more limited "channel-capacity" (i.e., the amount of stimuli they can absorb at a time) and, therefore, they have less practice in processing television information regardless of the amount of time they spend watching it. Channel-capacity is also dependent on competition with other sources of information that are in simultaneous operation. This may possibly explain why children perform better in an experimental situation; they are not distracted by competing sources of information typically available in home viewing, such as the presence of other conversations, music, phone calls, or street noises.[18]

The concept of Amount of Invested Mental Effort (AIME) discussed in Chapter 2 in relationship to attention to television is useful here, too. Here the assumption is that a greater AIME leads to improved learning skills, such as improvement of memory, comprehension, and ability to deduct conclusions. However, AIME is influenced, among other things, by the way children perceive what is expected of them, the level of difficulty of the content, the expected gratifications that may be yielded, and their self-confidence in their ability to make sense of it. Children perceive viewing television as a much less demanding assignment in comparison to reading books: it allows making meaning in a more sensory manner, it appears to be "self-explanatory" and "real," and it is easily enjoyable. However, viewing television is not a uniform experience and this discussion is an example of the multiple layers and complexities involved in it. For example, consider the differences in the levels of the program – entertainment versus educational, and adult programming versus children's. Children make use of different cues in the programs to estimate its level of difficulty and the AIME required to interpret it. In addition, environmental factors (e.g., seating arrangements, screen size, noise), social norms (e.g., the way others are treating the viewing situation), or their own motivation for viewing, also affect the level of AIME.[19]

As a result, studies have found that children with higher mental abilities who had negative attitudes toward television and invested less AIME in it were least able to learn from it. However, when children are directed to learn from viewing a particular program (i.e., their perception of the viewing situation is changed), they increase their AIME and the level of their mental functioning improves. That is to say, children are capable of employing the skills they already have in interpreting television content when they are motivated to do so. This conclusion may lead us to an intriguing hypothesis: perhaps the perception that television is an easy activity, one that requires limited exertion, is based (to some degree at least) on children's prior conceptions of what it means to view television, rather than on the nature of the medium itself. That is, until children are taught to treat viewing television seriously, they will continue to invest very limited effort in it and as a result gain less from the viewing. In Chapter 6, we will describe how many educational systems throughout the world are attempting to teach children to take their viewing seriously as well as to examine television programs with a critical eye.

However, even if children invested AIME in the viewing, the question still remains: Is learning from television different than any other form of learning? And, if so, does learning from television have any advantage over learning from other media, such as books or radio? Is it more – or less – effective? Do different media have relative advantages in regards to particular subject matter? Here, too, the evidence from research to date is equivocal.

For example, one line of research argued that if television presents behaviors in a dynamic way, when combined with the visual enrichment of the verbal content, it would increase the ability to understand characters' behavior. At the same time, the experience of looking at still pictures in a book read by a parent is visually limited thus allowing more attention to the audio channel and the verbal descriptions. In order to verify this hypothesis, a series of experiments were conducted in which two groups of children were presented with the same story – one via the television and the other by listening as the story was read to them – and then the children's memory and comprehension were tested.[20] The results suggested that television does make a difference in regard to what the children learned from the stories. It emphasizes learning of activities presented in the program in comparison to learning verbal information from a version read to them. This was expressed both in children's description of the story as well as in their own behavior while re-telling it, such as hand-motioning used in attempts to reconstruct it. Furthermore, when referring to the story, children who had viewed it employed more visually obtained content in comparison to those who had listened to it, who used more verbal information. That is to say, the medium through which a story is told is significant not only for what will be remembered from it, but also for the way children will make references based upon it.

Related to this is the concept known as the *visual superiority effect.* Here reference is made to the conclusion that young viewers remember visual information much better than audio information, particularly in situations where the two media are not compatible (what one sees is not what one hears); a very common characteristic of televised contents.[21] However, most effective learning occurs when the two systems support and reinforce one another; that is, when the same information is presented in both the visual and the audio channels, as is the case of programs designed especially for children. This *dual-coding hypothesis* suggests that audio-visual information is stored simultaneously in two separate reciprocal systems in the child's memory, each assisting the other in recalling relevant information. The visual superiority effect of television fades away when there is a gap between the visual and the audio (as in regular news programs).[22]

At this point, it is appropriate to interrupt our discussion to relate to several methodological considerations. It is possible to argue that the learning differences found are not necessarily a function of the different media, but of one from among many other elements: the differences in production elements of the two versions of the story; the impossibility of presenting exactly the same story visually and verbally; differences in the forms of testing of the learning from each version; differences in children's acquired cognitive skills; and the like. According to this line of argument, it is impossible to make a true comparison between different media.

Alternatively, perhaps it is not the medium itself that accounts for the differences, but the specific "teaching style" of each story. This argument is similar to focusing on teachers, rather than focusing on teaching: that is, it is possible that the differences in teaching effectiveness of one teacher in comparison to the other is not a matter of the teachers' personality, but rather of their different teaching styles. Obviously, it is impossible to separate the two in order to achieve clear-cut conclusions.[23]

As the central variable measured in most of these studies, recall of information is but one necessary skill, but not one that can be considered to be sufficient for completion of more complicated comprehension and learning processes. This leaves us with unsatisfactory answers regarding the unique contribution of television as a medium for learning in comparison with other media. Research findings suggest a rival possibility: rather than regarding visual culture and verbal culture as competing with or in contradiction with one another, perhaps learning requires integrating them in various forms of multimedia systems in order to exhaust the possibilities concealed within the use of varied forms of signification systems.

Learning from Educational Television

The inability of psychological studies so far to provide conclusive explanations in regard to audio-visual language and cognitive processes has contributed to the development of another body of knowledge that is concerned with educational television and the intentional employment of television to achieve specific educational and instructional goals. At the core of the endeavor is the claim that the content of popular television does not necessarily exhaust the potential of the

medium and that with appropriate professional investment it is possible to use it in significantly more valuable ways: to decrease social
knowledge gaps; to teach diverse subject matter; to convey value-laden
messages; or to develop specific skills. The findings regarding the
negative effects of television only served to reinforce these hopes: If
children are capable of learning negative messages from television, it
should be possible to use it to teach them some positive ones as well.

Varying cultural needs motivated the rise in interest in the educational potential of television. This interest developed in the USA during
the educational crisis of the 1950s that was spawned by an alleged
deterioration in the ability of American society to compete with the
technological and scientific development of the post-Second-World-
War industrialized countries. This situation was attributed to exist, in
part, due to a shortage of teachers, the claim of the low level of teacher
training, and outmoded curricula. In many developing countries, television was perceived as both a symbol and a potential catalyst of
national development, modernization, and progress. Furthermore, it
was argued that television was among the best means to be effective in
advancing social change through the educational system since it was
accessible, inexpensive, democratic, highly attractive, multi-sensual,
and felt to have other significant potential. Hence, many hopes were
invested in its ability to contribute to the resolution of a variety of
social hardships.

At the same time, since its onset, some of its critics have opposed
educational television claiming that it has a "robotic," non-personalized
nature, may undermine teachers' employment, has the potential to
damage interpersonal relationships between pupils and teachers, lacks
opportunities for feedback from and interaction with the television
teachers, and as well that pupils may come to perceive their classroom
teachers as boring and inferior in comparison with their television
counterparts. Many logistic concerns were voiced as well: the financial
expense involved in special productions, scheduling difficulties within
the school day, the problem of creating programs relevant to children's
lives, and the need for continuous updating.[24] Often recipients of a
complete infrastructure of educational television along with initial training and supervision of personnel as a donation by a former colonizer,
developing countries were wary of the possibility that educational television would stimulate a process of cultural intervention by outside
forces, as well as, inspire a takeover by commercial television.

As a result of the familiar tension between high aspirations and deep
fears that characterize the introduction of each new medium, two
different styles of educational television emerged: the first employed
excellent television teachers who led the educational process with the

assistance of less trained teachers in the classes themselves, thus overcoming problems such as large classes and shortage of well-educated teachers. This was particularly the case for many of the developing countries. Gradually becoming the preferred approach in the industrialized countries, a second style emphasized the need for a high quality, attractive form of educational television that can compete with commercial television – a format that serves as a complement to, rather than substitute for the classroom teacher.

We need to clarify that in our discussion here the term educational television is inclusive of instructional television. The two concepts often overlap or the boundaries blurred: Usually, educational television has more general, educational goals, while instructional television concentrates on specific subjects that are taught at school. Dwelling deeply into the discussion of educational television would require discussion of complicated educational/pedagogical issues, such as teaching methods, curricula development, learning principles, and the like that are not within the scope of this book. Thus, we will focus mainly on the characteristics of educational television as a medium, as a world of substance, and as a social resource – and in the contribution of research in this area to understanding the role of television in the lives of young children.

The development of educational television

Early educational television programs in the 1950s and 1960s where characterized by "talking heads:" a television teacher, usually assisted by simple teaching aids, such as blackboard and still pictures, talked directly to the camera, i.e., to the target audience of pupils. Production was simple, non-creative, and rarely realized the potential of the medium. However, the mere presence of television in the class had a novelty effect on the pupils, particularly in remote areas and in lower class neighborhoods, where children might not have had a television set at home.

The educational television of these early days had many obstacles to overcome. The television teachers, who might have been excellent in their fields and even in their classrooms, were not professional actors and actresses and often did not feel comfortable in front of a camera and away from the real children usually in front of them. Classroom teachers felt threatened by the television teachers and on many occasions did not integrate these lessons effectively into their teaching. And, indeed, evidence from the many studies that accompanied the early diffusion of educational television suggested that the benefits from the use of TV were negligible. The one difference was associated more with the specific teachers' style, rather than the medium used for teaching.

Of course, this argument does not negate the possibility that under specific learning conditions, certain children may learn better from television than from a teacher, or vice versa, but it re-emphasizes that as a general rule, the expectation to actually find dramatic differences between the two was not supported.[25]

At the same time, several experimental projects designed specifically to improve learning achievements proved to be beneficial – in a town in the eastern part of the USA in the late 1950s, in remote villages in Japan in the beginning of the 1960s, in Delhi India and in Columbia in the mid-1960s.[26] In these projects, the emphasis remained on the centrality of the classroom teacher with television serving only to complement them. Teachers were involved in the introduction and operation of the broadcasts and retained control over its use in their classroom. One might argue that it is the significant investment in innovative educational projects and in the teachers themselves that brought about the improvement in their teaching, and not television as a medium. Still, there is evidence to suggest that wise employment of educational television might be effective in pursuing educational goals. This can be the case particularly if the unique features and potential of television are maximized, rather than placing it in competition with teachers. For example, television can illustrate phenomena in ways that teachers are incapable; it can bring children to different places around the globe; it can bring experts or talents into the classroom; it can enrich the studying routine with a change of pace and style. It can introduce children to the world outside of their own world in a dynamic and attractive manner.

However, in its early days educational television did not soar. Viewing surveys suggested repeatedly that when given a choice, children preferred unequivocally to watch commercial over educational television. It became clear that in order for educational television to survive, it needed to undergo a dramatic transformation – from focusing on school instruction to a wider scope of offering children quality television that broadens their intellectual horizons and challenges them in enjoyable ways. A breakthrough in this new approach came about with the establishment of the Children's Television Workshop (CTW) in New York, best known for its revolutionary educational program – *Sesame Street*. We will discuss CTW in detail shortly, but suffice to mention at this point that CTW clearly led the turnaround in public awareness of the potential embodied in quality public television in the world.

The dramatic features of this change of approach included: the adoption of commercial formats and genres; involvement of psychologists and educational advisors in production stages; addressing unique issues with well-defined and attainable goals; targeting specific audiences; incorporating social as well as educational goals; and the like. As a result, innovative educational programs were designed that followed the patterns of commercials, quizzes, suspense movies, drama, and magazine programs. In doing so, they presented educational programming in an attractive and pleasurable manner that also integrated entertainment elements that make learning much more fun (such as, music, humor, rhyming, animation, and the like). The subject matter areas dealt with were limitless: from teaching numbers and letters, to social values such as tolerance, to all forms of "otherness;" from familiarity with the map of the globe to drug prevention programs. They dealt with learning and education in the realms of cognition, emotion, and behavior. The target audience included children and schools as well as programming for the entire family. In doing so, educational television moved from the classroom to the home in order to become part of the family routine.[27]

Theoretical models for evaluating learning from educational television

These developments were assisted by formative research, designed to provide feedback from children during the production stages along with summative evaluation research designed to provide feedback regarding the degree of success in achieving program goals. The body of knowledge that has accumulated through such studies is quite impressive. The positive effects that educational television had on young audiences were significant: from learning language; arithmetic; solving logical and mathematical problems; science and technology; civil studies and history; and general skills of school readiness. Before illustrating some of these findings in more detail, let us examine one theoretical model for assessing learning from educational television.[28]

The model assumes that educational content on television includes two major knowledge domains: formal information (such as historical facts) as well as procedural knowledge (such as problem-solving strategies). Like any other form of stimuli, the processing of televised stimuli is accomplished in the working memory and is thus restricted by its limited capacity and constraints in regard to the amount and depth of processing that can take place simultaneously. For example, the limitations of the working memory manifest themselves in the amount of time required by the viewer to process the televised information and/or the difficulties that can arise while completing various secondary tasks during the viewing. Since televised information (in contrast with reading, for example), consists of both visual and audio components, and since the viewer cannot set the pace of exposure to them, the child's working memory is bombarded with unique difficulties. When the viewer invests more mental effort (i.e., AIME), he or she assigns a larger part of working memory to making sense of television stimuli. However, the amount of AIME invested does not fully explain children's ability to simultaneously manipulate the two tasks during television viewing – the need to understand the program's narrative as well as the educational content embedded within it.

One possible proposition is that understanding television's narratives as well as educational content involve similar cognitive processes. However, the effort required to process them is increased the more they are removed from one another, that is, when the educational content is incidental to the main plot line of the program, for example, when during a drama on the life of a group of adolescents, marginal reference is made to problems arising from drinking alcohol. The two cognitive processes compete with each other over the limited capacity of working memory and thus the processing of the educational content is debilitated. However, when the distance between the narrative and the educational content is small (for example, when a drama on the life of a group of adolescents centers on problems arising out of drinking alcohol effecting many aspects of their lives), the educational content is integrated within the narrative and the processing reinforces and is complementary of both components.

Many factors may effect the processing of both narratives and educational content, as we have already indicated in our discussion of cognitive development in Chapter 2. Some are entangled in the characteristics of the children: their prior acquaintance with the subject matter; the story and the characters; the cognitive schemas they bring with them to understanding story lines and production features; their interest in the program; their verbal ability; their short-term memory, and the like. Other factors are related to the nature of the program: the clarity with which the messages are presented; the complexity and/or integrative nature of the story; the need to make references; the chronology; the hints embedded in the program to assist comprehension; and the like.

How does working memory allocate effort to processing both narratives and educational content? The hypothesis suggested is that children will prioritize investing in understanding the narrative when the two compete with each other, as this is a more familiar viewing task associated with their everyday experiences of watching television. The less the effort required for comprehending the narrative, the more resources are left for learning the educational ones. Other factors, such as individual interest in the subject matter of the program or mediation by other viewers may also effect the division of working memory resources between the two mental assignments. In summary, we can expect better comprehension of educational messages, as children grow older, when both the narrative and the educational content are not overly demanding, and when the distance between them is small. This model also leads us to suggest that children should be encouraged to show an interest in the subject matter and to invest more AIME during the viewing. In addition, educational television producers should attempt to decrease the demands placed on understanding the narratives, educational content, as well as the gap between them so to reduce the resources necessary for their processing, particularly for younger children.

Getting children motivated to learn from educational television is, of course, the task of parents and caregivers at home (as we have discussed in Chapter 1) as well as teachers at school. The latter can determine how to realize the educational potential embodied in television: they can decide whether and how to use a particular program; they can prepare their pupils for the viewing situation, assign viewing tasks, and direct follow up activities to reinforce learning. Teachers also determine criteria for program evaluation in grading pupils' learning achievements.

Experience with educational television in the school system led to the development of the following evaluative model that was applied by teachers.[29] First, the teacher evaluates: (a) the quality of the program (the television format as well as the nature of its contents, values, and the teaching method integrated within it); and (b) the program's potential contributions to children's cognitive, emotional, and behavioral worlds. Second, the teacher evaluates the degree to which the specific program is appropriate to the specific pupils in the specific classroom (e.g., knowledge level, task level, cultural background, teaching style). Finally, based on the above, the teacher decides whether and , if so, how to integrate the program in the class. The teacher evaluates the amount of investment required of her and from the pupils in processing the television content (before, during, and following the viewing session). This investment relates to the declared educational goals of the program, in terms of knowledge, skills, and attitudes. Put differently, the teacher balances the amount of investment required in relationship to the expected benefits. Here, too, it is both the characteristics of the children as the audience as well as those of the program that are being considered.

Clearly, this is quite an elaborate and demanding task for teachers whose daily lives are already over-crowded with responsibilities and demands. No wonder that many find themselves resorting to either not bothering with educational television at all or using it in class as a "foreign object" – barely turning it on and off.

Children's Television Workshop (CTW) (Sesame Workshop, SW)[30]

CTW is a public non-profit organization established in 1968 in New York, and re-named Sesame Workshop at the turn of the century, that has been producing educational television programs and supportive learning aids (such as magazines, videocassettes, and computer programs), as well as, a host of teaching materials and information for parents, teachers, and community organizations. The concept behind CTW has been that it is possible to create effective educational programs that are enjoyable through professional cooperation between educational and psychological experts, as well as, television producers. We will devote a separate discussion of CTW due to the popularity of its programs worldwide for the last several decades, the organization's unprecedented educational achievements, the vast body of research conducted on its work throughout the years, and the contribution of its educational model to shaping the role of educational television all over the world.

Sesame Street has been the flagship of all of CTW productions. In addition, it has been researched more than any other television series with publications numbering in the hundreds of articles, several books, and dozens of theses and dissertations. One might say that while the issue of television violence represents, in a nutshell, the negative potential of television, *Sesame Street* represents to a large degree the other side of the coin. When it was aired originally in 1969, it was targeted as a program for pre-school viewers whose goal was to decrease the gap between lower-class children and their peers from middle and higher classes in developing school-readiness skills, with the intention of giving all American children a more equal starting point in the educational system.

Originally, the program's educational goals were defined along five axes:

1 Social, moral, and emotional development (e.g., dealing with separation anxiety from a parent; coping with the loss of a pet);
2 Language and reading (e.g., enriching vocabulary, letter recognition);
3 Counting and arithmetic skills (e.g., number recognition, counting objects);
4 Logic and problem solving (e.g., making logical inferences in a given situation); and
5 Perception (e.g., recognizing shapes, colors, sizes).

Since those initial days, the program has exposed millions of children to a wide and rich range of ideas and experiences in a variety of realms of life: from nutrition to outer space, from producing colors to identifying words. At the same time, it has provided children with great pleasure, while cultivating their social skills in areas such as cooperation and relationships with all kinds of "others" (e.g., children from different ethnic origins, people with disabilities). *Sesame Street* has become not only the first place that many children encounter ballet dancing, for example, but also the only place, perhaps, where they could be introduced to a girl who is performing ballet dancing in her wheelchair.

The program has had a fixed format consisting of a mosaic of segments with varied production features: animation, puppets, nature and documentaries, dramatic episodes with actors and actresses (permanent and guests, adults and children) in several familiar stage-settings. Production was characterized by a fast tempo, colorfulness, humor, music, and special effects. The producers assumed that the attention and comprehension skills of young viewers develop gradually and could vary from one child to the other. Therefore, they established the rich magazine format of the program, similar to a long commercial break that allows each child to attend to it as they wished and to get out of it what each is capable of and needs.

The unique features of *Sesame Street* can be summarized as follows:

1 Well-defined and specific educational goals (e.g., to recognize a stop sign or to legitimize feelings of envy towards a new baby sister).
2 Production techniques employed are meant to be attractive to children.
3 Educational goals direct producers to focus on development of the audience's cognitive and emotional abilities.
4 Children are the center of attention and the focus is on the world relevant to them.
5 Repetitiveness and reinforcement of certain components were employed in accordance with developmental theory.
6 Children were offered role models for modeling and identification.
7 Children were invited to participate actively with the program by talking, singing, reading, exercising, and the like.

Sesame Street has won more American Emmy awards (i.e., awards given to leading television series) than any other series in the history of television. At the beginning of the twenty-first century, four decades after its inception, more than 120 million children in 140 countries in the world are estimated to be viewing it regularly. Broadcasting organizations in 20 of these countries collaborated in co-productions of the series, incorporating parts of the original programs side by side with locally produced segments of local flavor, in the spirit of Sesame Workshop and under its supervision.[31] Estimates of viewing habits in the USA suggest that about 95 percent of children are already viewing *Sesame Street* on a regular basis before they are 3 years old. The program is also supported and extended through an array of supportive educational materials: computer games, magazines, books, as well as training of caregivers' in young children's daycares.

Given the unprecedented popularity of *Sesame Street*, what can be said about its achievement record? The evaluative research that has followed the series from its onset has provided systematic evidence that viewing the program on a regular basis helped 3–5-year-olds perform better in tests of skills such as number and letter recognition and understanding various concepts (such as near–far, wide–narrow). Furthermore, the more children viewed the program, the more their scores improved. These findings were found to hold for all children – both boys and girls, from a variety of ethnic groups, cultures, and geographical areas.

Still, even with these impressive results, the series is not without strong critics. One line of argument claimed that it was really parents' intervention in encouraging viewing that was the main factor in improving performance and not the viewing itself. Further, since it can be assumed that more well-to-do families have encouraged their children to view the program more often than did those from lower-class families, not only did the gap between the two populations of children not narrow, on the contrary, it widened. Another line of criticism has referred to the fast pace of the program. It was argued that this pace does not allow children enough time to process information; that it encourages impatience towards the more structured and slow-paced school setting; and that it makes it harder for children to learn to delay the need for gratification. Finally, concern was also expressed that parents invest most of their efforts in assisting viewing of the program, rather than spending quality time with their young children away from television.

Two major research projects in the early 1990s in the USA challenged these critics. The first, "The Early Window Project," followed about 250 children from diverse backgrounds, aged two and four, for three years, until they reached the age of five and seven respectively.[32] The children's viewing habits, family characteristics, linguistic skills, and school-readiness were monitored and tested periodically. The results presented persuasive evidence that viewing *Sesame Street* did indeed improve viewers' achievements over time; and, indeed, the more the program was viewed the greater the achievement. The effect was stronger for the younger group, suggesting that viewing *Sesame Street* improves younger viewers' chances of success in the educational system. Positive achievements were documented even without parental intervention and children from lower classes benefited from viewing just as much as their peers from higher classes. The main difference, however, was that on the average children from lower-class backgrounds viewed the program less than children from higher socio-economic status classes. This lead to the conclusion that in order to narrow the knowledge gap, it is necessary to find more effective ways to encourage disadvantaged children to watch the program more often.

In concluding this project, the researchers suggested that television is not a monolithic entity that affects children in a unified manner. On the contrary, the content of viewing makes a big difference in children's lives. Heavy viewers of *Sesame Street* who were light viewers of other television content popular at that age group (particularly animation programs) benefited most from *Sesame Street*. Even more striking was the claim made possible due to the longitudinal nature of the study that the positive contribution of viewing *Sesame Street* (in interaction with other background variables, such as parents' education) reached beyond the specific skills acquired during those early viewing days: as they mature young viewers developed a more positive set of attitudes toward learning, in general, as well as a higher level of self-confidence in their ability to learn.

The second project applied a very different method of study – a phone survey of a representative sample of about 11,000 parents of kindergarteners, first-, and second-grade children.[33] The survey examined the more general issue of school readiness, but included some specific questions regarding viewing *Sesame Street*. The results suggested that most children in all demographic groups, including disadvantaged children, were viewing the program at the time. That is to say, in contrast to other educational means available at this young age group, *Sesame Street* is accessible to children even in areas of poverty and distress. Regular viewers demonstrated early signs of reading and writing skills already in kindergarten, were more able to read on their own in first and second grade, and needed less assistance when faced with reading difficulties. However, this did not hold true for children with particular low achievements or learning disabilities. The results of the survey thus reinforced the claim that viewing educational programs during the pre-school years is associated, even if only partially, with better scores on school-readiness tests, with the exception of children with particularly low achievements. This having been said, it seems that educational television is incapable of answering the deeper social and economical deprivation of disadvantaged groups in our respective societies.

Sesame Street also provided a unique opportunity to undertake a comparative examination of questions related to children and television in many other parts of the world.[34] When children in various countries are watching co-productions of the program, they are exposed to a program with the original American features that have proven to be effective that are embedded in a local cultural context, with local educational priorities, a local cast of characters, and the like. Thus, for example, the Chinese program devoted a section to aesthetics deemed missing from school curricula; special attention was given to the transition to an open society in Russia; an attempt was made to deal with the Israel–Arab conflict in the Middle East (as was discussed in Chapter 4); and mothers were addressed in an effort to eradicate illiteracy in Turkey. This approach of combining local cultural content and the *Sesame Street* format is said to be at the heart of program's unprecedented international success.

In addition to the formative research that accompanied these productions, unique local research projects have been undertaken. Several studies that focused mainly on the learning of skills, presented evidence that supported the body of knowledge accumulating in the USA – viewing *Sesame Street* was found to improve performance on specific skills, particularly in letter and number recognition, in Mexico, Turkey, Portugal, and Russia. One explanation for these systematic findings is that these skills are highlighted in all productions of the program: each episode presents at least one letter and one number that are reinforced more then once in different segments and styles. Social messages, on the other hand, are presented in less-specific a manner and are not re-inforced in the same ways. Here it should be noted that it is much easier to evaluate through research specific skills like learning numbers and letters than it is more complex and abstract notions of attitudes and emotions. This having been said, clearly there is a great need to develop research in these latter areas, as well.

In addition to *Sesame Street*, CTW was also responsible for the production of several other quality programs for older children, all nourished by the same educational conception: *Electric Company*, and *Ghostwriter* for the development of literacy in the elementary school years; *3-2-1 Contact* for the promotion of science and technology; and *Square One TV* for stimulating mathematical thinking and problem solving for higher elementary school grades. Various experiments that followed these and other series found, as was expected, positive findings: children who watch attractive educational television programs learn whatever it is they are taught.

The Teletubbies

Another outstanding example of educational television is the *Teletubbies*. Produced in the late 1990s by the British Broadcasting Corporation (BBC), this is their most profitable series to date having been purchased by many countries around the world, where it is dubbed in their own languages. This revolutionary series was unique in targeting, for the first time, a very young audience at the stage of language acquisition: babies and toddlers between a few months and 3 years old.

The *Teletubbies* series revolves around four child-like, non-human characters that differ from one another in size and color, known respectively as Tinky-Winky, Dipsy, Laa-Laa, and Po. Their catchy, easily pronounced names, and playful behavior represent the happy world of childhood. These cheerful characters, full of curiosity, live in an imaginary land consisting of two complementary environments: a pastoral landscape of green lawns, flowers, and rabbits; and the characters' underground home, which is technologically rich. They move about in childish clumsiness (the lower part of their bodies looks inflated like a toddler in diapers), they play with each other and with familiar objects, and they use a very limited vocabulary that is repeated continuously. Professionals and parents claim that the program presents very young viewers with a safe and secure world, void of violence, threat or pain that has no social stereotypes. The environment that combines nature and technology makes references to the reality of many of today's children who learn to maneuver in a technological world and yet to continue to enjoy the natural environment. In addition, the program has also blurred, consciously, cultural and social differences; minimized localized cultural references, a strategy that made it easy to sell it worldwide, turning it to an international icon.

Each episode in the series brings little new information that has been adapted to the young target audience and broadcast with a very high degree of repetitiveness. The vocabulary is limited and imitates the speech style of the very young: single words or combination of a few words. In addition, the *Teletubbies* make non-verbal sounds that are typical to babies. Several additional production features were adapted to the target audience: a smiling baby-face fitted within a rising and setting sun; permanent accessories such as a purse, a scooter, and a hat; a shower head that emerges from the ground; a background female voice; opening and closing rituals; and the like. An exceptional component is a documentary segment that is incorporated within each episode and repeated twice, portraying older children engaged in a familiar activity (e.g., playing a musical instrument, caring for pets, going to the beach).

The series has been highly popular among a wide audience in many countries in the world (indeed, in several societies, it has become a "cult" program for adolescents, who treat it, naturally, with amusement). Research that examined the series in several countries (including Australia, England, Germany, Israel, Norway, and the USA) found that the attitude toward it was mixed.[35] On one hand, the program was perceived as safe, relaxing, and stimulates happiness and a feeling of well being among its adoring viewers. On the other hand, it had been criticized for not being challenging enough and for not enriching the children's world, and thus reinforcing a status quo world without development or change. Observational evidence from these studies suggested that young viewers were very involved in viewing: making facial expressions, movements, singing and dancing, sound repetition, laughter, hand clapping, and the like. Parents and caregivers of these children reported that they had learned a vocabulary and basic concepts from the program (in a similar way to babies' viewing of *Sesame Street*) while the older children learned more complicated information from the documentary segments (e.g., caring for pets or making a list of things needed for a trip to the beach).

The most central criticism of the program is directed particularly at its verbal aspect. According to the critics, the limited vocabulary not only does not encourage language development, but on the contrary, it reinforces baby-like talk. Indeed several studies found that viewing the *Teletubbies* was negatively associated with both acquisition of vocabulary and expressive language use, and that viewers tended to imitate non-verbal vocalizations more than non-viewers.[36]

The popularity of the *Teletubbies* is of particular interest due to the growing number and range of programs designed for children of very young ages. Since its inception, the market for the very young has grown significantly, raising new questions about television and very early childhood. This trend was inspired by a highly controversial recommendation by the American Academy of Pediatrics (1999) that discouraged all forms of television viewing before the age of two.[37]

The value of such early viewing needs to be examined from a variety of points of view: parents, for example, may wish to examine the program from the point of view of "what is best for my child;" the child viewer is more concerned with the point of view of "what is fun to watch;" producers of the program may concentrate on the point of view of "what sells this program better." Which of these perspectives should determine the policy of broadcasting for children? We will return to this issue in Chapter 6.

Concluding Remarks

In summary, accumulative evidence suggests that educational television can and does teach. However, it does not provide convincing proof that educational television can succeed in place of other socializing agents in closing substantial gaps between different populations. Children from all strata of society and cultures are attracted to successful programs, but children who are living in more culturally enriched environments – and who receive parental as well as other types of reinforcement – seem to gain a lot more from sustained viewing. While many original educational projects have been developed worldwide that deserve our attention, few have been the focus of evaluative research that would enable us to assess and to discuss their contributions to children's development and pleasure.

The substantial achievements of educational television require a substantial investment of resources – economic, technological, and creative. The general crisis of public broadcasting worldwide and of educational television, in particular, threatens the continuity of such efforts. Educational broadcasting, which attempts to contribute among other things to the preservation of multiculturalism and local uniqueness, finds itself engaged in a difficult struggle to survive in a world of globalization and commercialization of television. As a result, although it is clear that the potential of educational television is high, its future remains unclear. Educational television can indeed educate, but will it be given the opportunity to do so in the complex world of the twenty-first century?

Notes

1 Meyrowitz (1995), Postman (1979).
2 Neuman (1991).
3 Van Evra (2004).
4 Jönsson (1986), Rosengren and Windahl (1989).
5 For an integrative discussion see Schmidt and Anderson (2006). For a few exemplary studies see Huston, Wright, Marquis and Green (1999), MacBeth (1996b), and van der Voort (2001). For some other recent studies coming from the medical literature see Borzekowski and Robinson (2005), Hancox, Milne, and Poulton (2005), and Zimmerman and Christakis (2005).
6 Lemish and Rice (1986), Singer, J.L. and Singer, D.G. (1998).
7 Naigels and Mayeux (2001), Selnow and Bettinghuas (1982), Singer and Singer (1981).

8 Rice and Woodsmall (1988), Rice, Buhr, and Oetting (1992), Rice, Oetting, Marquis, Bode, and Pase (1994).
9 Rice, Huston, Truglio, and Wright (1990).
10 Linebarger and Walker (2005).
11 Lemish and Rice (1986), Lemish and Tidhar (1999).
12 Blosser (1988).
13 Fisch (2004), Linebarger (2001).
14 Koolstra and Beentjes (1999).
15 Salomon (1994 [1979]).
16 Lonner, Thorndike, Forbes, and Ashworth (1985), MacBeth (1996a).
17 Messaris (1994).
18 This discussion is based on the work of Cohen and Salomon (1979), Salomon (1981).
19 Salomon (1983), Salomon (1984), Salomon and Leigh (1984).
20 Meringoff, Vibbert, Char, Fernie, Banker, and Gardner (1983).
21 Hayes and Birnbaum (1980), Zuckerman, Zeigler, and Stevenson (1978).
22 Macklin (1999), Walma van der Molen (1999).
23 Clark (1983).
24 O'Bryan (1980).
25 Schramm (1960).
26 Schramm (1977).
27 Tidhar (1990).
28 Discussion of the capacity model is based on Fisch (2004).
29 Based on the published work in Hebrew of Tidhar in Israel Educational Television.
30 The discussion of *Sesame Street* is based on Fisch (2004) and Fisch and Truglio (2001).
31 At the time of writing these are, in chronological order: Brazil. Mexico, Canada, Germany, The Netherlands, France, Kuwait, Spain, Sweden, Israel, The Philippines, Turkey, Portugal, Norway, Russia, Poland, China, Palestinian Territories, Egypt, and South Africa. See Cole, Richman, and McCann Brown (2001).
32 Wright, Huston, Scantlin, and Kotler (2001).
33 Zill (2001).
34 Cole, Richman, and McCann Brown (2001).
35 *The Teletubbies* (1999).
36 Linebarger and Walker (2005).
37 See special issue of *American Behavioral Scientist*, 2004.

6

Implications for Education and Policy

We discussed in previous chapters a variety of domains in the lives of children in which television has a central role. We discovered that television has many implications for their behavior and worldview, as well as their cognitive and emotional worlds. We emphasized, repeatedly, that viewing television is part of the routine everyday life of children and that it is contextualized within each viewer's culture, in general, and family, in particular.

Further, we highlighted that much of the literature on the relationships between children and television has focused on the more problematic aspects as well as on concern for the well being of children. In this regard, we pointed out the differences between the two major socializing agents in children's lives: the family environment, where most of children's leisure activities, television included, takes place; and formal educational institutions. These two systems that simultaneously serve such central roles in children's lives hardly ever refer to one another when it comes to television viewing. This being the case, the question remains: Does the educational system need to intervene in television viewing at home, and if so, in what ways?

We also pointed out that scholarly as well as popular writings often direct their critical arrows at broadcasting organizations, demanding that they demonstrate more social responsibility when it comes to children and accept – either voluntarily as a form of self-control or in response to formal regulations – various constraints that will protect young viewers from what are deemed potentially negative influences of television. Such demands may be seen to be in conflict with fundamental rights such as freedom of speech and the public's access to information that are at the heart of all media in democratic societies.

Following such considerations, the two central issues that remain for discussion in this chapter are: What are the implications of what we know about television and children for their formal education, on the one hand, and for the television industry, on the other hand?

Media Literacy

The term "media education," has been alternatively referred to as "media literacy," "critical viewing skills," and "media competencies." These terms have been used interchangeably and with little conceptual distinction to refer, first, to analyses of television texts, television audiences, and viewing contexts and cultures; and, second, to discussion of issues of public policy, domains of cultural criticism, as a set of pedagogical tools for teachers, as educational guidelines for parents, as hypotheses in the spirit of technological determinism, or as topics for research on cognitive processing of information. While discussions within these domains have also included those media that should be included in the center of the educational concern, television is undoubtedly perceived as the main focus in all approaches.[1] Since, therefore, the discussion of television education is part of the more general one on media education, we will refer to it here interchangeably.

Media literacy, in general terms, is commonly understood to refer to the ability to analyze and evaluate messages, as well as the ability to communicate in a variety of ways. It is perceived to be a form of literacy necessary for participation in civic and cultural life that requires an informed, critical, and creative citizenry. The goals of educational programs that advance media literacy as stated in the extensive, extant literature are diverse and not necessarily complementary. For some advocates and program developers, media literacy is a way to develop creativity in children by providing them with another domain within which they can be creative and have opportunities for self-expression. Others place a priority on media literacy's potential to empower children by allowing them to present their own voices, to pursue social and political goals, and to advance particularly those who are socially disadvantaged. For other analysts, media literacy's central feature is that it seeks to enable media consumers to have a critical perspective, to challenge mainstream media and the existing social order, to advance democratization and civic participation, as well as, to return some power to popular citizenry. Media literacy has also been employed to refer to vocational training for future employment and in the growing media saturated workplace. Finally, for some educators, media literacy is an opportunity to challenge traditional educational institutions by experimenting with alternative pedagogies.[2]

The variety of educational goals has led to the development of a host of curricula that employ different pedagogies, assessment practices of children's achievements, as well as approaches to institutionalization of media literacy programs in formal and non-formal settings. Though there are many differences, writers agree that media literacy skills incorporate at least an understanding of the following five elements:

1   Media messages are constructed and not merely a reflection of reality.
2   Messages are created in specific contexts that represent interests that are economic, social, political, historical, cultural, and aesthetic in nature.
3   The process of interpreting media messages is a product of an interaction between the interpreter, the text, and the cultural context.
4   Different media use various languages that are expressed in a variety of symbol systems, forms, and genres.
5   Different representations in the media have a role in the way we understand our social reality.[3]

Notice that all five characteristics are central issues in the study of media, in general, and of television, in particular, as we have discussed in the previous chapters. The ability to explain and apply these understandings in the process of interpretation, analysis, critique, as well as, creation of media messages is a life-long process. In the widest sense, we can define media literacy as a non-ending process of investigation into the ways in which we search for meaning and create it through media texts, and the investigation of the ways others do the same for us.

The central debates in media literacy

The demand for the incorporation of media literacy in the school systems in many countries around the world since the 1980s was greatly nourished by the studies on children and television discussed throughout the book. In countries where the dominant approaches were those of "direct (and mainly negative) effects" of television on children, it was commonly the case that media literacy programs were expected to teach critical skills that will allow learners to resist the temptation to enjoy much of their viewing, to change their attitudes and viewing preferences, and to immunize them against negative influences. As such, media literacy curricula were thus perceived to be a form of educational "immunization." An alternative approach suggests that media literacy programs build on an understanding of children's viewing preferences and knowledge about television content as a pre-requisite to communicating with them about their viewing.

Children-viewers' needs, interpretations, pleasures, and social contexts are at the center of this educational process. Clearly, these two approaches – the immunization versus the interpretive – are based upon different assumptions about the pupils, pursue different goals, and utilize an array of pedagogies.

In England, the cradle and current leader advancing media literacy in the school system, media literacy was strongly influenced by the development of cultural studies in the 1950s and 1960s. Cultural studies redefined the approach taken to culture so that it was perceived not only as a canon of preferred works of art, but as a way of life that includes a host of forms of expressions, including those that are part of everyday life such as television. Applied to media literacy, the cultural studies approach perceived the media to be part of a more general trend of democratization in which children's leisure is treated to be a relevant contributing factor to their education and a legitimate topic for study in school. At the same time, the early work of media literacy in England did develop the still dominant (in other places in the world) protective approaches that expect teachers to inculcate in pupils skills that immunize them from the negative effects of television, such as: protect the elitist culture with its valued qualities; protect moral values regarding such phenomena as violence, sex, consumerism; and political protection from false beliefs and discriminatory ideologies of enslavement expressed in the media in regard to ethnicity, class, and gender issues, for example. In all of these realms, media literacy was expected to struggle with vast and complicated social issues. The media were perceived to be the cause of both society and children's troubles, with education for media literacy as the solution. Teachers were expected to be able to place themselves outside of these processes of media influence and to be able to provide pupils with skills for critical viewing that empower them, too.[4]

This historical review of the early days of media literacy in England allows us to understand the changes that took place in this field and the principles underlying present efforts. Media literacy today is no longer defined in a narrow sense of opposition to children's viewing pleasures, neither is it a process of education that distinguishes between good or bad viewing, involves a de-mystification of the medium, or seeks to immunize against its negative effects. The studies presented in previous chapters assumed that children are active, conscious viewers, rather than passive and naive. Nor are children viewed anymore as a homogenous group. Rather, like any other social category, they are distinguished by their personality characteristics, age group, life experience, social and cultural background, and the like. Teachers, too, are not perceived to be omniscient purveyors of the magic key to the one and only "true" interpretation of media messages. Rather, teachers and pupils are assumed to be involved in a complicated process of negotiation that takes place, continuously, between audience and texts, a process characterized by the possibility that multiple readings and interpretations exist for each and every text.

Media literacy around the world

The differentiated development of media literacy throughout the world is due to the specific academic environment of media studies in each country as well as national goals, educational systems, media environments, and the like. A 2001 survey of 38 countries worldwide conducted on behalf of UNESCO revealed that the diffusion of media education has been uneven.[5] Countries seem to be going through different phases of development – from the initiation of activities some quite innovative, to decisions about programs that often result in removal of support or denial of proposals to advance programs and policies, all the way to well-established implementation of curricula. In addition, some countries who led the initial efforts in media education are now showing signs of weariness, while others are only just now developing a budding interest.

When examining the development in the USA, for example, we find that while it is the greatest producer and exporter of television programs, it lags far behind many other countries in developing media literacy programs in its school systems. This is surprising given the vibrant civic society in the USA and the many informal education and non-profit organizations engaged in media activism. How can we explain these limited educational efforts and what can we learn from them about the consequences of variables such as political, economic, cultural, and so forth on trends in the development of media literacy?

Several complementary explanations have been offered[6]:

- *Geography and organization*: Professionals engaged in media literacy find that it is easier to meet, exchange ideas, develop policy, and the like in small countries (such as Israel) or small educationally autonomous regions (such as Scotland). In contrast, in larger countries such as the USA, where each state has its independent educational authority as well as local school boards, media educators are quite isolated from each other and often lack public support locally.
- *Culture and educational systems*: The fact that the USA is a cultural super-power along with the disregard for "the rest of the world" said to be characteristic of much of the USA's ethnocentric attitude reinforces a situation where US citizens are much less aware of

their need to examine themselves and their culture critically. Further, the ethnic, racial, and cultural diversity of US society often inhibits, even prevents, the possibility of achieving consensus in regard to many aspects of children's education. This is one explanation for the preference for local educational pluralism over a centralized system. As a result, innovative initiatives, such as media literacy, need to struggle for recognition in each and every local educational system individually and often do not enjoy government support. Consequentially, private schools in the USA lead in the development of media literacy curricula as part of their more general openness to educational experimentation and innovation. Teachers in public schools, on the other hand, have to struggle to advance children's acquisition of the basic skills of reading, writing, and arithmetic in an over-crowded schedule, under difficult teaching conditions, and, thus, are not easily convinced of the merits of this "luxurious" subject matter. The absence of institutionalized teacher education and teacher-training programs in media literacy also contribute to the lack of interest and awareness, to difficulties in understanding the nature of media literacy and its goals, and to the lack of willingness to confront the subject and its unique pedagogical approaches. As a consequence, teachers often feel threatened and are resistant to local attempts to introduce media literacy classes into their schools.

- *Exclusivity of local culture*: One of the strongest motivations for the development of media literacy programs worldwide is the need to counter possible implications for their local cultures, traditions, and values of the heavy import of American programs. Indeed, many countries hope that media literacy will help youngsters understand that the value systems presented on American television does not necessarily represent or serve their interests. In contrast, in US homes almost all television fare is locally produced, therefore American viewers do not have to face this challenge, as they do not find themselves in a situation where they stand outside of their own culture and need to look at it reflectively.

- *A split between various approaches to media literacy*: In many leading countries in media literacy, such as England, the cultural studies' approach places children at the center of the educational process and sees as significant their interpretations and pleasures. In the USA, however, the protective approach is still dominant (following, among others, the research traditions discussed in previous chapters) with its harsh criticism of television for its supposed contribution to many social and educational ills (including violence, sexual permissiveness, and substance abuse). This approach seems to be supported by public opinion and governmental bodies, as part of a general worldview that is concerned about an alleged deterioration of morals in society, in general, and among the young, in particular. A deep chasm divides these two approaches and, as a result, discussion within the field of media literacy is often conflicted and problematic.

• *Capitalistic forces*: Some leaders view media literacy as a threat to the economic interests of powerful large corporations. This is due to the goal in media literacy of developing a critical understanding of the entertainment industry, in general, and commercials in particular and therefore is discouraged in a variety of subtle ways.

The above analysis of the US case serves to illustrate how many variables, including economic interests, politics, geography, demography, and culture are interlinked in the influence of worldviews on educational policy.

A very different case in point is the development of media literacy in South Africa, as it had a unique history. In this case, media literacy was assigned a central role in the advancement of a political agenda that sought to promote significant social changes in South Africa in the late 1980s and during the 1990s in regard to issues related to the abolishment of the Apartheid regime, the process of reconciliation between the races, and human rights. The experience of South Africa is of value not only in its own right, but also as an instructive role model for other societies undergoing political revolutions and national reformation.[7]

The development of media literacy in South Africa was directly influenced by the political struggles against the Apartheid regime and the media under its control, as well as, by the critical pedagogy entitled "the people's education." In contrast with the dominant approach to education up to the 1980s that encouraged passivity and non-critical viewing as a means of enabling whites to retain power and prevent change, people's education encouraged productive and creative education. Catalysts of change were the alternative media organizations that were established in South Africa in the second half of the twentieth century whose aim was to bypass censorship in mainstream media, to offer competitive information and perspectives, and to promote political resistance. Accordingly, media literacy was conceived to be a means to incorporate children's real-life experiences within the formal knowledge acquired in schools, allowing them to develop as citizens critical of their environment. Media activists encouraged teachers to adopt the various educational activities, teacher training workshops, and learning materials as subversive strategies. Often, these activists themselves became teachers of media literacy, thus blurring the boundaries between critical action and critical teaching. The development of "civic courage" – the courage to express an opinion, to resist, to offer alternatives, to act – was defined as a central goal for media literacy. Through this process, the curricula involving media literacy, encouraged discussion of social and moral issues, while encouraging freedom of speech and critical thinking skills. Empowering children became a key concept in the goals of media literacy within this perspective.

In the South African model of media literacy pupils are encouraged to be critical "readers" of media, able to identify biases, deceptions, and omissions in media coverage; and they develop an understanding of media production, the people involved in it, and their constructed or fictional nature. Media literacy programs were a safe educational environment that enabled pupils to investigate moral and social issues and to see the world through the perspectives of others – be it an "other" by nature of race, gender, class, or political stance. The creative component of media literacy enabled them to become more involved citizens who are capable of expressing their views through the media. On the other hand, the South African case is an example of how media literacy has the potential to develop a citizenry critical of a political regime that encourages and, indeed, guides children to become active citizens in their changing world.

A third example comes from Israel, where media literacy gained the status of a "much debated consensus" in the 1990s.[8] On the one hand, there seemed to be agreement about the importance of media literacy in children's education, yet, on the other hand, there was deep disagreement over almost every aspect of it. Understanding this peculiar situation requires familiarity with the nature of Israeli society as one deeply divided over many issues, including such difficult issues regarding the nature of Israel as a Jewish and democratic state as well as the future of the occupation of the Palestinian people and its land. Four particular issues influenced the development of media literacy in Israel:

1   *Media literacy as an issue of ethnic identity.* The concern over the potential Americanization of Israeli society, with its capitalistic values of commercialization, privatization, individualization and the like has been central in the history of the introduction and development of television in Israel. The demands for media literacy was an ancillary argument that emerged in the process of introducing television as a means of resisting Americanization and the primal threat it represents to the development of an authentic Israeli society and culture.

2   *Media literacy as a political issue.* Having to function in a society deeply divided over central issues, the media in Israel are attacked by opponents on all sides of the political map. Each side blames the media for leaning towards the other side and calls for media literacy

to demystify the news media for young people and to educate them to critical understandings of the sociology of news production as well as to the content, structural, and political constraints of the major sources of information.

3   *Media literacy as an ethical issue*: On occasion, various coalitions of interests have formed around ethical issues concerning media content such as representations of minorities and women, pornography and sexual promiscuity, violence, the glorification of drug and alcohol abuse, and the like. Educators, non-governmental activists concerned with human rights, child welfare, and social justice, religious leaders – while differing in ideological motivation – share the belief that the media function as socializing agents and that a literate audience can and should resist the value systems and behaviors that undermine proponents' ideological dispositions.

4   *Media literacy as a current affairs issue*: Educators feel that there is a desperate need for curricula, learning materials, and pedagogical tools that will enable classroom teachers to deal with the often highly charged events of the day that are affecting their pupils' every day life in an academic, nonpolitical way. Many teachers believe that focusing attention and analysis on media functioning and roles may be a mechanism to avoid the need to take sides and an easy solution to the anxiety of dealing with highly volatile topics in the classroom.

In summary, media literacy policies in Israel developed out of pressure from the public, the educational establishment, academia, and politicians. Within this broad consensus, alliances developed among persons whose political and ideological views differed on almost every other issue.

Similar to the Israeli case, many other countries are concerned with the tension between the more global concerns of media literacy advocates and their own unique local needs. For example, as noted, media literacy in Israel is largely influenced by the desire to resist a process of Americanization of Israeli culture. In India and Australia, media literacy has been seen as a way to engage pupils in examination of local issues related to class, gender, and ethnic differences. In South Korea, it is perceived to be a facilitator of technological education and social mobility. In Japan, it is related to the discourse of the rights of children as individuals. In Spain, the emphasis is being put on the development of democratic citizenship. In Sweden the concern is for children's ability for self-expression; and in South Africa it has been recruited in the struggle for HIV-AIDS education. Thus, in general, we can say that media literacy is involved in developing in young viewers an awareness of issues such as: whose voice is being heard and whose is not, and why? More specifically, which classes and ethnic groups in society are excluded from the public sphere?

Countries such as Italy, Denmark, India, Scotland, and South Africa have emphasized media literacy's potential contribution to civic education, originally formulated in the English tradition in the field. There they relate media literacy efforts to the burning ideological-political issues of their respective societies. The diverse national agendas in the areas of culture, society and politics have led to the development of a variety of educational programs. For some groups, media literacy serves to legitimate existing power structures and so to prevent social change. For example, such has been the case of media literacy programs developed by conservative-religious groups in several societies, such as the "moral majority" in England and the USA. For others, as the case of South Africa discussed previously above, media literacy served an important role in the anti-Apartheid movement and was assigned an educational role in advancing a national agenda that focused on human rights, equality, social change, and – later on – reconciliation. Clearly then, while many writers agree that media literacy should be part of civic education, they differ on what it means to be a "citizen."[9]

Practical aspects of media literacy

How do these theoretical and ideological issues translate into the practicality of educational work in formal institutions? The applications of the academic debate over the field focus on three educational areas: curriculum, teaching, and assessment.

The curriculum

Here there are several related questions, such as: What are the goals of the media literacy curriculum? How do we incorporate media literacy in the school program? What knowledge, skills, attitudes, and values should be taught?

Responses to such basic educational issues differ depending on the approach taken to media literacy, as well as, the stance taken in regard to more general educational tensions between the liberal desire to educate children to be literate citizens in the complex societies in which they live and the desire to equip them with practical production skills. These two approaches are perceived by many as complementary – the experience of producing media messages can assist children to understand better the processes of communication and to sharpen their critical skills in examining the relationships between media and reality. Here, it is important to note that involvement in production does not automatically elicit an analytical or critical perspective, as children may be tempted to imitate the genres and contents familiar to them on television rather than to challenge them.

A second concern relates to the placement of media literacy within the general school curriculum. Here educational systems have adopted one of four approaches: (1) media literacy as an independent discipline; (2) media literacy as a component of another discipline (e.g., civic education, art); (3) integration of media literacy across the entire spectrum of the school curriculum (i.e., each discipline integrates aspects of media literacy deemed relevant); and (4) media literacy as part of an integrative inter-disciplinary curriculum (e.g., contemporary society, "humanity and culture").

Teaching

Teaching media literacy raises serious questions in regard to the traditional role teachers play in the educational process. Many writers argue that media literacy requires an innovative teaching style, one that is more democratic and egalitarian, since the teacher does not own knowledge and is a partner in the dialogic process. The mere engagement with media can thus assist in the democratization of the relationships between pupils and teachers that require reflection and critique. In general, media literacy poses many challenges and opportunities for teachers: integration of many subjects; open-ended teaching that encourages tolerance and interpretation over the transmission of knowledge; as well as a need to relate media literacy studies to children's life experiences.

The re-examination of the nature of pupil–teacher relationships required by media literacy brings to the forefront not only the variety of teaching styles, but also the variety of pupils' learning styles. Children bring to the study of media a host of personal interests, needs, goals, experiences, prior knowledge, and motivations. For example, sometimes they expect to be entertained in class, while at other times they may feel that their personal taste and self-worth are being threatened, or that they are expected to become television producers against their will.

Assessment

How can the educational effectiveness of the various media literacy curricula be evaluated? What do children need to express in order for us to define them as media literate? Should we test their knowledge? Skills? Behaviors? Attitudes? Emotions? Values? Indeed, those involved in media literacy wrestle with the problem of whether to require knowledge tests, critical analysis of television texts, production of a text, or a combination of all of the above. Some models of evaluation base their concepts on literary and artistic forms of critique, others on the capability for self-reflection. Clearly, the issue of assessment of the success of media literacy curricula in general, and pupils' achievements in particular, is a thorny issue.

Let us consider now, as an illustration, one of the most popular models of media literacy that has served as a basis for many curricula around the world. Developed by the British Film Institute in London in the 1980s, This model extends a curriculum framework that revolves around central concepts, rather than educational goals or skills. The framework of this model is shown in Box 6.1.

Box 6.1 The BFI model of areas of knowledge and understanding in media education[10]

Media Agencies
Who is communicating, and why?

Who produces a text; roles in the production process; media institutions; economics and ideology; intentions and results

- -

Media Categories
What type of text is this?

Different media (television, radio, cinema, etc); forms (documentary, advertising, etc); genres (science fiction, soap opera, etc); other ways for categorizing texts; how categorization relates to understanding.

- -

Media Technologies
How is it produced?

What kind of technologies are available to whom; how to use them; the differences they make to the production processes as well as the final product.

- -

Media Languages
How do we know what it means?

How do the media produce meanings; codes and conventions; narrative structures.

- -

> ## Media Audiences
> ### Who receives it, and what sense do they make of it?
>
> How audiences are identified, constructed, addressed and reached; how audiences find, choose, consume, and respond to texts.
>
> -
>
> ## Media Representations
> ### How does it present its subject?
>
> The relation between media texts and the actual places, people, events, ideas; stereotyping and its consequences.

The components of the model are not a "grocery list" required of each media literacy program, nor are they hierarchical or mutually exclusive. On the contrary, they are understood to be interdependent – each presents an alternative means of entry into the study of media, and at the same time requires addressing the other issues. Each of these topics also has an additional value for applied production work. In addition, the advantage of this model is that it does not list facts to be memorized or point to a list of canonic texts that need to be studied. On the contrary, it allows media literacy to be adapted to different cultures and to changes in the experiences and interests that children have within them. In addition, this model offers a theoretical framework that can be applied to a variety of media, old and new, in order to understand the interrelationships between them, and to transfer knowledge and understanding between them. For example, it is expected that children will apply the knowledge acquired in their studies of the construction of stereotypes in a television situation comedy to the analysis of a literary work; or, to use their skills for critical analysis of persuasive messages in television advertising in their engagement with pop-up commercials that appear in favorite Internet sites.[11]

Evaluating media literacy curricula

As we can see, there are high expectations for media literacy curricula around the world. There are at least four different approaches applied in scholarly evaluation of the merits of media literacy curricula: focus on the curricula; the teachers; the pupils; and the relationship with other disciplines.[12] :

1   Evaluation of the suitability of the educational goals for the specific child-audiences of different ages can be achieved through conventional pre-post studies; that is, a study that compares the achievements of children before the introduction of the curriculum and after it has been implemented over a period of time. Such studies seek to identify the nature and effectiveness of learning processes. Comparisons with control groups of pupils who do not study media literacy can sharpen our understanding of how children spontaneously apply skills in analyzing and creating media messages in comparison to those acquired through formal learning.
2   Studies of teachers' experiences and attitudes toward teaching media literacy ask questions such as: Are teachers resistant or do they raise objections to teaching media literacy? What motivates those teachers that are enthusiastic about teaching media literacy? How do they apply the curricula? What is the nature of such applications?
3   Studies of children's experiences and attitudes toward learning media literacy complement our understanding by posing questions such as: What do they think they gain from it? Do they feel it "spoils" their viewing pleasures or adds to it? What are their attitudes toward such studies – do they feel enthusiasm, resentment, or boredom? What would they like to study in their media literacy classes?
4   Finally, evaluation of the inter-relationships between media literacy studies and other disciplines focus on the question: Does media literacy advance skills in other areas, such as civic studies, art, science, literature, technology?

Surprisingly, very little is actually known about the real influence of media literacy efforts in the world. Although there is great need to examine the different curricula, the ideologies embedded in them, and their effectiveness in achieving their goals, there is hardly any accumulative evaluative research. The few studies in this area have mainly tested acquired knowledge through a comparison of different teaching methods. The few attempts to relate media literacy programs to actual modifications in children's viewing habits, for example, have not revealed any significant insights.

Several studies conducted in this area can illuminate the potential of this unexplored territory. A large-scale study in Australia examined the development of analytical skills in children aged 8 to 15 following systematic media literacy training.[13] The results suggested that children did indeed acquire basic skills: they were able to identify visual and audio codes and conventions, and they succeeded in analyzing familiar stereo-types and connotations aroused by specific images. However, at the same time, they did not demonstrate a more general understanding of the social context and implications of media that were expected to assist them in developing strategies for applying these skills in everyday situations out of the classroom. Children, so it seems, learn those skills taught in class, but the degree to which this learning is relevant to their everyday experiences is unclear.

A different kind of an experiment conducted in the USA examined the effectiveness of a specific media literacy program developed for purpose of study by the researchers that included program-designed teacher training and parental involvement.[14] This framework allowed the researchers to attain significant control of all elements of the experiment, including the learning materials, the program's concrete goals, teaching style in class, and pupils' achievements. A comparison between the achievements of pupils in the experimental and control groups demon-strated that the former improved their skills significantly following the media literacy classes (for example, they demonstrated a better ability to understand various elements of the television production process as well as a capability to distinguish between fantasy and reality on television. These gains were maintained even following a period of three months after the program had been concluded. Similar experimental studies applied this format, including studies of children with learning disabil-ities and emotional disorders, and the results reinforced this basic principle: children learn skills that are taught to them through a structured formal educational process.

A study conducted in The Netherlands was an examination of a specific educational intervention that promoted understanding the process of television news production.[15] In the experiment, children aged 10 to 12 viewed a six-part television series supported by a workbook for independent study. The issues of study included a discussion of "what is news," the selection process of news, verbal and visual elements of news, the editorial process, news delivery, and comparisons between different news broadcasts. An evaluation of pupils' achievements based on a pre-post intervention test revealed that children in the experimental group improved their understand-ing of the process of news production, but not their abilities to critique the reliability of news reports. On the contrary, the children in the experimental group assigned more credibility to the news reports than their counterparts who did not go through the educa-tional intervention. It seems, once again, that while educational intervention may be effective in transmitting knowledge, the ability to develop critical skills in relation to the world of television requires a much more complex educational process.

Our last example comes from an experiment in Israel with pre-school children who were taught specific skills via educational television programs and with the aid of teachers trained for this specific experiment.[16] Following the intervention, pres-school viewers were better able to identify fiction elements in the programs, to understand time and logic gaps in the narrative, as well as to identify specific camera shots as they relate to specific meanings.

Overall, then, it seems that media literacy interventions that are well designed and executed have the potential of helping even young viewers overcome some of their developmental barriers (discussed in Chapter 2). Undoubtedly, there is an absence of studies in this field. This may be due to the difficulties involved in evaluating media literacy efforts. Among the difficulties is a concern that research findings that do not demonstrate significant achievements will weaken efforts to introduce media literacy into the school system and will dry out funding resources. For their part, many educators are concerned that researchers will intrude into their classroom, intervene in their educational work, and undermine their professional actions.[17]

The definitions of the goals of media literacy and of what constitutes the "media literate child" are very complex endeavors. The result is an unfortunate vicious circle, as only the development of a systematic and accumulative body of research regarding the teaching and learning of media literacy can help clarify the goals, define a clear policy, identify effective teaching practices and teacher education, and explain the educational process that pupils undergo when they study media. All forms of research methodologies can be applied to contribute in such an effort. Furthermore, there is an acute need for longitudinal studies that will follow closely, perhaps through ethnographic methods, educational processes taking place in classrooms from the points of view of both pupils and teachers. There is also a need for large-scale surveys, which measure changes in achievements, attitudes, perspectives, viewing habits, and the like, to take place in schools that go through such an educational intervention in comparison to those who do not. Finally, tightly planned small-scale experiments can best fit the study of effectiveness of specific teaching methods or teaching aids.

In summary, media literacy is a dynamic, developing, and complicated field. Those who promote it expect that it will have far-reaching influences on the definition of schooling, democracy, and even on our understanding of knowledge all together. Whether it will live up to these ambitious promises has yet to be seen. In addition, we need to remember that media literacy can be understood to be a life-long process that is not confined to the school system: parents, caregivers, siblings, peers – all have the potential to contribute to the development of media literacy, as indicated in our discussion in Chapter 1.

Policy of Broadcasting for Children

The pressure on broadcasters to control their programming for children constitutes the second route of attempts at intervening on behalf of children's rights and needs. For a host of reasons, civic pressure groups, politicians, legislators, and scholars have called for both external regulation (enforced by legislation) as well as internal regulation (voluntarily) over programming for children. As a result, many countries eventually developed broadcasting policies, including regulations and agreements that benefit children, but also compromise the needs and constraints imposed by the broadcasting industry. Several countries including in Europe and Australia have been also experimenting with a more recent model of co-regulation, i.e., cooperation between the authorities and the broadcast industry.[18]

What are the considerations that influence the development of broadcast policy for children? We can organize such considerations into four groups. First, there are structural considerations related to the type of broadcast systems of each country (i.e., private or public) and the responsibility each type has for a variety of national populations. Second, there are ideological considerations that are central to national identity, including self-definitions in terms of culture, traditions of freedom of speech, society's willingness to impose restrictions on its television industry, and the like. Third, there are economical considerations that are related to the economic power held by the broadcast industry; its dependency on other sources of financial support (such as governmental budgets, advertisers, user fees); and its ability to influence policy decisions. Finally, we can point to political considerations that are motivated by those in power who benefit from the media and wish to maintain their power.

These four groups of considerations are, naturally, interdependent, and require deeper investigation. However, they serve as a starting point in our attempt to understand how various countries have developed different broadcasting policies.[19] At the same time, since television programs are distributed around the globe – through cable, satellites, videotapes, CDs, computers, and cellular phones – their broadcast policy becomes a global issue. A case in point is the action-adventure animation series popular around the world in the 1990s – *The Power Rangers*. Due to its violent nature, attempts were undertaken to limit its broadcast in many countries, including Australia, Canada, Denmark, and New Zealand. In turn, this forced the producers in the USA to re-examine its content and their own broadcasting policy. The fact that children around the world often view the same programs creates an urgent need to develop an international broadcasting policy that abides by similar criteria. Indeed, several such attempts have been advanced by voluntary organizations.

A comparative analysis of broadcast policy for children worldwide suggests three central themes: content related issues; advertising for children and during children hours; and issues related to the sponsorship of programs for children.

Central content-related policy issues

Many countries have attempted to monitor television content that targets children. Most of these efforts are aimed at limiting children's exposure to content that is deemed inappropriate for their age, their emotional and cognitive abilities, as well as the content that presents a social world based on a-social values and behaviors that might have a negative impact on children. Policies in this realm are directed at limiting broadcast hours of such content to parts of the day when children are supposedly not around television (e.g., late night hours), particularly in relation to violent and stereotypical content that raises ethical issues. Complementary content-related policies are directed toward the encouragement of broadcasting quality programs for children that have an added educational and social value.

The struggle over the regulation of children's television in the USA is a particularly interesting case, due to the fact that, first, many programs for children are produced there and exported globally; and, second, the USA is a point of reference for other regulatory systems, as well as for the nature of the broadcast system that is mostly commercial and privately owned. Without going into detail about the evolution of the regulatory system, we can pinpoint many of the central issues by examining the Children's Television Act (CTA) legislated by the American Congress in 1990. Following many years of public debate and many attempts at legislation, this act restricted the amount of advertising time allowed during children's programs, required broadcasters to televise programs of educational and informative value for children, and allocated a budget for production of children's programs. Fulfilling these requirements became a prerequisite for the renewal of the broadcast license (at the time, every five years, and since 1996 every eight years). The Federal Communication Commission (FCC), the supervising body of the US broadcast system, was charged with enforcing these requirements.

As appealing as this act may seem at first glance, it raises some of the most primary difficulties in broadcast regulations, the most central of which is the vagueness of the concept of "quality television." As we have noted repeatedly, "quality" is in the eyes of the beholder. According to children, for example, a quality program is one that attracts and interests them; for parents and public organizations, quality may be determined on its educational value; and for industry professionals, quality is measured by its production values (such as famous actors, advanced technology camera work and effects, music, humor, and the like) as well as the rating measures it receives with the audiences. Accordingly, broadcasters often include popular cartoons and popular prime time series in their definition of "quality" television. In appealing for license renewal, broadcasters justify such programs in a variety of creative, yet some might say cynical ways. An action-adventure cartoon is perceived as having positive value, because the protagonists defend their universe from others who want to destroy it thus demonstrating concern for others and a distinction between good and bad; and a stereotypical situation comedy is presented as educational since it deals with everyday conflict within families.[20]

Interviews with industry broadcasters for children in the USA suggest that they have quite clear-cut opinions about their target audience, which dictates their policies.[21] In their view, children around the age of six lose interest in quality educational programs when they enter the school system; the only way to bypass children's resentment of instructional content is to focus on social aspects of the programs; and it is more expensive to produce educational programs. In addition, they argue that it is better to target programs for boys rather than to girls or to a mixed audience, for several reasons: boys control the remote-control at home and dictate viewing habits of the family; girls would watch boys' programs but not vice versa; and boys are more easily persuaded to purchase program-related merchandise. Putting all of these together, broadcasters, on their own account, do not believe in producing educational programs for children over pre-school years and prioritize action and adventure genres with male protagonists that appeal traditionally to boys.

The debate over the definition of "quality" in children's television has taken many turns over the years. For educational broadcasters, public or private, the question of broadcasting policy for children is very different since their view of educationally oriented television is usually influenced by the realities of functioning under severe financial constraints and in an aggressively competitive market. Quality television, according to many of such efforts, is expected to abide by several principles (see Box 6.2).[22]

Box 6.2 Principles of quality television

- To provide children with programs prepared especially for them without taking advantage of them; programs that entertain, but at the same time try to advance child viewers physically, mentally and socially.
- To allow children to hear, see and express themselves, their culture, their language and their life experiences through television programs that affirm their personal identity, community, and place.
- To encourage awareness and appreciation of other cultures as well as the child's own.
- To offer a variety of genres and content and not just reproduce programs according to a successful formula.
- To be broadcast at times that children are available to watch and through accessible technologies.
- To recognize differences between children that are a result of their cognitive and emotional development, their talents, interests, personality characteristics, interpersonal relationships and their social environment.
- To take steps to protect and encourage programs that reflect local cultures and those with minority languages.
- To avoid unnecessary presentation of violence and sex in the programs.

In examining educational television programs, many criteria are often applied. Some examples are shown in Box 6.3.

Box 6.3 Criteria for examining educational television programs

- Does the program invite children to see things they have not seen in the past, hear things they haven't heard, and most importantly – to think or imagine things that they would not have thought or imagined without television?
- Does the program tell a good story? Does it rely on the familiar in order to bridge the new and unfamiliar for young children? Are the verbal and visual components compatible?

- Does the program offer characters that children really care about? Is there a struggle between good and bad that is not too extreme? Are the children in the program capable of overcoming difficulties in a reasonable manner? Is the end of the story dependent on the generosity, fairness, honesty, caring, and responsibility of the main characters?
- Does the program avoid preaching to children or talking to them in a condescending manner? Does it avoid presenting adults as behaving in an unfair, irrational or foolish manner that undermines children's trust in the adult world?
- Does the program expand the children's world of experiences in an aesthetically attractive way?
- Does the program include a degree of wittiness and humor that is not exploitive of others?

Another attempt at defining quality television has suggested that programs that have educational values should be examined according to the following criteria[23]:

- Is the educational lesson clear, so the audience can understand it?
- Is the educational lesson prominent, presented systematically, or as an integral part of the program?
- Is the educational lesson engaging and challenging of the audience?
- Is the educational lesson presented in a way that is deemed applicable by the audience?

An analysis of children's programs according to these criteria in one Midwest American city during one broadcast season in 1996–7 revealed that while about 40 percent of the programs broadcast (mainly in the public broadcasting service PBS) were highly educational, the same rate of 40 percent had no educational value whatsoever.

When we move away from the American case to other countries, we find that an additional policy concern becomes prominent – the requirement that broadcasters offer children locally produced programs that take into consideration the cultural context in which they are raised. In Australia, for example, in the late 1990s, the Children's Advisory Committee (CAC) reached an agreement with broadcasters that requires them to offer a minimum of 390 hours of children's programs per year (with at least 130 for pre-schoolers), with 55 percent of them locally produced. These programs are to be broadcast during realistic viewing times of children (before and after school hours, and during the weekends). A children's program was defined to be: produced especially with children in mind; entertaining; of high quality and well produced; seeks to advance the understanding and experience of children; and appropriate for Australian children.[24]

Concerns over the infiltration of US programs into other societies and cultures as well as a desire to protect local production are strongly evident in many other countries as well. In Canada, for example, the requirement was set at 60 percent local programming. The Canadian Association of Broadcasters developed a self-regulatory mechanism that included a request that programs for children should reflect the social and ethical standards of the Canadian society. In addition, they were required to deal specifically with issues of morals, violence, and stereotypes, including reference to gender portrayals.[25]

Many European countries regulate their children's programs and have adopted the "watershed" guideline that specifies those broadcast hours before and during which broadcasters need to adapt their contents to an audience that includes children. Some countries refer specifically to the need to protect young viewers from exposure to inappropriate content such as pornography, racism, and violence.[26] Still, to date, many countries around the world have not been able to keep up with technological developments and to develop a clear and binding regulation-policy to regulate broadcasting to children.

Policy regarding television violence
Not surprisingly, the issue of television violence is central to the discourse of broadcasting policy worldwide. The fierce debate over this issue in the USA is particularly illuminating due to the deeply engrained tradition of freedom of speech in that country. According to the First Amendment to the American constitution "Congress shall make no law ... abridging the freedom of speech, or the press ..." The American legislature can only intervene in regulating any forms of expression, including television broadcasts, when there is a "compelling interest." When it comes to television violence, only clear evidence of a causal relationship between viewing television violence and violent behavior constitutes a compelling interest that justifies formal intervention. As we have seen in Chapter 3, presenting such evidence is quite problematic. The judicial discussion regarding this issue, therefore, distinguishes between "immediate and clear danger," when there is a high certainty that indeed watching violence has harmful effects, and research evidence that suggests such possible relationships, but can not prove "immediate and clear danger."[27] Decades of transferring the responsibility for this issue back and forth between the broadcasting industry and the American Congress resulted in the development of several strategies for the supervision of violence on television. Many

countries around the world have adopted some of these strategies, adapted to the needs of their own societies. While none of these have actually proven to provide a fully satisfactory solution, they nevertheless deserve our attention[28]:

1 *Banning and zoning*: Limiting the broadcast of violent content to particular strips of broadcast hours.
2 *Balancing*: A requirement to balance each violent program with the broadcast of a non-violent one. This proposal assumes that it is possible to "counteract" harmful content by broadcasting "corrective" programs.
3 *Labeling*: Broadcasting a warning announcement before each program deemed problematic ("parental and viewer discretion is advised") or rating programs according to a scale (for example: G – suitable for a general audience; PG – Parental guidance is advised; PG13 – Parental guidance for children under 13; R – a rated program that is unsuitable for children).
4 *User block*: Using various technological means to block reception of programs at the individual home. This can be achieved through blocking a particular channel (Lockbox), blocking particular hours, or using a violence chip (the V-chip) that is inserted into the television set and allows blocking programs selectively.

Each of these strategies presents different challenges to the freedom of speech and at the same time does not offer a comprehensive solution to the complexity of the issues involved. Children view television at all hours of the day; labeling programs as violent may have the opposite effect of attracting them even more; rating and blocking programs is dependent on predetermined criteria enforced by others and not by the viewers themselves; the ratings that appear on printed television-programs' guides are not always comprehensible to parents; and the like.

Policy regarding television advertising
Advertising is a second very central concern of policy for broadcasting to children. Here, too, the American example stands out, as it relates to a highly commercialized television environment that serves as an example for other countries, as well. The Children's Television Act of 1990 limits the amount of time dedicated to commercials during children's hours: no more than 10.5 minutes per hour during the weekend and not more than 12 minutes per hour during weekdays. Programs that constitute a commercial in and of themselves are prohibited (such as program hosts promoting products during the show). Other requirements include banning of advertising presented by celebrities broadcast during their

own programs; and a requirement that advertisements must include disclaimers (such as: "assembly required;" "parts sold separately;" "batteries required"). All these regulations are directed at restricting the exploitive nature of advertising for young children who may find it difficult to understand the persuasive intent of advertising and assign it high credibility, as we have discussed in Chapter 2.

In an attempt to prevent legislative intervention, the Association of National Advertisers, Inc. (ANA) offered a substantive list of guidelines for advertisers for children, as long ago as 1972. These guidelines are of interest to us even though they have no legal force, are hardly applied, and cannot be enforced, because they acquaint us with what advertisers define for themselves as problematic issues in advertising for children. These guidelines can be divided into several areas of concern.[29] The first area is concerned with values contained in advertising. The ANA recommended, for example, that commercials should not present unacceptable behaviors from the point of view of social, legal, religious, institutional, or family values; should not present disrespect for parents and/or other authorities responsible for children; should not present bad habits; and avoid suggesting that ownership of a product will improve the child's social position, or that without it the child will be a target of ridicule or contempt.

Guidelines concerned with protecting children from exploitation include demands to avoid all attempts to exploit the fact that children experience difficulties in distinguishing between reality and fantasy; to strive to direct children's imagination toward healthy and productive growth; to guarantee that each component of the commercial – verbal, audio, and visual – as well as the commercial in its entirety do not deceive the children in regards to the functioning of the product (such as speed, size, color, durability, nutrition value, noise, and the like) or in regard to the perceived benefits (such as gaining power, popularity, growth, exper- tise, intelligence, and the like); to guarantee that the commercial will clearly explain what is included in the original purchase price, including clear statements regarding the items sold separately and for products that require assembly of parts needs to be stated so explicitly; to present products clearly; and demonstrations of how to use the product or the prize should be done in a way that the average target child would be able to model it.

Guidelines concerning the difficulties of young children to distinguish between commercials and programs demanded that no actors and char- acters from children's programs (real or animated) should be employed in commercials in order to encourage the selling of products, prizes, or services during, right before or after, a program in which that character appears; that actors and characters as above who are identified with a product could be employed only under the condition that they are not committing any misleading acts that are intended for imitation by children in regards to the product's or service's characteristics; and that national celebrities will only be employed when they are identified as having the authority to talk about the topic involved in the commercial, and only when they are considered credible.

Guidelines concerning pressuring parents prescribed that commercials should encourage children to consult their parents about purchasing the product rather than exerting pressure on them; should not approach children in regards to products that are not intended for them, and children should not be encouraged to purchase them; should present the products' prices clearly and without any pressure, and no use should be made of terminology suggesting a discounted price (e.g., the price is only so and so).

Finally, guidelines concerning the safety of children stated that with the exception of public announcement broadcasts, it is forbidden to present in commercials adults or children involved in unsafe activities, situations, or conditions of any kind; that commercials should avoid demonstration or presentation of any product in a way that encourages inappropriate use or use that exceeds accepted safety regulations.

Close study of these recommendations, as well as of many others that were not detailed here, demonstrates the breath of concerns regarding advertising for children. In practice, however, there is a huge gap between the official discourse of good intentions of the advertisers and their everyday practices.[30]

Policy regarding sponsorship of children's programs

The need for sponsorship of quality programming for children is a reality of a competitive commercial market and is a major concern for broadcasters, educators, and activists as one. It is often raised as a major topic discussed at international events, such as the World Summit on Media for Children. This organization brings together representatives of the television industry, public organizations, and scholars to discuss, among other issues, policy recommendations that will encourage quality programming, cultural diversity, and advances the possibility that children's voices will be heard.[31]

In the 1980s, Australia was among the first countries to recognize the importance of governmental support for educational broadcasting and several countries since then have followed suit. The frameworks offered for such sponsorship are varied: the establishment of independent funds for the production of quality programs for children; requiring advertisers and commercial broadcasters to allocate a certain percentage of their income to quality productions; government sponsorship; and private philanthropic funds.

Clearly, there are many outstanding television programs for children produced worldwide. The *Prix Jeunesse*, for example, an international gathering of hundreds of professionals from dozens of countries that takes place in Munich Germany every two years since 1964 as well as the Japan Prize in Tokyo since 1965 provide such market places and show cases of quality television for children and youth.[32] However, all persons involved agree that there is a huge need to secure a lot more funding for realizing the potential of television to improve the quality of children's lives.

Convention on Television Broadcasting for Children and Youth

Box 6.4 gives an example of a convention on television broadcasting for children and youth that is a result of a combined effort by academics and broadcasters in Israel – both public and private – who are concerned with the well being of children. Framed as the "Ten Commandments of Broadcasting" they specify 5 principles of "thou shalt do" and 5 principles of "thou shalt not do."

Box 6.4 Convention on Television Broadcasting for Children and Youth[33]

We are committed to the happiness and welfare of all the children from all social classes and sectors without distinction in regard to gender, ethnicity, or religion, as delineated in the UN Convention Regarding the Rights of Children and Youth ratified by the state of Israel.

In view of our understanding of the important role that the medium of television plays in shaping the spiritual, emotional, and behavioral lives of children and youth; and

In accordance with the basic laws, legislation, regulations, as well as, ethical codes that apply to the different broadcasting authorities; and

In view of our strong sense of responsibility for our roles as creators, producers, and broadcasters of television programs;

We have committed ourselves, collectively, as the representatives of those involved in the production and broadcast of programs for children and youth, in consultation with relevant members of the academic and educational communities, and in recognition of our right to preserve the distinctive uniqueness of each constituent organization, to this convention regarding television broadcasting.

In the spirit of this joint agreement, we proclaim that we shall act:

1   *To promote the presentation of a social world based upon humanitarian principles of human rights, tolerance towards difference, social justice, freedom of religion, conscience, and belief, the dignity and freedom of mankind, the authority of the law and the status of the court of justice, in the spirit of the basic values and laws of the State of Israel.*

    We shall act to promote the production of TV programs and the acquisition of foreign programs that profess this worldview and present it as desirable, conceivable, and positive embodiment of ideas.

    We shall act to promote, actively, programs that seek to develop social awareness in the fields of social justice, as well as, those that encourage social involvement and responsibility. Programs that deviate from the spirit of this commitment will be presented in a context that conveys a clearly critical message regarding negative projections broadcast to young viewers and society, in general.

2   *To promote presentation of a multicultural world in which the distinctive characteristics of local culture are valued along with trends in the creation of a global culture, while observing openness towards diversity and the expression of different opinions.*

    We shall act to promote the production of TV programs and the acquisition of foreign programs that represent a variety of cultural worlds that characterize the different ethnic, cultural, linguistic, and religious backgrounds that are present in Israeli society and beyond. We shall act to promote the production of original programs reflective of the society and contemporary affairs of Israel, as well as, to advance understanding of the heritage of the Jewish people over the generations and in all countries of the Diaspora.

    We shall provide for appropriate expressions of all facets of the Israeli society and the diverse groups that compose it as well as their culture, language, and heritage. We shall enable children and youth with the opportunity to become acquainted with the diversity of human life in regard to physical properties (such as color of the skin, pronunciation)

(continued)

and the cultural attributes (such as clothing, cultural and religious ceremonies, philosophy and art, etc).

3 *To advance addressing the specific needs of children and youth of different ages living under different circumstances.*

We shall act to promote the production of TV programs and the purchase of foreign programs that appropriately address the needs, abilities, and life experiences of children of different age groups and genders living under different cultural and social circumstances. We will relate to the mental and emotional needs that arise due to contemporary events. We shall devote special attention to populations whose alternatives for leisure activities are the most limited. We shall endeavor to help children and youth who suffer from psychological, cognitive, and physical handicaps.

4 *To assist children and youth to offer their own views and to enable them to present their views of the world on television.*

We shall act to promote the production of TV programs that enable children and youth from all sectors of the population with opportunities to express themselves, their worldviews, and relate to issues of concern to them, in the production process as well as during the broadcast. We shall listen to their voices respectfully and shall take note of their wishes, keeping in mind that at every stage of their development they are persons in their own right with their own views.

5 *To promote quality productions for children and youth characterized by investment, audio-visual richness, and by a high level of content that will enrich their aesthetic and creative world.*

We shall act to promote the production of television programs and acquisition of foreign programs that are rich in quality in every domain of production and genre: in their linguistic richness; presentation of appropriate and well-developed humor; high standards of acting or moderation; quality of musical performances, photography, and editing; as well as the profundity of ideas. We will take into account that, in spite of their young age, all audiences acquire their own cultural tastes and should be honored with programs of high production quality.

And, based upon such agreements, we shall act in order to:

6 *Refrain from presenting the world as a place of violence, cruelty, and inhumanity, as well as, one where violence is presented positively and as the only way to solve problems.*

We shall act to promote the production of TV programs and acquisition of foreign programs that lack violence, of any kind – physical, emotional and verbal, that is directed against people, other living creatures, nature, and property. In the event that acts of violence are present, as an integral part of the description of reality or an essential component in a plot that is deemed to be of value, we shall refrain from glorifying and presenting it humorously, as enjoyable, and inconsequential. We shall avoid the presentation of content that encourages destructive behavior and unnecessary physical risks.

7 *Refrain from overemphasizing or presenting sex and sexuality as a means of titillation or as an expression of a power relationship that involves the domination of others.*

We shall act to promote the production of TV programs and acquisition of foreign programs that contribute to the equality of the genders and presentation of human sexuality as a natural and worthy aspect of human relations, and not as a means for achieving objectives, domination, exploitation, and oppression. We shall avoid using sexuality as a means of titillating children and youth and attracting their attention. We shall refrain from presenting content that combines violence and sexuality as well as common stereotypes of femininity and masculinity.

8 *Refrain from a stereotypical presentation of groups according to their religious background, ethnicity, gender, as well as, physical attributes of age, disability, or appearance.*

We shall act to promote the production of TV programs and acquisition of foreign programs that present humanity with all its diversity, without use of stereotypes regarding difference and otherness of any kind whatsoever. We shall be particularly aware of stereotypes that portray central divisions within Israeli society. We shall refrain from presenting contents that may encourage physical and mental self-affliction.

9 *Refrain from presenting consumption and materialism as an ultimate value, as a means of self-satisfaction, or solving human problems.*

(continued)

We shall act to promote the production of TV programs and acquisition of foreign programs that abstain from presenting materialism and persistent consumerism as a way to cope with individual and social hardships, as a means of competition applied to advance personal aims, and as a manifestation for self-esteem. We shall abstain from making a connection between the possession of property and individual self-worth. We shall present the diversity of other resources that exist for use by the individual, such as education, family, friends, positive activity, and so forth.

10 *Refrain from exploitation of children and youth in the process of production and in TV programs proper.*

We shall relate to children and youth who participate in the production of programs or who appear in them in a variety of roles as we relate to mature adults – as persons with rights, their own will, and value. We shall insure appropriate working conditions, rest, food, and beverage. We shall honor the aspirations of employees and not exploit them. We shall not present them in programs in a way that might impair them or their reputation, even if their consent has been obtained. It is our duty to encourage them to consult with persons who fulfill a meaningful role in their lives and not to take advantage of their feelings in situations of weakness.

Notes

1 Chris and Potter (1998).
2 For discussions see Buckingham (1993), Hobbs (1998), Kubey (1998), Lewis and Jhally (1998), and Potter (2001).
3 Aufderheide (1997), Kubey (1998).
4 Based on Buckingham (1998).
5 Buckingham and Domaille (2003).
6 Based on Kubey (1998).
7 Based on Criticos (1997) and Prinsloo and Criticos (1991).
8 Lemish and Lemish (1997).
9 Tufte, Lavender, and Lemish (2003).
10 Based on Bazalgette (1989, p. 8) and Bowker (1991, p. 17).
11 Buckingham (1998).

12 Adopted from Bazalgette (1989).

13 Quin and McMahon (1993).

14 Singer, D.G. and Singer, J.L. (1998).

15 Vooijs, van der Voort, and Hoogeweij (1995).

16 Tidhar (1996).

17 Bazalgette (1997), Kubey (1998).

18 von Feilitzen and Bucht (2001), von Feilitzen and Carlsson (2003).

19 Lisosky (1997).

20 Alexander, Hoerrner and Duke (1998), Kunkel (1998).

21 Jordan and Woodward (1997).

22 The discussion is based slight modification of Lesser (1996).

23 Jordan and Woodward (1997), Kunkel (1998).

24 Lisosky (1997), Shipard (2003).

25 Ibid.

26 Aroldi (2003), Blumler (1992).

27 Ballard (1995).

28 Edwards and Berman (1995), Price (1998), Price and Verhulst (2002), Simpson (2004).

29 The original guidelines have been re-ordered and slightly reworded.

30 See also the Advertising Education Forum (AEF) website: www.aeforum.org

31 The first World Summit took place in Melbourne Australia in 1995, followed by London UK in 1998, Thessaloniki Greece 2001, and Rio de Janeiro Brazil 2004. As these lines are being written, the next is scheduled to take place in Johannesburg South Africa in 2007.

32 The *Prix Jeunesse* is sponsored by the Bavarian Broadcasting Corporation (BR) in Munich Germany (see Kleeman, 2001). The Japan Prize is organized by the Japan Broadcasting Corporation (NHK) in Tokyo Japan.

33 The Convention on Television Broadcasting for Children and Youth was signed in July 2002 by representatives of all Israeli broadcasters for children and youth, in the Israeli Knesset (Parliament). It was initiated by the Israel Educational Television and written by Lemish, Damari, Limor, and Segal.

7

Conclusion: Growing up in a Global Screen Culture

Throughout this book we have seen how television is integrated in children's everyday lives and the many roles it has in their families, as well as, in their social life and leisure activities. We reviewed television's interaction with children's development and its implications for three complementary realms of life: behavior, social construction of reality, and learning. All this led us to ask complicated questions regarding the consequences of this accumulated knowledge for education for media literacy, as well as, broadcasting policy for children. Many questions still remain open for further intellectual engagement, academic research, and civic activism.

Several major themes were interwoven throughout the book. We can summarize them in the following five principles:

Principle 1 *Age*: Age is a significant indicator of children's possible relationship with television, as it points to many of the changes that may take place within children as they grow up. Development of cognitive, emotional, and behavioral skills, as well as the accumulated everyday experience with both mediated and unmediated reality, all interact as the child grows, develops, and matures.

Principle 2 *Gender*: Understood to be a socially constructed set of identities and expectations, gender is a central predictor of the nature of much of children's relationships with television.

Principle 3 *Context*: The social and cultural contexts within which childhood is constructed and the individual child situated are crucial to our understanding of the complex roles television plays in children's lives.

Principle 4 *Content*: It is not the amount of television viewed alone that needs to be considered in attempting to evaluate the centrality of television in children's lives, but mainly the diverse forms and content offered by television worldwide.

Principle 5 *Potential*: Television is neither the childhood "messiah" nor its "devil," but rather a medium important in many peoples' lives that has great potential and a range of influential qualities, from good to bad.

Furthermore, we have demonstrated how in many countries around the world media activists and educators have sought to confront the consequences of children's viewing in two central ways: attempts to educate children, teachers, parents, and others to be literate and critical viewers; and attempts to supervise and control the broadcasts. Programs in media education, as well as specific broadcast policies, are a result of a variety of unique characteristics of each society, but all efforts and such struggles are anchored in the recognition that young viewers have complex relationships with the medium of television and it is adults' duty to pay attention to this medium as well as to all of the other central socializing agents. At the same time, many inherent conflicts are involved in intervention attempts: the conflict with such basic rights as freedom of speech; the tension between paternalistic and liberal approaches to child-rearing; tension between high and popular culture in the education of the young; lack of agreement on the appropriate balance between "knowledge" and "pleasure" involved in viewing; and the like. There is also a tendency by all involved to divert responsibility for children's media education and behavior: the school system places it on parents and broadcasters; parents claim that schools and broadcasters are responsible; and broadcasters argue that they are only responsible for presenting programs while schools and parents need to assist children to choose their own viewing preferences.

Globalized Screen Culture

Our discussion of television's role in children's lives would not be complete without locating it within the more general context of trends of globalization, changes in youth culture, and the implications of these processes for young viewers. The adoption of television, initially as a technology, is accompanied by introduction of an entire value system and political economy that are quite often foreign to the receiving country.[1] At the same time, television has also been among the interventions employed in nation building and cultural preservation. Do children live today in a global village á la McLuhan's vision? Children around the world are being entertained through popular television programs originating primarily in the USA or in other parts of the world, but diffused through a process coined "The Megaphone Effect."[2]

As a result, children all over the world sing similar pop tunes, wear similar clothing, and drink the same soft drinks. Can we argue that they are living in a shared global culture whose cultural values learned through a process that has been referred to as "McDonalization?" As a result, do they perceive the social world in similar ways? Is their local identity being erased? Are they evolving the same vision of themselves as consumers, individuals, and citizens of the world?

The academic debate on globalization as well as its economic and cultural characteristics is broad in scope and multi-disciplinary. Among the leading perspectives is one that suggests that globalization is a form of Western, ethnocentric, patronizing cultural imperialism that invades local cultures and lifestyles, deepens the insecurities of indigenous identities, and contributes to the erosion of national cultures and historical traditions. This definition of globalization focuses on the processes in which countries lose their independence, perhaps informally, through transnational powers in various dimensions of life: economics, culture, information, production, ecology, and the like. Media, and mostly television, are blamed for being the central mobilizers of these globalization processes, as they serve as a channel for transmitting Western worldviews, including values, cultural tastes, economic and political interests. In contrast to this process, or perhaps as a complementary force, there is the strengthening of the development of self-awareness of local sub-cultures that are striving for recognition and an opportunity to flourish, who demonstrate strong resistance to what they perceive to be a takeover by a super-power Western culture. The result of this tension is the process of glocalization, a combination of the global and the local. This is the process through which the consumption of global cultural products by local audiences that are embedded in specific cultural contexts creates the meanings that serve their needs.

What, then, are the expressions and implications of these processes on young viewers around the world? How do they struggle with cultural tension and what role do they assign themselves in this world? Although there is an abundance of theoretical writing on this topic, there are very few studies that actually offer empirical data that can shed some light on these questions. One such study that examined the leisure culture of children and youth in 12 European countries in the mid-1990s found that children used a variety of criteria to distinguish between local and imported programs.[3] For example, in Denmark and Israel, the use of subtitles marked programs as foreign, but children used other markers: Israeli children noticed the blond hair of the actors and actresses, unlike most of their own darkish colored hair; Danish children pointed out the quick editing style and special effects that characterize an American program; and French children related to the different skin color and eating habits of the Japanese animation series.[4] Chinese children, in another study, pointed out the educational quality of their national television programs in comparison to the entertaining markers of foreign ones.[5]

Interestingly, in this European study, children's identification of programs as foreign was not related to the degree of their viewing pleasure. Sometimes it was actually the contrary. Foreign programs, particularly those imported from the USA, were often identified as those of higher quality, more original, "cooler." Their own local programs were often perceived as less professional, with bad acting, and even as less realistic. For example, local soap operas were criticized for being non-realistic, while the popular American ones at the time (e.g., *Beverly Hills*; *Bay Watch*) were evaluated as more realistic. One possible explanation, already suggested, is that the perception of "realism" is, among others, a result of a critical view that emerges from the degree of familiarity with the world presented in the program. When this world is more familiar to viewers (e.g., their own local soap opera), they are more capable of comparing it to their own reality and, therefore, to identify more easily the constructed and unreal nature of television. However, when this world is more distant (e.g., imported soap-operas), familiarity with it is almost solely based on previous television encounters, so children are less able to look at it critically.

An additional aspect that surfaced in the European study related to the feeling of a "utopian common world" that was created as a result of the global culture. Popular television content, for example, is that which centers on universal interests such as interpersonal relationships, feelings, and interpersonal struggles. These children were not concerned with where the program originated, but rather that it dealt with humanity. The researchers impression was that television offered children a symbolic sphere of a common world populated by people and relationships that are disconnected from defined contexts and cultural borders. It seemed to connect children to an illusion of a social universal "center," similar to the interest of children and young adolescents in science fiction and magic programs that relate to a "different" world, to which all belong.

The creation of a hybrid culture, that is, a culture that is a combination of different cultural characteristics, was an additional aspect of this struggle between the local and global. Popular music, such as that offered on MTV and other music channels, is an illustration of this trend. Many children worldwide seem to prefer foreign music, particularly American and English pop and rock music – that symbolize for them innovativeness and style, even if the English lyrics are incomprehensible (as is often the case for the younger viewers).

Thus, the words are of secondary significance in comparison to the "English sound" of the songs. Popular local bands are often an imitation of that style. However, at the same time, children also express a strong attraction to their local ethnic music. Children demonstrate a preference for a variety of musical styles simultaneously without any sign of uneasiness or internal contradiction.

Interestingly, the older children are, the more they seem to be attracted to global culture, as expressed in programs originating in the USA. Globalization also seems to be associated with socio-economic status, with mastery of the English language, and preference for American content characteristic of the higher classes.

Globalization, so it seems, is not a matter of oppositions for young viewers: it is not globalization in contrast with localization, internalization in contrast with nationality, universalism in contrast with particularism; but, rather, globalization is integrated within the specific location of the child in the world at large. We may conclude that the two processes live side by side: on the one hand, adoption of a global perception of social life, while at the same time also the existence of multiculturalism, even hybrid cultures, in the lives of children. The meeting between the global and local is a meeting of integration and co-existence, and not a choice between two contradictory options. It's a dialectic process of "push and pull" between the two poles.

But the media-landscape is a constantly changing one. It is impossible today to discuss television and its place in children's lives in complete isolation from current debates about other media, particularly the computer and the Internet. "Screen culture," shared by all, is active and interactive, as well as developing through the screens of television, computers, movie theaters, mobile-phones, game consoles, and many other technologies that are developing at a much faster pace than the printing of this book. This culture offers children an integrated reality with subjects, celebrities, and social environments existing in various media worlds that are enjoyed by children as they integrate them in their everyday routines.

In the yet to be foreseen future, academic, educational, and policy efforts may become engaged with new concerns given the new trends of "open skies," growth of global commercial corporations, and expanding viewing alternatives available to children, as well as the development of convergence of television, computers, and mobile phones; the growing possibilities for interactive usage; and the improvement of reception qualities. As the ability to control content available to children becomes more restricted, so demands to empower the viewers themselves as critical consumers of the media and the expectation for self-regulation by producers and broadcasters become more urgent.

The Changing of Childhood

One of the central aspects of the discussion of the processes of globalization in regards with the construction of reality and youth culture focuses on the concept of "disappearance of childhood," inspired by technological determinists.[6] The disappearance of childhood, or at least the shortening of this period (and more critical writers would say – the changing of its nature) is suggested to be a process stimulated by television's central role in children's lives. "Childhood," as a social construction, according to this perspective, is a by-product of the print era and the gradual need to separate children from the world of adults in order to prepare them to function in a book-culture world based on reading and writing skills at its center. Before the invention of print in the fifteenth century followed by the gradual development of modern Western enlightenment, children were not perceived as a unique group of people deserving special attention. They were regarded as physically "small" people who had no specific needs or rights of their own. The development of print culture brought with it the institution of the school, among other things, and the growing interest in children, in the need to legally protect them (for example, by setting laws in many – but not all – countries, that protect children from labor and sexual exploitation, and setting mandatory education), and the formation of professional fields of expertise that are related to the education of children, their health, their mental and cognitive development, culture, fashion, and the like. According to this view, the twentieth century represents the golden age of the recognition and protection of childhood in this sense.

However, according to this approach (which is highly Western-centric), media, and television in particular, gradually eroded this protection. Through television, as we have already discussed, children are exposed to the world of adults that was largely concealed from them in earlier modern times for the purpose of protecting them from sensitive domains of life, for which they were perceived to be too immature to handle: death and disasters, physical and mental sicknesses, sexual intimacy, and the like. However, all these realities have been exposed to them on the television screen: sexual acts, blown up bodies, atrocities, and hunger – all have become accessible to children with the push of a button. No more a world that is unveiled gradually as children grow up, but a world without protective walls. Accordingly, the medium of television and its content deprive children of a naive childhood and the gradual process necessary for healthy mental development. Furthermore, this approach also argues that the television world that exposes adults at their weaknesses – meanness, intrigues, crime, injustices, dangers, insecurities – undermines parental authority and the basic trust in adults as knowledgeable and responsible people who can guard children from harm. As a result, so goes the argument, children are growing up with distrust, hopelessness, and absence of borders. The social knowledge that children acquire from hours of watching television, as well as, the values and perspectives they internalize, are frequently in contradiction with the ideals and myths that traditional socializing systems seek to cultivate. The disappearance of childhood is, thus, a threat not only to children and the construction of childhood as a period of life, but also to human society as a whole.

The glorification of youth culture that television advances also encourages children to rush into adolescence and adults to toil at preserving their youth, according to this perspective. Both groups try to belong to that seemingly "ideal" age, the age of attractiveness and adventures, age of sexual blossoming and romance, the age when the interesting life-stories supposedly happen – the age of youth. This is not necessarily an age defined by a specific counting of years, but rather it is an abstract concept. The attempt at blurring those different periods of life can be observed through fashion, musical tastes, and forms of leisure, speech styles, as well as preferences for television programs. The focus on this age period in the life cycle at the expense of the period of adulthood characterized by maturity, life experience, accumulated knowledge, and wisdom is also typical of much of television content.

The "disappearance of childhood" hypothesis has received a great amount of public and academic exposure accompanied by lively debates. Many find its commonsense approach appealing due to being similar to their own experiences. However, others argue that external attempts to imitate adults through clothing styles or behaviors are not necessarily an indication of serious psychological changes. At the same time, the fact that adults wear T-shirts with favorite cartoon figures is no proof that they are indeed childish or that they do not apply their many years of experience in their own handlings of their life affairs. Furthermore, there is no evidence that heavy exposure to television fundamentally transforms processes such as childish egocentrism or the ability to distinguish between reality and fantasy. Neither is there evidence that heavy viewers are more emotionally mature than lighter viewers due to their accumulated exposure to the adults' world.

A different line of critique suggests that even before the television era children found ways to "peek" into adults' worlds of secrets, through eavesdropping on conversations, following older siblings, reading adult books, and the like. Furthermore, the assumption that children are better off staying ignorant about the physical and emotional world of adults, too, is debatable. Perhaps it is better for children and healthy emotional development to challenge adults' monopoly of knowledge. Children in all societies and throughout history were always smaller, weaker, less developed, and less experienced than adults, regardless of whether they lived with or without television. Further, as children have grown, changed, and developed they have always required care and supervision, with or without television.

A Research Agenda

Interestingly enough, we know very little about how children feel about this hypothesis, and a growing number of researchers are now advocating the need to allow young viewers to express their own voices; that is, to listen closely to the views of the subjects they study. This recommendation has both theoretical and methodological implications. Accordingly, we need not only examine children's perceptions and analyze them in comparison with our adult values and assumptions as well as criteria of right or wrong. Rather, children have their own experiences and perspectives and we need to hear their point of view, stated in their own words, without assuming a judgmental stance. The aspiration of this kind of research is not to study THE children, but to study WITH them and FOR them. At the same time, it does not mean that children's perspectives should be accepted uncritically, but rather they need to be interpreted critically.

Thus, the dynamic discussion of the meaning of "childhood" continues with the growing concern for children's rights and the claim that each child should be perceived as a creative and autonomous person in his and her own right, as one entitled to voice their own perspective – whatever the stage of development. Concomitantly, media are expected to bolster the process of children and youth's empowerment in the third millennium by providing them with access and production skills. Accordingly, the expectation is that children throughout the world are becoming active creators, as well as, consumers of screen culture.

Research, too, is adopting changing technologies and public agenda that follows suit. Intrigued by the forces of globalization, many researchers are engaged in multinational projects examining children's culture around the world. Studies of the unprecedented commercial success of the *Pokémon* phenomenon in various countries (with its television series, movies, computer games, cards, toys, and ancillary products) are one such an example.[7] The global audiences study of the

Disney culture phenomenon that has dominated children's culture for many decades (with its movies, theme parks, and blooming industry of related products) is another impressive effort at examining the similarities and differences in the reception of media products worldwide.[8]

At the same time, another line of research is taking the opposite direction, investigating in depth in an attempt to make sense of individual children's everyday life experiences through small-case ethnographic studies that facilitate the possibility of giving voice to children. Such is the study of a handful of adolescents in the urban east coast of the USA who shared their everyday learning experiences while growing up with television[9]

Box 7.1 The Children's Television Charter of the World Summit on Media for Children[10]

1 Children should have programs of high quality that are produced specifically for them, and that do not exploit them. In addition to entertaining, these programs should allow children to develop physically, mentally, and socially to their fullest potential.

2 Children should hear, see, and express themselves, their culture, their language, and their life experiences, through television programs that affirm their sense of self, community, and place.

3 Children's programs should promote awareness and appreciation of other cultures in parallel with the child's own cultural background.

4 Children's programs should be wide-ranging in genre and content, but should not include gratuitous scenes of violence and sex.

5 Children's programs should be aired in regular slots, at times when children are available to view and/or distributed via other widely accessible media and technologies.

6 Sufficient funds must be made available to make programs that are of the highest possible standards.

7 Governments as well as production, distribution and funding organizations should recognize both the importance and vulnerability of indigenous children's television and take steps to support and protect it as well as promoting children's programs in minority languages and/or dialects.

Between these two ends of a research continuum, there are many more studies taking place using a variety of methodologies – experiments, surveys, focus groups, interviews, observations, employment of art work – all of them conducted in the hope of enriching our understanding of what it means to grow up today in a technologically saturated environment. Box 7.1 presents the Children's Television Charter of the World Summit on Media for Children, which has been used in a variety of ways to influence funding and broadcasting policy.

We can conclude, therefore, that the many current changes taking place in the screen culture combined with the changing construction of childhood present us with many challenges in a variety of areas: academic, moral, educational, cultural, political and the like. We will continue to face them not only as students and researchers of media, but also as parents and citizens concerned with the well being of our children worldwide.

Notes

1 For a discussion of such issues see von Feilitzen and Carlsson (2002). Also, read about local experiences, such as Agrawal, Karnik, Lal, and Vishwanath (1999), and Goonasekera, Chung Zhu, Eashwer et al. (2000).
2 Bloch and Lemish (2003).
3 Livingstone and Bovill (2001).
4 Lemish, Drotner, Liebes, Maigret, and Stald (1998).
5 Hemelryk (2005).
6 Meyrowitz (1985), Postman (1982).
7 Tobin (2004).
8 Wasko, Phillips, and Meehan (2001).
9 Fisherkeller (2002).
10 Online at: http://www.childrensmediasummit.com. The charter was presented by Anna Home at the First World Summit in 1995 and initially endorsed by signatories in 38 countries. It was later revised and further amended at the Second World Summit. Its objectives have been included in other declarations as well.

Recommended Sources for Additional Readings

Books

Berry, G.L. and Asamen, J.K. (eds) (1993) *Children and television in a changing socio-cultural world.* Newbury Park, CA: Sage

Buckingham, D. (1993) *Children talking television.* London: Falmer.

Buckingham, D. (2000) *After the death of childhood: Growing up in the age of electronic media.* Cambridge: Polity.

Calvert, S.L., Jordan, A.B., and Cooking, R.R. (2002) *Children in the digital age: Influences of electronic media on development.* Westport, CT: Greenwood.

Comstock, G. (1991) *Television and the American child.* New York: Academic Press.

Drotner, K. and Livingstone, S. (eds) (forthcoming) *International Handbook of Children, Media and Culture.* Thousand Oaks, CA: Sage.

Fisch, S. (2004) *Children's learning from educational television: Sesame Street and beyond.* Mahwa, NJ: Lawrence Erlbaum.

Fisherkeller, J. (2002) *Growing up with television: Everyday learning among young adolescents.* Philadelphia, PA: Temple University Press.

Gunter, B. and McAleer, J. (1997) *Children and television.* Routledge: London.

Kinder, M. (ed.) (1999) *Kids' media culture.* Durham, NC: Duke University Press.

Livingstone, S. (2002) *Young people and new media.* Thousand Oaks, CA: Sage.

Livingstone, S. and Bovill, M. (eds) (2001) *Children and their changing media environment: A European comparative study.* Mahwah, NJ: Lawrence Erlbaum.

MacBeth, T.M. (ed.) (1996) *Tuning in to young viewers: Social science perspectives on television.* Thousand Oaks, CA: Sage.

Mazzarella, S.R. (ed.) (forthcoming) *20 Questions about youth and the media.* New York: Peter Lang.

Pecora, N., Murray, J.O., and Wartella, E. (eds) (2006) *Children and television: 50 years of research.* Mahwah, NJ: Lawrence Erlbaum.

Postman, N. (1982) *The disappearance of childhood.* NY: Vintage Books.

Roberts, D.F. and Foehr, U.C. (2004) *Kids and media in America.* Cambridge, MA Cambridge University Press.

Singer, D.G. and Singer, J.L. (eds) (2001) *Handbook of children and the media.* Thousand Oaks, CA: Sage.

Strasburger, V.C. and Wilson, B.J. (2002) *Children, adolescents, and the media.* Thousand Oaks, CA: Sage.

Valkenburg, P.M. (2004) *Children's responses to the screen: A media psychological approach.* Mahwah, NJ: Lawrence Erlbaum.

Van Evra, J. (2004) *Television and child development* (3rd edn). Mahwah, NJ: Lawrence Erlbaum.

Zillman, D., Bryant, J., and Huston, A.C. (eds) (1994) *Media, children, and the family: Social scientific, psychodynamic and clinical perspectives.* Hillsdale, NJ: Lawrence Erlbaum.

Websites

International Center Institute for Youth and Educational Television (IZI), of the Bavarian Broadcasting Corporation: http://www.izi-datenbank.de/en/

Media Education at the UNESCO Moscow Office: http://www.unesco.ru/eng/pages/bythemes/stasya29062005124316.php

The International Clearinghouse on Children, Youth and Media: http://www.nordicom.gu.se/clearinghouse.php

World Summit on Media for Children: http://www.childrensmediasummit.com

References

Abelman, B. (1995) *Reclaiming the wasteland: TV and gifted children.* Cresskill, NJ: Hampton.

Adler, R.P., Friedlander, B.Z., Lesser, G.S., Meringoff, L., Robertson, T.S., Rossiter, J.R., and Ward, S. (1980) *Research on the effects of television advertising on children: A review of the literature and recommendation for future research.* Washington, DC: US Government Printing Office.

Adoni, H. (1979) The functions of mass media in the political socialization of adolescents. *Communication Research,* 6(1), 84–106.

Advertising Education Forum (AEF) website www.aeforum.org

Agrawal, B.C., Karnik, K.S., Lal, C., and Vishwanath, K. (1999) *Children's television in India: A situational analysis.* New Delhi: Conceptual Publishing Company.

Alexander, A., Hoerrner, K., and Duke, L. (1998) What is quality children's television? *The Annals,* 557(May), 70–82.

Alexander, A., Sallayanne Rayan, M., and Munoz, P. (1984) Creating a learning context: investigations on the interaction of siblings during television viewing. *Critical Studies in Mass Communication,* 1(4), 358, 446–53.

Anderson, D. and Lorch, E.P. (1983) Looking at television: Action or reaction? In Bryant, J. and Anderson, D.R. (eds), *Children's understanding of television: Research on attention and comprehension* (pp. 1–33). New York: Academic Press.

Anderson, D.R. and Field, D.E. (1986) Children's attention to television: Implications for production. In Meyer, M. (ed.), *Children and the formal features of television* (pp. 56–96). Munich: K.G. Saur.

Anderson, D.R. and Pempek, T.A. (2005) Television and very young children. *American Behavioral Scientist,* 48(5), 505–22.

Anderson, R.E., Crespo, C.J., Barlett, S.J., Cheskin, L.J., and Pratt, M. (1998) Relationship of physical activity and television watching with body weight and level of fatness among children: Results from the Third National Health and Nutrition Examination Survey. *JAMA – Journal of the American Medical Association,* 279, 938–42.

Andreason, M.S. (2001) Evaluation in the family's use of television: An overview. In Bryant, J. and Bryant, J.A. (eds), *Television and the American family second edition* (pp. 3–30). Hillsdale, NJ: Lawrence Erlbaum.

Ang, I. (1985) *Watching Dallas: Soap opera and the melodramatic imagination.* London: Methuen.

Aitken, P., Aitken, P.P., Eadie, D.R., Leathar, D.S., McNeill, R.E.J., and Scott, A.C. (1988) Television advertisements for alcoholic drinks do reinforce under-age drinking. *British Journal of Addiction,* 83(12), 1399–419.

Aroldi, P. (2003) Television and protection of minors in some European countries: A comparative study. In von Feilitzen, C. and Carlsson, U. (eds), *Promote or protect? Perspectives on media literacy and media regulations* (pp. 179–95). Göteborg University, Sweden: The International Clearinghouse on Children, Youth and Media.

Atkin, C.K. (1980). Effects of television advertising on children. In Palmer, E.L. and Dorr, A. (eds), *Children and the faces of television: Teaching, violence, selling* (pp. 287–305). New York: Academic Press.

Atkin, C.K. (1990) Effects of televised alcohol messages on teenage drinking patterns. *Journal of Adolescent Health Care,* 11(1), 10–24.

Atkin, C., Greenberg, B., and McDermott, S. (1979) Television and race role socialization. *Journalism Quarterly,* 60(30), 407–14.

Atkin, C.K., Hocking, J., and Block, M. (1984) Teenage drinking: Does advertising make a difference? *Journal of Communication,* 34(2), 157–67.

Aufderheide, P. (1997) Media literacy: From a report of the national leadership conference on media literacy. In Kubey, R. (ed.), *Media literacy in the information age* (pp. 79–86). New Brunswick, NJ: Transaction Publishers.

Bachen, C.M. and Illouz, E. (1996) Imagining romance: Young people's cultural models of romance and love. *Critical Studies in Mass Communication,* 13(4), 279–308.

Ballard, I.M. (1995) See no evil, hear no evil: Television violence and the first amendment. *Virginia Law Review,* 81, 175–85.

Bandura, A. (1965) Influence of models' reinforcement contingencies on the acquisition of imitative responses. *Journal of Personality and Social Psychology,* 1, 589–95.

Bandura, A., Ross, D., and Ross, S.A. (1963) Imitation of aggression through imitation of film-mediated aggressive models. *Journal of Abnormal and Social Psychology,* 67, 601–7.

Baran, S.J. (1976) Sex on TV and adolescent sexual self-image. *Journal of Broadcasting,* 20(1), 61–74.

Barky, S.L. (1988) Foucault, femininity, and the modernization of patriarchal power. In Diamond, I. (ed.), *Feminism and Foucault* (pp. 61–86). Boston, MA: Northeastern University Press.

Barner, M.R. (1999) Sex-role stereotyping in FCC-mandated children's educational television. *Journal of Broadcasting and Electronic Media,* 43(4), 551–64;

Bazalgette, C. (ed.) (1989) *Primary media education: A curriculum statement.* London: British Film Institute.

Bazalgette, C. (1997) An agenda for the second phase of media literacy development. In Kubey, R. (ed.), *Media literacy in the information age* (pp. 15–68). New Brunswick, NJ: Transaction Publishers.

Berry, G.L. and Asamen, J.K. (1993) *Children and television: Images in a changing sociocultural world*. Newbury Park, CA: Sage.

Bickham, D.S., Wright, J., and Huston, A.C. (2001) Attention, comprehension, and the educational influences of television. In Singer, D.G. and Singer, J.L. (eds), *Handbook of children and the media* (pp. 101–19). Thousand Oaks, CA: Sage.

Bloch, L-R. and Lemish, D. (2003) The Megaphone Effect: The international diffusion of cultural media via the USA. In Kalbefleisch, P.J. (ed.), *Communication Yearbook 27* (pp. 159–90). Mahwah, NJ: Lawrence Erlbaum.

Blosser, B. (1988) Television, reading and oral language development: The case of the Hispanic child. *NAEB Journal*, 21–42.

Blumler, J.G. (1992) *Television and the public interest: Vulnerable values in West European broadcasting*. London: Sage.

Borzekowski, D.L.G. and Robinson, T.N. (2001) The 30-second effect: An experiment revealing the impact of television commercials on food preferences of preschoolers. *Journal of the American Dietetic Association*, 101(1), 42–6.

Borzekowski, D.L.G. and Robinson, T.N. (2005) The remote, the mouse, and the No. 2 pencil: The household media environment and academic achievement among third grade students, *Archives Pediatrics and Adolescent Medicine*, 159, 607–13.

Botta, R.A. (1999) Television images and adolescent girls' body image disturbance. *Journal of Communication*, 49(2), 22–41.

Bowker, J. (ed.) (1991) *Secondary media education: A curriculum statement*. London: The British Film Institute.

Brenick, A., Lee-Kim, J., Killen, M., Fox, N., Raviv, A., and Leavitt, L (forthcoming) Social judgments in Israeli and Arabic children: Findings from media-based intervention projects. In Lemish D. and Götz, M. (eds), *Children and media at times of war and conflict*. Cresskill, NJ: Hampton.

Brown, J.D. and Newcomber, S.F. (1991) Television viewing and adolescents' sexual behavior. In Wolf, M. and Kielswasser, A. (eds), *Gay people, sex and the media* (pp. 77–91). New York: The Haworth Press.

Browne, B.A. (1998) Gender stereotypes in advertising on children's television in the 1990s: A cross-national analysis. *Journal of advertising*, 27(1), 83–96.

Buckingham, D. (1993) *Children talking television*. London: Falmer.

Buckingham, D. (1998) Media education in the UK: Moving beyond protectionism. *Journal of Communication*, 48(1), 33–43.

Buckingham, D. (2000) *The making of citizens: Young people, news and politics*. London: Routledge.

Buckingham, D. and Bragg, S. (2004) *Young people, sex and the media: The facts of life?* New York: Palgrave Macmillan.

Buckingham, D. and Domaille, K. (2003) Where are we going and how can we get there? General findings from the UNESCO Youth Media Education

Survey 2001. In von Feilitzen, C. and Carlsson, U. (eds), *Promote or protect? Perspectives on media literacy and media regulations* (pp. 41–54). Göteborg University: The International Clearinghouse on Children, Youth and Media.

Buerkel-Rothfuss, N.L. and Buerkel, R.A. (2001) Family mediation. In Bryant, J. and Bryant, J.A. (eds), *Television and the American family* (2nd edn) (pp. 355–76). Hillsdale, NJ: Lawrence Erlbaum.

Buerkel-Rothfuss, N.L. and Strouse, J.S. (1993) Media exposure and perceptions of sexual behaviors: The cultivation hypothesis moves to the bedroom. In Greenberg, B.S., Brown, J.D., and Buerkel-Rothfuss, N.L. (eds), *Media, sex and the adolescent* (pp. 225–47). Cresskill, NJ: Hampton.

Bushman, B.J. and Huesmann, L.R. (2001) Effects of televised violence on aggression. In Singer, D.G. and Singer, J.L. (eds), *Handbook of children and the media* (pp. 223–54). Thousand Oaks, CA: Sage.

Calvert, S.L. and Huston, A.C. (1987) Television and children's gender schemata. In Liben, L. and Signorella, M. (eds), *Children's gender schemata: Origins and implications: New directions in child development* (38, 75–88). San Francisco: Jossey-Bass.

Cantor, J. (1994) Confronting children's fright responses to mass media. In Zillman, D., Bryant, J., and Huston, A.C. (eds), *Media, children and the family: Social scientific, psychodynamic and clinical perspectives* (pp. 87–116). Thousand Oaks, CA: Sage.

Cantor, J. (1996) Television and children's fear. In MacBeth, T. (ed.), *Tuning in to young viewers: Social science perspectives on television* (pp. 87–115). Thousand Oaks, CA: Sage.

Cantor, J. (2001) The media and children's fears, anxieties, and perceptions of danger. In Singer, D.G. and Singer, J.L. (eds), *Handbook of children and the media* (pp. 207–221). Thousand Oaks, CA: Sage.

Cantor, J. (2002) Fright reactions to mass media. In Bryant, J. and Zillmann, D. (eds), *Media effects: Advances in theory and research* (pp. 287-306). Mahwah, NJ: Lawrence Erlbaum;

Cantor, J., Mares, M.L., and Oliver, M.B. (1993). Parents and children's emotional reactions to TV coverage of the Gulf War. In Greenberg, B.S. and Gantz, W. (eds), *Desert Storm and the mass media* (pp. 325–40). Cresskill, NJ: Hampton.

Carlsson, U. and von Feilitzen C. (eds) (1998) *Children and media violence.* Göteborg University: The UNESCO International Clearinghouse on Children and Violence on the Screen.

Carter, C. and Steiner, L. (2004) *Critical readings: Media and gender.* Maidenhead, England: Open University Press.

Chaffee, S.H. and McLeod, J.M. (1972) Adolescent television use in the family context. In Comstock, G.A. and Rubinstein, E.A. (eds), *Television and social behavior* (vol. 13, pp. 149–72). Washington, DC: U.S. Government Printing Office.

Chaffee, S.H. and Yang, S-M. (1990) Communication and political socialization. In Ichilov, O. (ed.), *Political socialization, citizenship education and democracy* (pp. 37–157). New York: Teachers College Press.

Chafee, S.H., McLeod, J.M., and Wackman, D. (1973) Family communication patterns and adolescent political participation. In Dennis, J. (ed.), *Socialization to politics: A reader* (pp. 349–64). New York: Wiley.

Chandler, D. (1997) Children's understanding of what is 'real' on television: A review of the literature. *Journal of educational Media*, 22(1), 65–80;

Chris, W.G. and Potter, J. (1998) Media literacy, media education, and the academy. *Journal of Communication*, 48(1), 5–15.

Christakis, D.A., Zimmerman, F.J., DiGiuseppe, D.L., and McCarthy, C.A. (2004) Early television exposure and subsequent attentional problems in children. *Pediatrics*, 133(4), 708–13.

Clark, R.E. (1983) Reconsidering research on learning from media. *Review of Educational Research*, 53(4), 445–59.

Cline, V.B. (1994) Pornography effects: Empirical and clinical evidence. In Zillman, D., Bryant, J., and Huston, A.C. (eds), *Media, children and the family: Social scientific, psychodynamic and clinical perspectives* (pp. 229–47). Hillsdale, NJ: Lawrence Erlbaum.

Cohen, A.A. and Salomon, G. (1979) Children's literate television viewing: Surprises and possible explanations. *Journal of Communication*, 29(3), 156–63.

Cole, C., Arafat, C, Tidhar, C., Zidan, W.T., Fox, N., Killen, M., et al. (2003) "So they will be friends": The educational Impact of Rechov Sumsum/ Shara'a Simsim, A Sesame Street television series to promote respect and understanding among children living in Israel, the West Bank, and Gaza. *International Journal of Behavioral Development*, 27(5), 409–22.

Cole, C.F., Richman, B.A., and McCann Brown, S.K. (2001) The world of *Sesame Street* research. In Fisch, S.M. and Truglio, R.T. (eds) *"G" is for growing: Thirty years of research on children and Sesame Street* (pp. 147-79). Mahwah, NJ: Lawrence Erlbaum.

Collins, W.A. (1981) Schemata for understanding television. In Kelly, H. and Gardner, H. (eds), *Viewing children through television: New directions for child development* (vol. 13, pp. 31-45). San Francisco, CA: Jossey-Bass.

Collins, W.A. (1983) Interpretation and inference in children's television viewing. In Bryant, J. and Anderson, D.R. (eds), *Children's understanding of television: Research on attention and comprehension* (pp. 125–50). New York: Academic Press.

Collins, W.A. and Wellman, H.M. (1982) Social scripts and developmental patterns in comprehension of televised narratives. *Communication Research*, 9(3), 380–98.

Collins, W.A., Sobol, B.L., and Westby, S. (1981) Effects of adult commentary on children's comprehension and inferences about a televised aggressive portrayal. *Child Development*, 52, 158–63.

Comstock, G. (1991) *Television and the American child.* New York: Academic Press.

Coon, K.A., Goldberg, J., Rogers, B.L., and Tucker, K.L. (2001) Relationships between use of television during meals and children's food consumption patterns. *Pediatrics*, 107(1), e7.

Cortés, C.E. (2000) *The children are watching: How the media teach about diversity.* New York: Teachers College, Columbia University.

Criticos, C. (1997) Media education for a critical citizenry in South Africa. In Kubey, R. (ed.), *Media literacy in the information age* (pp. 229–40). New Brunswick, NJ: Transaction.

Currie, D. H. (1997) Decoding femininity: Advertisements and their teenage readers. *Gender and Society,* 11(4), 453–77.

Das, U. (1999) What does America symbolize to the urban, educated youth in India? In Kamalipour, Y.R. (ed.), *Images of the U.S. around the world: A multicultural perspective* (pp. 209–20). New York: State University of New York Press.

De Beauvoir, S. (1989[1952]) *The second sex.* New York: Vintage Books.

Deitz, W. H. (1990) You are what you eat – what you eat is what you are. *Journal of Adolescent Health Care,* 11(1), 76–81.

Ditsworth, D. (2001) The portrayal of gender in the children's program *Sesame Street* and its effect on the intended audience. *New Jersey Journal of Communication,* 9(2), 214–26.

Dobrow, J.R. and Gidney, C.L. (1998) The good, the bad, and the foreign: The use of dialect in children's animated television. *Annals of the American Academy of Political and Social Sciences,* 557, 105–19.

Donnerstein, E., Slaby, R., and Eron, L. (1994) The mass media and youth violence. In Murray, J., Rubinstein, E., and Comstock, G. (eds), *Violence and youth: Psychology's response 2* (pp. 219–50). Washington, DC: American Psychological Association.

Dorr, A. (1983) No shortcuts to judging reality. In Bryant, J. and Anderson, D.R. (eds), *Children's understanding of television: Research on attention and comprehension* (pp. 190–220). New York: Academic Press.

Dorr, A., Kovaric, P., and Doubleday, C. (1990) Age and content influences on children's perceptions of the realism of television families. *Journal of Broadcasting and Electronic Media,* 34(4), 377–96.

Douglas, S. (1994) *Where the girls are: Growing up female with the mass media.* New York: Penguin Books.

Drabman, R., Robertson, S., Patterson, J., Jarvie, G., Hammer, D., and Cordua, G. (1981) Children's perceptions of media-portrayed sex- roles. *Sex Roles,* 7, 379–89.

Durham, M.G. (2004) Constructing the "New ethnicities": Media, sexuality and diaspora identity in the lives of South Asian immigrant girls. *Critical Studies in Media Communication,* 21 (2), 140–61.

Durkin, K. (1985) *Television, sex roles and children: A developmental social psychological account.* Philadelphia, PA: Open University Press.

Durkin, K. and Low, J. (1998) Children, media and aggression. In Carlsson, U. and von Feilitzen, C. (eds), *Children and media violence* (pp. 107–24). Götteborg University, Sweden: The International Clearinghouse on Children, Youth and Media.

Dyson, A. H. (1997) *Writing superheroes: Contemporary childhood.* New York: Columbia University, Teachers College Press.

Edwards, H.T. and Berman, M.N. (1995) Regulating violence on television. *Northwestern University Law Review*, 89(4), 1487–566.

Elias, N. and Lemish, D. (under review) The roles of mass media in the lives of immigrant children and adolescents: A case of immigrants from the Former Soviet Union in Israel and Germany.

First, A. (1997) Television and the construction of social reality: An Israeli case study. In McCombs, M.E., Shaw, D.L., and Weaver, D. (eds), *Communication and democracy* (pp. 41–50). Hillsdale, NJ: Lawrence Erlbaum.

Fisch, S. (2004) *Children's learning from educational television: Sesame Street and beyond.* Mahwah, NJ: Lawrence Erlbaum.

Fisch, S.M. (forthcoming) Using television to promote respect and understanding: Impact of past projects and implications for the future. In Cole, C. and Lesser, G.S. (eds), *Begin with children.* Mahwah, NJ: Lawrence Erlbaum.

Fisch, S.M. and Truglio, R.T. (eds) (2001) *"G" is for growing: Thirty years of research on children and Sesame Street.* Mahwah, NJ: Lawrence Erlbaum.

Fisherkeller, J. (2002) *Growing up with television: Everyday learning among young adolescents.* Philadelphia, PA: Temple University Press.

Fiske, J. (1989) *Understanding popular culture.* Boston: Unwin Hyman.

Fitch, M., Huston, A.C., and Wright, J.C. (1993) From television forms to genre schemata: Children's perceptions of television reality. In Berry, G.L. and Asamen, J.K. (eds), *Children and television in a changing socio-cultural world* (pp. 38–52). Newbury Park, CA: Sage.

Frazer, E. (1987) Teenage girls reading *Jackie. Media, Culture, and Society,* 9, 407–25.

Frueh, T. and McGhee, P.E. (1975) Traditional sex role development and amount of time spent watching television. *Developmental Psychology,* 11(1), xx- 109.

Fujioka, Y. (1999) Television portrayals and African American stereotypes: Examination of television effects when direct contact is lacking. *Journal of Mass Communication Quarterly,* 76(1), 52–75.

Gerbner, G., and Gross, L. (1976) Living with television: The violence profile. *Journal of Communication,* 26(2), 172–99.

Gillespie, M. (1995) *Television, ethnicity and cultural change.* London: Routledge.

Gilligan, C. (1982) *In a different voice: Psychological theory and women's development.* Cambridge, MA: Harvard University Press.

Gobod, L.C. and Pfau, M. (2000) Conferring resistance to peer pressure among adolescents: Using inoculation theory to discourage alcohol use. *Communication Research,* 27(4), 411–37.

Goonasekera, A., Chung Zhu, H., Eashwer, L., Guntarto, B., Balraj-Ambigapathy, J.O., Ai-Leen, L., Chung, A., and Minn Hanh, V.T. (2000) *Growing up with TV: Asian children's experience.* Singapore: Asia Media Information and Communication Centre.

Gorn, G. and Goldberg, M. (1982) Behavioral evidence of the effects of televised food messages on children. *Journal of Consumer Research,* 9(3), 200–5.

Gortmaker, S.L., Cheung, L.W.Y., Peterson, K.E., Chomitz, G., Cradle, J.H., Dart, H., Fox, M.K., Bullock, R.B., Sobol, A.M., Colditz, G., Field, A.E., and Laird, N. (1999) Impact of a school-based interdisciplinary intervention on diet and physical activity among urban primary school children. *Archives of Pediatrics Adolescent Medicine*, 153(9), 957–83.

Gortmaker, S.L., Must, A., Sobol, A.M., Peterson, K.E., Colditz, G., and Deitz, W.H. (1996) Television viewing as a cause of increasing obesity among children in the United States, 1986–1990. *Archives of Pediatrics Adolescent Medicine*, 150(4), 356–62.

Götz, M. (2004) "Soaps want to explain reality." Daily soaps and big brother in the everyday life of German children and adolescents. In von Feilitzen, C. (ed.), *Young people, soap operas and reality TV* (pp. 65–80). Göteborg University, Sweden: The international Clearinghouse on Children, Youth and Media.

Götz, M., Lemish, D., Aidman, A., and Moon, H. (2005) *Media and the make believe worlds of children: When Harry Potter met Pokémon in Disneyland.* Mahwah, NJ: Lawrence Erlbaum.

Graves, S.B. (1993) Television, the portrayal of African Americans, and the development of children's attitudes. In Berry, G.L. and Asamen, J.K. (eds), *Children and television: Images in a changing socio-cultural world* (pp. 179–90). Newbury Park, CA: Sage.

Graves, S.B. (1999) Television and prejudice reduction: When does television as a vicarious experience make a difference? *Journal of Social Issues*, 55(4), 707–25.

Gray, A. (1987) Behind closed doors: Video recorders in the home. In Baehr, H. and Dyer, G. (eds), *Boxed-in: Women and television* (pp. 38–54). London: Pandora Press.

Greenberg, B.S. and Brand, J.E. (1994) Minorities and the mass media: 1970s to 1990s. In Braynt, J. and Zillamn, D. (eds), *Media effects advances in theory and research* (pp. 315–63). Hillsdale, NJ: Lawrence Erlbaum.

Greenberg, B.S., Brown, J.D., and Buerkel-Rothfuss, N.L. (1993) *Media, sex and the adolescent.* Cresskill, NJ: Hampton.

Greenberg, B.S., Linsangan, R., and Soderman, A. (1993) Adolescents' reactions to television sex. In Greenberg, B.S., Brown, J.D., and Buerkel-Rothfuss, N.L. (eds), *Media, sex and the adolescent* (pp. 196–24). Cresskill, NJ: Hampton.

Greenfield, P. and Beagles-Roos, J. (1988) Radio vs. television: Their cognitive impact on children of different socio-economic and ethnic groups. *Journal of Communication*, 38(2), 71–2.

Greenfield, P., Farrer, D., and Beagles-Roos, J. (1986) Is the medium the message? An experimental comparison of the effects of radio and television on imagination. *Journal of Applied Developmental Psychology*, 7(4), 237–55.

Groebel, J. (1998) The UNESCO global study on media violence: Report presented to the Director General of UNESCO. In Carlsson, U. and von Feilitzen, C. (eds), *Children and media violence* (pp. 181–99). Göteborg

University: The UNESCO International Clearinghouse on Children and Violence on the Screen.

Grube, J. and Wallack, L. (1994) Television beer advertising and drinking knowledge, beliefs, and intentions among schoolchildren. *American Journal of Public Health*, 84(2), 254–9.

Gultig, J. (2004) "This is it" – South African youth's reading of Yizo Yizo 2. In von Feilitzen, C. (ed.), *Young people, soap operas and reality TV* (pp. 227–41). Göteborg University, Sweden: The International Clearinghouse on Children, Youth and Media.

Gunter, B. (1995) *Television and gender representation*. London: John Libbey and Company.

Gunter, B. (2002) *Media sex: What are the issues?* Mahwah, NJ: Lawrence Erlbaum.

Haeffner, M.J. and Wartella, E.A. (1987) Effects of sibling coviewing on children's interpretations of television programs, *Journal of Broadcasting and Electronic Media*, 31(2), 153–68.

Hancox, R.J., Milne, B.J., and Poulton, R. (2005) Association of television viewing during childhood with poor educational achievement. *Archives Pediatrics and Adolescent Medicine*, 159, 614–18.

Hansen, F., Rasmussen, J., Martensen, A., and Tufte, B. (eds) (2002) *Children – Consumption, advertising and media*. Copenhagen: Copenhagen Business School Press.

Harrison, K. (2000a) The body electric: Thin-ideal media and eating disorders in adolescents. *Journal of Communication*, 50, 119–43.

Harrison, K. (2000b) Television viewing, fat stereotyping, body shape standards and eating disorder symptomatology in grade school children. *Communication Research*, 27(5), 617–40.

Harrison, K. and Cantor, J. (1997) The relationship between media consumption and eating disorders. *Journal of Communication*, 47(1), 40–67.

Hawkins, R. (1977) The dimensional structure of children's perceptions of TV reality. *Communication Research*, 4(3), 299–320.

Hayes, D.S. and Birnbaum, D.W. (1980) Preschoolers' retention of televised events: Is a picture worth a thousand words? *Developmental Psychology*, 16(5), 410–16.

Hearold, S. (1986) A synthesis of 1,043 effects of television on social behavior. In Paik, H. and Comstock, G. (1994) The effects of television violence on antisocial behavior: A meta-analysis. *Communication Research*, 21(4), 516–46.

Heintz-Knowles, K.E. (1992) Children's interpretations of television families: An examination of the influence of family structure on children's perceptions of real-life and TV families and parents. Paper presented at the annual meeting of the International Communication Association, Miami Florida.

Heintz, K.E., Shively, A., Wartella, E., and Oliverez, A. (1995) Television advertising and childhood: Form, function and future uses. Paper presented at the annual meeting of the International Communication Association, Albuquerque, NM.

Hemelryk D.S. (2005) *Little friends: Children's film and media culture in China.* Oxford, UK: Rowman and Littlefield Publishers.

Himmelweit, H.T., Oppenheim, A.N., and Vince, P. (1958) *Television and the child.* London: Oxford University Press.

Hobbs, R. (1998) The seven great debates in the media literacy movement. *Journal of Communication,* 48(1), 16–32.

Hoffner, C. (1996) Children's wishful identification and para-social interaction with favorite television characters. *Journal of Broadcasting and Electronic Media,* 40, 289–402.

Hoffner, C. and Cantor, J. (1991) Perceiving and responding to mass media characters. In Bryant, J. and Zillman, D. (eds), *Responding to the screen: Reception and reaction processes* (pp. 63–101). Hillsdale, NJ: Lawrence Erlbaum.

Hoffner, C. and Haefner, M. (1993) Children's affective responses to news coverage of the war. In Greenberg, B.S. and Gantz, W. (eds), *Desert Storm and the mass media* (pp. 364–80). Cresskill, NJ: Hampton.

Huesmann, L.R. and Eron, L.D. (eds) (1986) *Television and the aggressive child: A cross-national comparison.* Hillsdale, NJ: Lawrence Erlbaum.

Huston, A.C., Wright J.C., Marquis, J., and Green, S.B. (1999) How young children spend their time: Television and other activities. *Developmental Psychology,* 35, 912–25.

Jenkins, H. (1990) "Going Bonkers!:" Children, play and *Pee-wee.* In Jenkins, J. (ed.), *Camera Obscura* (pp. 169–93). New York: Johns Hopkins University Press.

Jones, G. (2002) *Killing monsters: Why children need fantasy, super heroes, and make-believe violence.* New York: Basic Books.

Jönsson, A. (1986) TV: A threat or a complement to school? *Journal of Educational Television,* 12(1), 29–38.

Jordan, A. (1992) Social class, temporal orientation, and mass media use within the family system. *Critical Studies in Mass Communication,* 9, 374–86.

Jordan, A.B. and Woodward, E.H. (1997) *The 1997 state of children's television report: Programming for children over broadcast and cable television.* University of Pennsylvania: The Annenberg Public Policy Center.

Kamalipour, Y.R. (ed.) (1999) *Images of the U.S. around the world: A multicultural perspective.* New York: State University of New York Press.

Kelly, J., Logue, P., and McCully, A. (1996) Speak Your Piece/Off the Walls. Channel 4 Schools. England.

Kielwasser, A.P. and Wolf, M.A. (1992) Mainstream television, adolescent homosexuality, and significant silence. *Critical Studies in Mass Communication,* 9, 350–73.

Killen, M. and Fox, N. (2003) Evaluations of children's reactions to Israeli–Palestinian Sesame Street. *Maryland International,* 2, 12.

Killen, M., Fox, N.A., and Leavitt, L. (2004) Stereotypes and conflict resolution in the Mid-East: Young children's social concepts as a function of exposure to a media intervention. Paper presented at the Annual Meeting of the Jean Piaget Society: Society for the Study of Knowledge and Development. Toronto, Canada.

Kleeman, D.W. (2001) Prix Jeunesse as a force for cultural diversity. In Singer, D.G. and Singer, J.L. (eds), *Handbook of children and the media* (pp. 521–31). Thousand Oaks, CA: Sage.

Kohlberg, L. (ed.) (1984) *The psychology of moral development: The nature of validity of moral stages.* Cambridge, MA: Harper and Row.

Kodaira, S.I. (1998) A review of research on media violence in Japan. In Carlsson, U. and von Feilitzen, C. (eds), *Children and media violence* (pp. 81–106). Götteborg University, Sweden: The International Clearinghouse on Children, Youth and Media.

Koolstra, C.M. and Beentjes, J.W.J. (1999) Children's vocabulary acquisition in a foreign language through watching subtitled TV programs at home. *Educational Technology Research and Development,* 47, 51–60.

Kubey, R. (1998) Obstacles to the development of media education in the U.S. *Journal of Communication,* 48(1), 58–69.

Kunkel, D. (1998) Policy battles over defining children's educational television. *The Annals of the American Academy of Political and Social Science Special Issue: Children and Television,* 557, 39–53.

Kunkel, D. (2001) Children and television advertising. In Singer, D.G. and Singer, J.L. (eds), *Handbook of children and the media* (pp. 375–93). Thousand Oaks, CA: Sage.

Kunkel, D., Cope, K.M., and Biely, E. (1999) Sexual messages on television: Comparing findings from three studies. *The Journal of Sex Research,* 36(3), 230–6.

Lee, A.Y.L. (2004) Critical appreciation of TV drama and reality shows: Hong Kong youth in need of media education. In von Feilitzen, C. (ed.), *Young people, soap operas and reality TV* (pp. 117–27). Göteborg University, Sweden: The International Clearinghouse on Children, Youth and Media.

Lefkowitz, N.M., Eron, L.D., Walder, L.O., and Huesmann, L.R. (1977) *Growing up to be violent: A longitudinal study of the development of aggression.* Elmsford, NY: Pergamon.

Lemish, D. (1987) Viewers in diapers: The early development of television viewing. In Lindlof, T. (ed.), *Natural audiences: Qualitative research of media uses and effects* (pp. 33–57). Norwood, NJ: Ablex.

Lemish, D. (1997) Kindergartners' understandings of television: A cross-cultural comparison. *Communication Studies,* 48(2), 109–26.

Lemish, D. (1998a) What is news? A cross-cultural examination of kindergartners' understanding of news. *Communications: European Journal of Communication Research,* 23, 491–504.

Lemish, D. (1998b) Spice Girls' talk: A case study in the development of gendered identity. In Inness, S.A. (ed.), *Millennium girls: Today's girls around the world* (pp. 145–67). New York: Rowman and Littlefield.

Lemish, D. (1999) "America the beautiful": Israeli children's perception of the U.S. through a wrestling television series. In Kamalipour, Y.R. (ed.), *Images of the U.S. around the world: A multicultural perspective* (pp. 295–308). New York: State University of New York Press.

Lemish, D. (forthcoming) "This is our war": Israeli children's domestication of the war in Iraq. In Lemish, D. and Götz, M. (eds), *Children and media in times of conflict and war.* Cresskill, NJ: Hampton.

Lemish, D. and Götz, M. (eds) (forthcoming) *Children and media at times of war and conflict.* Cresskill, NJ: Hampton.

Lemish, D. and Rice M. (1986) Television as a talking picture book: A prop for language acquisition. *Journal of Child Language,* 13, 251–74.

Lemish, D. and Lemish, P. (1997) A much debated consensus: Media literacy in Israel. In Kubey, R. (ed.), *Media literacy in the information age* (pp. 213–28). New Brunswick, NJ: Transaction.

Lemish, D. and Tidhar, C.E. (1999) Mothers close to life: An Israeli case study. *TelevIZIon,* 12(2), 39–46.

Lemish, D., Drotner, K., Liebes, T., Maigret, E., and Stald, G. (1998) Global culture in practice: A look at children and adolescents in Denmark, France and Israel. *European Journal of Communication,* 13(4), 539–56.

Lemish, D., Liebes, T., and Seidmann, V. (2001) Gendered media meanings and uses. In Livingstone, S. and Bovill, M. (eds), *Children and their changing media environment: A European comparative study* (pp. 263–82). Mahwah, NJ: Lawrence Erlbaum.

Lesser, G.S. (1996) Programmes for young children. Paper presented at the EBU workshop, Montreal.

Lewis, J. and Jhally, S. (1998) The struggle over media literacy. *Journal of Communication,* 48(1), 109–20.

Lichter, S.R. and Lichter, L. (1988) *Television's impact on ethnic and racial images: A study of Howard Beach adolescents.* New York: American Jewish Committee, Institute of Human Relations.

Liebert, R.M. and Sprafkin, J. (1988) *The early window.* New York: Pergamon.

Liebes, T. and Ribak, R. (1992) The contribution of family culture to political participation, political outlook, and its reproduction. *Communication Research,* 19(5), 618–41.

Linebarger, D.L. (2001) *Summative evaluation of* Dora the Explorer, *Part 1: Learning outcomes.* Kansas City, KS: Media and Technology Projects, ABCD Ventures, Inc.

Linebarger, D.L. and Walker, D. (2005) Infants' and toddlers' television viewing and language outcomes. *American Behavioral Scientist,* 48(5), 624–45.

Lisosky, J.M. (1997) Controlling children's channels: Comparing children's television policies in Australia, Canada, and the United States. Dissertation, University of Washington.

Livingstone, S. (1992) The meaning of domestic technologies: A personal construct analysis of familial gender relations. In Silverstone, R. and Hirsch, E. (eds), *Consuming technologies: Media and information in domestic spaces* (pp. 113–30). London: Routledge.

Livingstone, S. (2005) Assessing the research base for the policy debate over the effects of food advertising to children. *International Journal of Advertising,* 24(3), 273–93.

Livingstone, S. and Bovill, M. (2001) *Children and their changing media environment: A European comparative study.* Mahwah, NJ: Lawrence Erlbaum.

Lonner, W.J., Thorndike, R.M., Forbes, N.E., and Ashworth, C. (1985) The influence of television on measured cognitive abilities: A study with Native Alaskian children. *Journal of Cross-Cultural Psychology,* 16(3), 355–80.

Lull, J. (1980a) The social uses of television. *Human Communication Research,* 6(3): 197–209.

Lull, J. (1980b) Family communication patterns and the social uses of television. *Communication Research,* 7(3), 319–34.

Lull, J. (1988) *World families watch television.* Newbury Park, CA: Sage.

Lyons, J.S., Anderson, R.L., and Larson, D.B. (1994) A systematic review of the effects of aggressive and nonaggressive pornography. In Zillman, D., Bryant, J., and Huston, A.C. (eds), *Media, children and the family: Social scientific, psychodynamic and clinical perspectives* (pp. 271–310). Hillsdale, NJ: Lawrence Erlbaum Associates.

MacBeth, T.M. (ed.) (1996a) *Tuning in to young viewers: Social science perspectives on television.* Thousand Oaks, CA: Sage.

MacBeth, T.M. (1996b) Indirect effects of television: Creativity, persistence, school achievement, and participation in other activities. In MacBeth, T.M. (ed.), *Tuning in to young viewers: Social science perspectives on television* (pp. 149–219). Thousand Oaks, CA: Sage.

McKee, N., Aghi, M., and Shahzadi, N. (2004) Cartoons and comic books for changing social norms: *Meena,* the South Asian girl. In Singhal, A., Cody, M.J., Rogers, E.M. and Sabido, M. (eds), *Entertainment-education and social change: History, research, and practice* (pp. 331–49). Mahwah, NJ: Lawrence Erlbaum.

Macklin, M.C. (1999) The impact of audiovisual information on children's product-related recall. *Journal of Consumer Research,* 21(1), 154–64.

Macklin, M.C. and Carlson, L. (eds) (1999). *Advertising to children: Concepts and controversies.* Thousand Oaks, CA: Sage.

Mander, J. (1978) *Four arguments for the elimination of television.* New York: Quill.

Mares, M.-L. and Woodard, E. (2005) Positive effects of television on children's social interactions: A meta analysis. *Media Psychology,* 7, 301–22.

Mazzarella, S. and Pecora, N. (eds) (1999) *Growing up girls: Popular culture and the construction of identity.* New York: Peter Lang.

Meringoff, L.K., Vibbert, M., Char, C.A., Fernie, D.E., Banker, G.S., and Gardner, H. (1983) How is children's learning from television distinctive? Exploiting the medium methodologically. In Bryant, J. and Anderson, D.R. (eds), *Children's understanding of television: Research on attention and comprehension* (pp. 151–79). New York: Academic Press.

Messaris, P. (1983) Family conversations about television. *Journal of Family Issues,* 4(2), 293–308.

Messaris, P. (1994) *Visual literacy: Image, mind and reality.* Boulder, CO: Westview Press.

Messenger Davies, M. (1989) *Television is good for your kids.* London: Hilary Shipman.

Messenger Davies, M. (1997) *Fake, fact, and fantasy: Children's interpretations of television reality.* Mahwah, NJ: Lawrence Erlbaum.

Meyers, M. (ed.) (1999) *Mediated women: Representations in popular culture.* Cresskill, NJ: Hampton.

Meyrowitz, J. (1985) *No sense of place: The impact of electronic media on social behavior.* Oxford: Oxford University Press

Meyrowitz, J. (1995) Taking McLuhan and "medium theory" seriously: Technological change and the evolution of education. In Kerr, S.T. (ed.), *Technology and the future of schooling* (pp. 73–110). Chicago, IL: The University of Chicago Press.

Modleski, T. (1984) *Loving with a vengeance: Mass-produced fantasies for women.* London: Methuen.

Morgan, M. (1987) Television, sex-role attitudes and sex-role behavior. *Journal of Early Adolescence,* 7(3), 269–82.

Morley, D. (1986) *Family television: Cultural power and domestic leisure.* London: Comedia Publishing.

Myers, P.N. and Biocca, F.A. (1992) The elastic body image: The effect of television advertising and programming on body image distortions in young women. *Journal of Communication,* 43(3), 108–33.

Naigels, L.R. and Mayeux, L. (2001) Television as incidental language teacher. In Singer, D. and Singer, J. (eds), *Handbook of children and the media* (pp. 135–52). Thousand Oaks, CA: Sage.

National Television Violence Study (1996) *National television violence study* (vol 1). Thousand Oaks, CA: Sage.

Newcomb, A.F. and Collins, W.A. (1979) Children's comprehension of family role portrayals in televised dramas: Effects of socioeconomical status, ethnicity, and age. *Developmental Psychology,* 15, 417–23.

Neuman, S.B. (1991) *Literacy in the television age.* Norwood, NJ: Ablex.

NIPPA, The Early Years Organization (2004) Respecting difference: The media initiative for children. Unpublished working paper. Northern Ireland: Peace Initiatives Institute.

O'Bryan, K.C. (1980) The teaching face: A historical perspective. In Palmer, E.L. and Dorr, A. (eds), *Children and the faces of television: Teaching, violence, selling* (pp. 5–17). New York: Academic Press.

Paik, H. and Comstock, G. (1994) The effects of television violence on antisocial behavior: A meta-analysis. *Communication Research,* 21(4), 516–46.

Palmer, A.W. and Hafen, T. (1999) American TV through the eyes of German teenagers. In Kamalipour, Y.R. (ed.), *Images of the U.S. around the world: A multicultural perspective* (pp. 135–46). New York: State University of New York Press.

Pasquier, D. (2001) Media at home: Domestic interactions and regulation. In Livingstone, S. and Bovill, M. (eds), *Children and their changing media environment: A European comparative study* (pp. 161–77). Mahwah, NJ: Lawrence Erlbaum.

Peterson, E.E. (1987) Media consumption and girls who want to have fun. *Critical Studies in Mass Communication*, 4(1), 37–50.

Peterson, J.L., Moore, K.A., and Furstenberg, F.F. (1991) Television viewing and early initiation of sexual intercourse: Is there a link? In Wolf, M. and Kielswasser, A. (eds), *Gay people, sex and the media* (pp. 93–118). New York: The Haworth Press.

Piaget, J. (1969) *The origins of intelligence in the child.* New York: International University Press.

Piaget, J. and Inhelder, B. (1969) *The psychology of the child.* New York: Basic Books.

Pingree, S. (1978) The effects of nonsexist commercials and perceptions of reality on children's attitudes about women. *Psychology of Women Quarterly*, 2, 262–77.

Pollack, W. (1998) *Real boys: Rescuing our sons from the myths of boyhood.* New York: Henry Holt and Co.

Posavac, H.D., Posavac, S.S., and Posavac, E.J. (1998) Exposure to media images of female attractiveness and concern with body weight among young women. *Sex Roles*, 38(2/4), 187–201.

Postman, N. (1979) The first curriculum: Comparing school and television. *Phi Delta Kappan*, November, 163–8.

Postman, N. (1982) *The disappearance of childhood.* New York: Vintage Books.

Potter, W.J. (2001) *Media literacy.* Thousand Oaks, CA: Sage.

Price, M.E. (ed.) (1998) *The V-Chip debate: Content filtering from television to the Internet.* Mahwah, NJ: Lawrence Erlbaum.

Price, M.E. and Verhulst, S.G. (ed.) (2002) *Parental control of television broadcasting.* Mahwah, NJ: Lawrence Erlbaum.

Prinsloo, J. and Criticos, C. (eds) (1991) *Media matters in South Africa.* Durban, South Africa: University of Natal.

Quin, R. and McMahon, B. (1993) Monitoring standards in media studies: Problems and strategies. *Australian Journal of Education*, 37(2), 182–97.

Radway, J. (1984) *Reading the romance: Women, patriarchy, and popular literature.* Chapel Hill, NC: University of North Carolina Press.

Raviv, A., Bar-Tal, D., Raviv, A., and Ben-Horin, A. (1996) Adolescent idolization of pop singers: Causes, expressions, and reliance. *Journal of Youth and Adolescence*, 25(5), 631–750.

Reeves, B. (1979) Children's understanding of television people. In Wartella, E. (ed.), *Children communicating: Media and development of thought, speech, understanding* (pp. 115–55). Beverly Hills, CA: Sage.

Reiser, R.A., Tessmer, M.A., and Phelps, P.C. (1984) Adult–child interaction in children's learning from "Sesame Street." *Educational Children and Television Journal*, 32(4), 217–23;

Ribak, R. (1997) Socialization as and through conversation: Political discourse in Israeli families. *Comparative Education Review*, 41(1), 71–96.

Rice, M.L. and Woodsmall, L. (1988) Lessons from television: Children's word learning when viewing. *Child development*, 59, 420–9.

Rice, M.L., Buhr, J., and Oetting, J.B. (1992) Specific language-impaired children's quick incidental learning of words: The effect of a pause. *Journal of Speech and Hearing Research*, 35, 1040–8.

Rice, M.L., Huston, A.C., Truglio, R. and Wright, J. (1990) Words from "Sesame Street": Learning vocabulary while viewing. *Developmental Psychology*, 26(3), 421–8.

Rice, M.L., Oetting, J.B., Marquis, J., Bode, J., and Pase, S. (1994) Frequency of input effects on word comprehension of children with specific language impairment. *Journal of Speech and Hearing Research*, 37, 106–22.

Robinson, T.N. (1999) Reducing children's television viewing to prevent obesity: A randomized controlled trial. *JAMA – Journal of the American Medical Association*, 282, 1561–7.

Rolandelli, D.R. (1989) Children and television: The visual superiority effect reconsidered. *Journal of Broadcasting and Electronic Media*, 33(1), 69–81.

Rosengren, K.E. and Windahl, S. (1989) *Media matter: TV use in childhood and adolescence*. Norwood, NJ: Ablex.

Rosenkoetter, L.I. (2001) Television and morality. In Singer, D.G. and Singer, J.L. (eds), *Handbook of children and the media* (pp. 463–73). Thousand Oaks, CA: Sage.

Ross, K. and Byerly, C.M. (2004) *Women and media: International perspectives*. Oxford: Blackwell.

Salomon, G. (1977) Effects of encouraging Israeli mothers to co-observe "Sesame Street" with their five-year-olds. *Child Development*, 48, 1146–58.

Salomon, G. (1981) Introducing AIME: The assessment of children's mental involvement with television. In Kelly, H. and Gardner, H. (eds), *Viewing children through television: New directions for child development* 13 (pp. 89–102). San Francisco, CA: Jossey-Bass.

Salomon, G. (1983) Television watching and mental effort: A social psychological view. In Bryant, J. and Anderson, D.R. (eds), *Children's understanding of television: Research on attention and comprehension* (pp. 181–98). New York: Academic Press.

Salomon, G. (1984) Investing effort in television viewing. In Murray, J.P. and Salomon, G. (eds), *The future of children's television* (pp. 125–33). Boys Town, NE: Father Flanagan's Boys' Home.

Salomon, G. (1994 [1979]) *Interaction of media, cognition, and learning*. San Francisco, CA: Jossey-Bass.

Salomon, G. and Leigh, T. (1984) Predispositions about learning from print and television. *Journal of Communication*, 34, 119–35.

Schmidt, M.E. and Anderson, D.R. (2006) The impact of television on cognitive development and educational achievement. In Pecora, N., Murray, J.O., and Wartella, E. (eds), *Children and television: 50 years of research* (pp. 65–87). Mahwah, NJ: Lawrence Erlbaum.

Schramm, W. (ed.) (1960) *The impact of educational television*. Urbana, IL: University of Illinois.

Schramm, W. (1977) *Big media little media: Tools and technologies for instruction*. Beverly Hills, CA: Sage.

Schramm, W., Lyle, J., and Parker, E.B. (1961) *Television in the lives of our children*. Stanford, CA: Stanford University Press.

Schwichenberg, C. (1993) *The Madonna connection: Representational politics, subcultural identities, and cultural theory*. St. Leonards, Australia: Allen and Unwin.

Seidler, V.J. (1997) *Man enough: Embodying masculinities*. London: Sage.

Selnow, G.W. and Bettinghuas, E.P. (1982) Television exposure and language development. *Journal of Broadcasting*, 26(1), 469–79.

Shanahan, J. and Morgan, M. (1992) Adolescents, families and television in five countries: Implications for cultural educational research. *Journal of Educational Television*, 18(1), 35–55.

Shannon, B., Peacock, J., and Brown, M.J. (2001) Body fatness, television viewing and caloric intake of a sample of Pennsylvania sixth grade children. *Journal of Nutrition Education*, 23(6), 262–8.

Sherry, J.L. (1997) Pro-social soap operas for development: A review of research and theory. *The Journal of International Communication*, 4(2), 75–102.

Shipard, S. (2003) A brief look at the regulation in Australia: A co-regulatory approach. In von Feilitzen, C. and Carlsson, U. (eds), *Promote or protect? Perspectives on media literacy and media regulations* (pp. 237–41). Göteborg University: The International Clearinghouse on Children, Youth and Media.

Shochat, L. (2003) Our neighborhood: Using entertaining children's television to promote interethnic understanding in Macedonia. *Conflict Resolution Quarterly*, 21(1), 79–93.

Signorielli, N. (1990a) Television's mean and dangerous world: A continuation of the cultural indicators perspective. In Signorielle, N. and Morgan, M. (eds), *Cultivation analysis: New directions in media effects research* (pp. 85–106). Newbury Park, CA: Sage.

Signorielli, N. (1990b) Children, television and gender roles. *Journal of Adolescent Health Car*, 11(1), 50–8.

Signorielli, N. (2001) Television's gender role images and contribution to stereotyping: Past, present, future. In Singer, D.G. and Singer, J.L. (eds), *Handbook of children and the media* (pp. 341–58). Thousand Oaks, CA: Sage.

Signorielli. N. and Lears, M. (1992) Children, television and conceptions about chores: Attitudes and behaviors. *Sex Roles*, 27(3/4), 157–70.

Simpson, B. (2004) *Children and television*. New York: Continuum.

Singer, D.G. (1993) Creativity of children in a television world. In Berry, G.L. and Asamen, J.K. (eds), *Children and television: Images in a changing sociocultural world* (pp. 73–86). Newbury Park, CA: Sage.

Singer, D.G. and Singer, J.L. (1990) *The house of make-believe*. Cambridge, MA: Harvard University Press.

Singer, D.G. and Singer, J.L. (1994) Evaluating the classroom viewing of a television series: "Degrassi Junior High." In Zillmann, D., Braynt, J. and Huston, A.C. (eds), *Media, children and the family: Social scientific, psychodynamic, and clinical perspectives* (pp. 97–115). Hillsdale, NJ: Lawrence Erlbaum.

Singer, D.G. and Singer, J.L. (1998) Developing critical viewing skills and media literacy in children. *The Annals of the American Academy of Political and Social Science Special Issue: Children and Television* 557, 164–79.

Singer, J.L. and Singer, D.G. (1976) Can TV stimulate imaginative play? *Journal of Communication*, 26, 74–80.

Singer, J.L. and Singer, D.G. (1981) *Television, imagination, and aggression: A study of preschoolers.* Hillsdale, NJ: Lawrence. Erlbaum.

Singer, J.L. and Singer, D.G. (1983) Implications of childhood television viewing of cognition, imagination and emotion. In Bryant, J. and Anderson, D.R. (eds), *Children's understanding of television: Research on attention and comprehension* (pp. 265–95). New York: Academic Press.

Singer, J.L. and Singer, D.G. (1998) "Barney and Friends" as entertainment and education: Evaluating the quality and effectiveness of a television series for preschool children. In Asaman, J. and Berry, G. (eds), *Research paradigms, television, and social behavior* (pp. 305–67). Thousand Oaks, CA: Sage.

Smith, R. (1986) Television addiction. In Bryant, J. and Zillman, D. (eds), *Perspectives on media effects* (pp. 109–28). Hillsdale, NJ: Lawrence Erlbaum.

Smith, R. (2004) Yizo Yizo: This is it? A critical analysis of reality-based drama series. In von Feilitzen, C. (ed.), *Young people, soap operas and reality TV* (pp. 241–51). Göteborg University, Sweden: The international Clearinghouse on Children, Youth and Media.

Smith, S.L., and Moyer-Guse, E. (Forthcoming) Children and the war on Iraq: Developmental differences in fear responses to TV news coverage. *Media Psychology.*

Smith, S.L. and Wilson, B.J. (2000) Children's reactions to a television news story: The impact of video footage and proximity of the crime. *Communication Research*, 27(5), 641–73.

Smith, S.L. and Wilson, B.J. (2002) Children's comprehension of and fear reactions to television news. *Media Psychology*, 4, 1–26.

Smith, S.L., Moyer, E., Boyson, A.R., and Pieper, K.M. (2002) Parents' perceptions of children's fear responses. In Greenberg, B.S. (ed.), *Communication and terrorism* (pp. 193–208). Cresskill, NJ: Hampton.

Sontag, S. (2003) *Regarding the pain of others.* New York: Farran, Straus and Giroux.

Sprafkin, J., Gadow, K.D., and Abelman, R. (1992) *Television and the exceptional child: A forgotten audience.* Hillsdale, NJ: Lawrence Erlbaum.

Stein, A.H. and Freidrich. L.K. (1972) Television content and young children's behavior. In Murray, J.P., Rubinstein, E.A., and Comstock, G.A. (eds), *Television and social behavior* vol 2: *Television and social learning (Surgeon General Report)* (pp. 203–317). Washington, DC: US Government Printing Office.

Stice, E., Schupak-Neuberg, E., Shaw, H.E., and Stein, R.I. (1994) Relation of media exposure to eating disorder symptomatology: An examination of mediating mechanisms. *Journal of Abnormal Psychology*, 13(4), 836–40.

Story M. and French S. (2004) Food advertising and marketing directed at children and adolescents in the U.S. *International Journal of Behavioral Nutrition and Physical Activity*, 1(3).

Stroman, C.A. (1986). Television viewing and self-concept among black children. *Journal of Broadcasting and Electronic media, 30*(1), 87–93.

The Teletubbies (1999) *TelevIZIon,* 12(2).

Thomsen, S.R., and Rekve, D. (2003) The influence of religiosity on reaction to alcohol advertisements on drinking among seventh and eight graders. *Journal of Media and Religion,* 2(2), 93–107.

Tidhar, C.E. (ed.) (1990) *ETV broadcasting research in the nineties: Readings from the Tel Aviv Seminar.* Tel Aviv: Israel Educational Television.

Tidhar, C.E. (1996) Enhancing television literacy skills among preschool children through an intervention program in the kindergarten. *Journal of Educational Media,* 22(2), 97–110.

Tidhar, C.E. and Levinson, H. (1997) Parental mediation of children's viewing in a changing television environment. *Journal of Educational Media, 23*(2/3), 141–55.

Tiggermann, M. and Pickering, A.S. (1996) Role of television in adolescent women's body dissatisfaction and drive for thinness. *International Journal of Eating Disorders,* 20(2), 199–203.

Tobin, J. (2000) *"Good guys don't wear hats": Children's talk about the media.* New York: Columbia University, Teachers College Press.

Tobin, J. (ed.) (2004). *Pikachu's global adventure: The rise and fall of Pokémon.* Durham, NC: Duke University Press.

Tufte, T. (2003) Entertainment-education in HIV/AIDS communication. Beyond marketing, towards empowerment. In von Feilitzen, C. and Carlsson, U. (eds), *Promote or protect? Perspectives on media literacy and media regulations* (pp. 85–97). Göteborg University, Sweden: The international Clearinghouse on Children, Youth and Media.

Tufte, B., Lavender, T., and Lemish, D. (eds) (2003) *Media education around the world: Promise and practice.* NJ: Hampton.

Uddén, G. (n.d.) *Want to be a hero: Young criminals' thoughts about real violence and film violence.* The National Council for Crime Prevention, Sweden: Våldsskildringsrådet. Online at: www.medieradet.se/upload/rapporter_pdf/youWant.pdf

Valkenburg, P.M. (2001) Television and the child's developing imagination. In Singer, D.G. and Singer, J.L. (eds), *Handbook of children and the media* (pp. 121–34). Thousand Oaks, CA: Sage.

Valkenburg, P.M. (2004) *Children's responses to the screen: A Media psychological approach.* Mahwah, NJ: Lawrence Erlbaum.

Valkenburg, P.M. and Cantor, J. (2000) Children's likes and dislikes of entertainment programs. In Zillman, D. and Vorderer, P. (eds), *Media entertainment: The psychology of its appeal* (pp. 135–52). Mahwah, NJ: Lawrence Erlbaum.

Valkenburg, P.M. and Cantor, J. (2002) The development of a child into a consumer. In Calvert, S.L., Jordan, A.B., and Cocking, R.R. (eds), *Children in the digital age: Influences of electronic media on development* (pp. 201–14). Westport, CT: Praeger.

Valkenberg, P.M. and van der Voort, T.H.A (1994) Influence of TV on day-dreaming and creative imagination: A review of research. *Psychological Bulletin*, 116, 316–39.

Valkenburg, P.M. and Vroone, M. (2004) Developmental changes in infants' and toddlers' attention to television entertainment. *Communication Research*, 31(1), 288–311.

Valkenburg, P.M., Krcmar, M., Peetrs, A.L., and Marseille, N.M. (1999) Developing a scale to assess three styles of television mediation: "Instructive mediation," "restrictive mediation," and "social coviewing." *Journal of Broadcasting and Electronic Media*, 43(1), 52–66.

Van der Voort, T.H.A. (1986) *Television violence: A child's-eye view*. Amsterdam: North-Holland.

Van der Voort, T.H.A. (2001) Television's impact on children's leisure-time reading and reading skills. In Verhoeven, L. and Snow, C. (eds), *Literacy and motivation: Reading engagement in individuals and groups* (pp. 95–119). Mahwah, NJ: Lawrence Erlbaum.

Van der Voort, T.H.A. and Valkenburg, P.M. (1994) Television's impact on fantasy play: A review of research. *Developmental Review*, 14, 27–51.

Van Evra, J. (2004) *Television and child development* (3rd edn). Mahwah, NJ: Lawrence Erlbaum.

Van Zoonen, L. (1994) *Feminist media studies*. London: Sage.

Vandewater, E.A., Park, S-E, and Wartella, E. (2005) "No – you can't watch that": Parental rules and young children's media use. *American Behavioral Scientist*, 48(5), 608–23.

Von Feilitzen, C., and Bucht, C. (2001) *Outlooks on children and media*. Göteborg University: The International Clearinghouse on Children, Youth and Media.

Von Feilitzen, C. and Carlsson, U. (eds) (2002) *Children, young people and media globalisation*. Göteborg University: The International Clearinghouse on Children, Youth and Media.

Von Feilitzen, C. and Carlsson, U. (eds) (2003) *Promote or protect? Perspectives on media literacy and media regulations*. Göteborg University: The International Clearinghouse on Children, Youth and Media.

Vooijs, M.W., van der Voort, T.H.A. and Hoogeweij, J. (1995) Critical viewing of television news: The impact of a Dutch schools television project. *Journal of Educational Television*, 21, 23–36.

Walker, A.J. and Bellamy, R.V. (2001) Remote control devices and family viewing. In Bryant, J. and Bryant, J.A. (eds), *Television and the American family* (2nd edn) (pp. 75–89). Hillsdale, NJ: Lawrence Erlbaum.

Walma van der Molen, J.H. (1999) *Children's recall of television and print news*. Leiden, The Netherlands: Center for Child and Media Studies.

Walma van der Molen, J.H. (2004) Violence and suffering in television news: Toward a broader conception of harmful television content for children. *Pediatrics*, 113, 1771–5.

Walma van der Molen, J.H. (forthcoming) Dutch children's emotional reactions to news about the Second Gulf War: Influence of media exposure, identification, and empathy. In Lemish, D. and Götz, M. (eds), *Children and media in times of conflict and war.* Cresskill, NJ: Hampton.

Walma van der Molen, J.H., Valkenburg, P.M., and Peeters, A.L. (2002) Television news and fear: A child survey. *Communication: The European Journal of Communication Research,* 27(3), 303–17.

Ward, S., Wackman, D.B., and Wartella, E. (1977) *How children learn to buy: The development of consumer information-processing skills.* Beverly Hills, CA: Sage.

Warren, R. (2003) Parental mediation of preschool children's television viewing. *Journal of Broadcasting and Electronic Media,* 47(3), 394–417.

Wartella, E. and Alexander, A. (1978) Children's organization of impressions of television characters. Paper presented at the annual meeting of the International Communication Association, Chicago.

Wartella, E., Scantlin, R., Kotler, J., Huston, A.C., and Donnerstein, E. (2000) Effects of sexual content in the media on children and adolescents. In von Feilitzen, C. and Carlsson, U. (eds), *Children in the new media landscape: Games, pornography, perceptions* (pp. 141–53). Göteborg University: The UNESCO International Clearinghouse on Children and Violence on the Screen.

Wasko, J., Phillips, M., and Meehan, E.R. (eds) (2001) *Dazzled by Disney?: A global Disney audiences project.* London: Leicester University Press.

Weaver, J.B. (1994) Pornography and sexual callousness: The perceptual and behavioral consequences of exposure to pornography. In Zillman, D., Bryant, J., and Huston, A.C. (eds), *Media, children and the family: Social scientific, psychodynamic and clinical perspectives* (pp. 215–28). Hillsdale, NJ: Lawrence Erlbaum.

Weimann, G. (2000) *Communicating unreality: Modern media and the construction of reality* (pp. 79–121). Thousand Oaks, CA: Sage.

Williams, T.M. (1986) *The impact of television: A natural experiment in three communities* (pp. 361–93). Orlando, FL: Academic Press.

Wilson, B., Kunkel, D., Kintz, D., Potter, J., Donnerstein, E., Smith, S., Blumenthal, E., and Gray, T. (1996) *National television violence study.* Thousand Oaks, CA: Sage.

Winn, M. (1977) *The Plug in Drug.* New York: Viking.

Wober, M. and Young, B.M. (1993) British children's knowledge of, emotional reactions to, and ways of making sense of the war. In Greenberg, B.S. and Gantz, W. (eds), *Desert Storm and the mass media* (pp. 381–94). Cresskill, NJ: Hampton.

Wolf, N. (1992) *The beauty myth: How images of beauty are used against women.* New York: Doubleday.

Wright, J.C., Huston, A.C., Scantlin, R., and Kotler, J. (2001) The Early Window Project: *Sesame Street* prepares children for school. In Fisch, S.M. and Truglio, R.T. (eds), *"G" is for growing: Thirty years of research on children and Sesame Street* (pp. 97–114). Mahwah, NJ: Lawrence Erlbaum.

Wroblewski, R. and Huston, A.C. (1987) Televised occupational stereotypes and their effects on early adolescents: Are they changing? *Journal of Early Adolescence*, 7(3), 283–97.

Zaharoponlous, T. (1999) Television viewing and the perception of the United States by Greek teenagers. In Kamalipour, Y.R. (ed.), *Images of the U.S. around the world: A multicultural perspective* (pp. 279–94). New York: State University of New York Press.

Zill, N. (2001) Does *Sesame Street* enhance school readiness: Evidence from a national survey of children. In Fisch, S.M. and Truglio, R.T. (eds), *"G" is for growing: Thirty years of research on children and Sesame Street* (pp. 115–30). Mahwah, NJ: Lawrence Erlbaum.

Zillman, D. (1994) Erotica and family values. In Zillman, D., Bryant, J. and Huston, A.C. (eds), *Media, children and the family: Social scientific, psychodynamic and clinical perspectives* (pp. 199–213). Hillsdale, NJ: Lawrence Erlbaum.

Zimmerman, F.J. and Christakis, D.A. (2005) Children's television viewing and cognitive outcomes. *Archives Pediatrics and Adolescent Medicine*, 159, 619–25.

Zohoori, A.R. (1988) A cross-cultural analysis of children's television use. *Journal of Broadcasting and Electronic Media*, 32(1), 105–13.

Zuckerman, P., Zeigler, M., and Stevenson, H.W. (1978) Children's viewing of television and recognition memory of commercials. *Child Development*, 49(1), 96–104.

Index